P9-EMB-714

DISCARDED

ACCOUNTABILITY,
ASSESSMENT, AND
TEACHER COMMITMENT

SUNY series, Restructuring and School Change
H. Dickson Corbett and Betty Lou Whitford, editors

ACCOUNTABILITY, ASSESSMENT, AND TEACHER COMMITMENT

Lessons from Kentucky's Reform Efforts

EDITED BY
Betty Lou Whitford
and Ken Jones

STATE UNIVERSITY OF NEW YORK PRESS

Published by
State University of New York Press, Albany

Printed in the United States of America

For information, address State University of New York Press,
State University Plaza, Albany, N.Y., 12246

Production by Cathleen Collins
Marketing by Patrick Durocher

Library of Congress Cataloging in Publication Data

Accountability, assessment, and teacher commitment : lessons from
    Kentucky's reform efforts / edited by Betty Lou Whitford and Ken
    Jones.
        p.   cm — (SUNY series, restructuring and school change)
    Includes bibliographical references and index.
    ISBN 0-7914-4409-0 (alk. paper). — ISBN 0-7914-4410-4 (pbk. :
    alk. paper)
        1. Educational accountability—Kentucky—Case studies.
    2. Educational tests and measurements—Kentucky—Case studies.
    3. School improvement programs—Kentucky—Case studies.
    4. Teachers—Kentucky—Case studies.   I. Whitford, Betty Lou.
    II. Jones, Ken, 1949-   .   III. Series.
    LB2806.22.A249   2000
    379.1'58'09769—dc21   99-21286
                                                                        CIP

10 9 8 7 6 5 4 3 2 1

Contents

Figures

Tables

Foreword

PATRICIA A. WASLEY

In recent years, all across our country, educators, legislators, and policymakers have been dreaming of better schools and smarter, more highly skilled public school graduates. In some places, dreams have moved to action. Kentucky was one of the first states in the nation to embrace a very important set of ideas as a means by which to improve student achievement statewide.

Those ideas, articulated in the Kentucky Education Reform Act, or KERA, were based on solid research about practices that foster productive teaching and learning. They included multi-age grouping for youngsters, teacher development, and performance assessments so that everyone would actually be able to see what our children knew and could do. Legislators and the commissioner of education were bold, and promised appropriate funding and new assessments that would help the country at large know whether their dreams were possible.

Kentucky Instructional Results Information System, or KIRIS, was the assessment system built to test the efficacy of such courageous and ambitious goals. Some initial reports indicated that scores came up and that many schools were improving. The authors of the chapters that follow suggest less positive outcomes. They deduce that as so often happens in public education, powerful dreams have been deferred.

Langston Hughes's poem, "Dreams Deferred," suggests that dreams, left untended and unsupported, will eventually die. In this case, important dreams have shriveled under the glare of an accountability system that turned from its original challenge—to build a new kind of performance based system—to adopt a more expedient and familiar form. The implications of this particular decision have been far-reaching. It is not that the dreams are not worth having nor that they are impossible to realize. Instead, the implication is that given the form KIRIS has taken, we still don't know whether the strategies outlined in KERA might give us the kind of system that really catapults our students into better educational skill and knowledge.

To test KERA's promise, Kentucky would had to have built the accountability system they first described, one that promised high-stakes accountability after moving teachers and principals to performance-based instruction and assessment. These chapters suggest that this is not what happened. Instead, as Seymour Sarason has reminded us so many times, the decisions made were unfortunately predictable. Instead of pushing for new forms and correcting for a stronger assessment system, test designers and legislators determined that the reliability of the test was the most important determinant in test construction. As a result, the test has turned from more open-ended performance assessments—of the kind that France and Japan use to a much greater extent than we do—toward greater dependence on an objective format. With this decision alone, a number of the KERA strategies were denied a real opportunity to come to life.

For instance, KERA hoped to move teachers to authentic instruction, but several of the authors herein describe that while they were looking forward to that challenge, the move toward objective tests also emphasizes coverage of the curriculum on the test and de-emphasizes authentic instruction or assessment. Two of the teachers profiled, Katherine Futrell and Mary Jo Foster, are constructivist teachers who focus on their own professional growth as a means by which to better enable them to reap benefits for kids. Both of them were concerned with issues of quality and accountability before KERA, and felt enthusiastic about KERA; it raised their consciousness, and provided them with resources and colleagues to explore more promising accountability. However, both noted the contradictions between its promises and the realities.

Many of the researchers and practitioners who've written about their KERA/KIRIS experiences concur with them, indicating that the most profound change sponsored by KIRIS was that more people were teaching to the test than working for more beneficial teaching practices.

Further, KERA also promised high-stakes accountability. In order to establish the high stakes, authors in the following chapters outline that a set of criteria were established that plummeted some schools that were making enormous progress into crisis. The criteria for successful schools did not take in to account differences in socioeconomic status of the students served or prior educational achievement, placing disadvantaged schools at greater risk.

While the aim to secure a fine education for all children is one we all share, when high stakes are put into place, the starting line has to be considered; otherwise, we continue to punish the disadvantaged yet again.

While KERA had more important dreams in mind, what it and KIRIS seems to have done very well is to educate teachers and administrators more thoroughly about the difficulties and limits of narrow testing, of accountability systems that use only one form of data as a means by which to determine the success of a

school. The teachers involved in these schools, engaged by the promise of performance based assessments, have been made ever more clearly aware of the effects
of easily scored and reliable tests on teachers work and children's skills and interests. Such tests turn teachers and principals toward teaching to the test, and cov-
erage-oriented curriculum. And it leaves the authentic tasks, the kind that
engage students, behind.

The implications of the realities of KERA and KIRIS outlined in this volume point to important lessons:

1. Nationally we need to be clear about what it is we want from our
   students. If we want to see the skills they have developed, then we
   need to test for those. For years, the American educational community has succumbed to old criteria for reliability and validity and
   valued those over tests that allow us to know more about our students actual performance.
2. We need to think very seriously about what we mean by high stakes.
   Nothing will be gained if schools that have always had fewer
   resources and students with greater need are penalized.
3. The stakes need to ensure potential for positive growth. We need to
   develop criteria for supporting schools in crisis that are in keeping
   with good research practices and that simultaneously honor positive
   changes that faculty and administration were working on.
4. Teachers and principals are interested in achieving more for their
   students. Accountability systems need to harness their interest as
   well as holding them accountable. To do less is to create a system
   that feels punishing, and that diminishes incentives.

Ultimately, all of us hope that Kentucky and other states interested in serious reform will dream marvelous dreams of high-stakes accountability systems
that allow us to push all of our students toward greater competence and that will
simultaneously restore public confidence in education while enabling teachers
and administrators to feel a strong sense of accomplishment. We know that to do
so will require courage to turn away from what we've always known, to build
something that can tell us things we need to know. We need not to defer any
longer. We need solid support for real and important dreams.

Bank Street College of Education
New York City, Fall 1998

Acknowledgments

Where would we be without each other? We would like to express our deep gratitude to the contributors to this volume, all of whom took on this project with great commitment, despite being busy enough to plead overload. Sharing experiences and insights helped all of us make sense out of our reform turmoil.

Priscilla Ross and Jennie Doling at SUNY Press have been wonderfully encouraging and a joy to work with. Three anonymous reviewers provided additional insights and helped improve the work presented here by raising significant questions. Kristine Thiess at the University of Louisville did most of the tedious parts of assembling the final manuscript, always working with meticulous care and good humor. We also appreciate the cooperation of the Center for Leadership in School Reform and the Southern Maine Partnership in allowing us to include the copyrighted figures appearing in chapters 8 and 9.

We are very grateful that the Ohio Valley Supervisors Organization (OVSO) formed a study group to focus on issues of accountability and assessment. All of those sessions were stimulating and informative and spurred our work on this book. In particular, two members of that group, Steve Frommeyer and Ken Draut, have been key in helping to develop an ongoing conversation about the issues in this book.

Two administrators deserve special thanks—Dean Ray Nystrand of the School of Education at the University of Louisville for his willingness to wrestle with the ideas in this book and for his thoughtful feedback, and OVEC Executive Director John Rosati for valuing and supporting the stance of "critical friend."

Ken expresses thanks and love to his family—Ronni and Meghan—for all the sharing and caring and for understanding and nurturing his relentless pursuit of truth, justice, and an American Way. Betty Lou appreciates the support of her University of Louisville doctoral students and the local and national colleagues who responded enthusiastically to participation in this project. Her parents, Louis and Mary Whitford, have always "been there," encouraging and loving.

Finally, the two of us want to thank each other. Collaborating on a complex and controversial project like this has been work that both of us care about deeply, and we have found in each other great sources of questioning, perspective, and understanding.

Introduction

BETTY LOU WHITFORD AND KEN JONES

This book is a collection of essays, cases, and proposals focused on the effects of making high-stakes accountability the centerpiece of state-mandated education reform. In 1989, when the Kentucky Supreme Court struck down over 700 laws governing elementary and secondary education, many in the state gasped and wondered what additional surprises were in store. Would the legislature replace the existing system with more of the same? Would it be better or worse that what we had? Would poor districts gain sorely needed resources? Would wealthy districts lose? What would be the effects on school governance? On teaching and learning?

In 1990, the legislature passed a massive reform package known as KERA—the Kentucky Education Reform Act—and many in Kentucky were gleeful as a result. Reform-minded educators viewed the innovations included as progressive, even cutting edge:

- A long-needed appointed (rather than elected) chief state school officer and antinepotism measures;
- An ungraded primary program;
- A new financing formula;
- Family resource and youth service centers;
- School-based decision making councils;
- Performance assessments including group problem-solving tasks and an emphasis on writing;
- School accountability for student learning rather than for how schools and teachers were to go about the context-laden tasks of improving teaching and learning.

These changes were dramatic, putting Kentucky in the forefront of state reform. Many were proud and excited to be involved in such reforms as the eyes

1

of the nation turned toward Kentucky, a state that typically has ranked near the bottom on most measures of educational quality and near the top on factors contributing to educational failures.

In the eight years since the passage of KERA, we have had opportunities to examine closely what has become the centerpiece of Kentucky's approach to reform, high-stakes school accountability, and some of the effects that can be observed in classrooms and schools. Divided into five parts, the book presents various perspectives on this approach to accountability by considering school and classroom cases, several alternative ways of approaching accountability, some of which are in use in other regions of the country, and essay reactions offered by others actively engaged in reform from different vantage points: two researchers, a former high school principal turned national consultant, and a private foundation grantmaker.

Part I introduces issues related to accountability, assessment, and teacher commitment in an essay by the editors, Betty Lou Whitford and Ken Jones. Here we present an argument for how Kentucky's linking of performance assessment with high stakes accountability has undermined the value of performance assessment as a strategy for improving teaching and learning. This linkage, we argue, has forced compliance with several state mandates but has not developed commitment to the vision of learner-centered, performance-oriented teaching and learning described in KERA.

The six chapters in part II are drawn from long-term case studies of teachers, classrooms, and schools. They move from the classroom level (chapters 2, 3, and 4), to a high school department (chapter 5), to a whole school view of change (chapter 6), and finally to a discussion of the reactions of teachers across four districts (chapter 7). Chapter 2, by Terry I. Brooks, describes two primary teachers who work as a team with the same group of different aged children for several years. At the time of his study, Brooks had just left a deputy superintendent position in a large, urban district where he had provided support for many cutting-edge reforms. His close look at the classroom of Jodie McKnight and Demi Kidd led him to question previously held perspectives on change, which he relates following a description of the classroom. In chapter 3, Christy McGee captures how another primary teacher, veteran Katherine Alexander Futrell, has constructed teaching and learning opportunities for a multi-age, multi-ability group of children beginning in 1991, just after KERA passed. The editors contribute chapter 4 about how 27-year veteran high school mathematics teacher Mary Jo Foster's quest for better learning experiences for her students led her to focus on professional development. In chapter 5, Letitia Hockstrasser Fickel captures the professional community developed by a high school social studies department and discusses the impact of high-stakes accountability on their practice. West Middle School, a low-income urban school with its fourth principal in six years, is the focus of chapter 6, written by Jan Calvert, Donna Gaus, and Gordon Ruscoe.

Calvert is now (fall, 1998) into her fourth year as principal of the school, while Gaus and Ruscoe have served as evaluators of various reform initiatives operating in the school during Calvert's tenure. This chapter is a story of how the school's efforts at reform clashed with the state's in the context of declining test scores and state intervention. Chapter 7 comes from a longitudinal study by a team of researchers from the Appalachian Education Laboratory who have been follow-ing KERA since 1990 in 26 schools comprising four mostly rural/small town dis-tricts. Patricia Kannapel, Pam Coe, Lola Aagaard, Beverly Moore, and Cynthia Reeves report on teachers' responses to the high- stakes accountability and some of the effects they have observed.

Part III, composed of three chapters, invites the reader to leave Kentucky for a time in order to consider three alternatives to Kentucky's high-stakes approach to accountability. Linda Shelor, in chapter 8, describes a teacher appraisal system that is focused on professional growth. Early evidence from its operation in dis-tricts in several states indicates that the model is effective at building commit-ment rather than just compliance to administrative mandates. In chapter 9, David Ruff, Debra Smith, and Lynne Miller of the Southern Maine Partnership describe how performance assessment can be used effectively for accountability in a state that values local rather than centralized control. Part III concludes with chapter 10, an essay from Anne Wheelock about how states might share power with local districts in a model of accountability that blends professional needs with state management responsibilities.

For part IV, we invited reactions to the first three parts of the book from a thoughtful group of individuals with different perspectives, all vitally engaged in education reform. In chapter 11, Jon Snyder discusses accountability by analyz-ing the book's cases and proposals. Currently director of teacher education at the University of California–Santa Barbara and senior researcher for the National Commission on Teaching and America's Future, Synder has written extensively about education reform and accountability. The views of a private foundation grantmaker, A. Richardson Love Jr., constitute chapter 12. As education pro-gram director for the John S. and James L. Knight Foundation, Love has closely observed KERA as a funder for a curriculum and staff development program used extensively in Kentucky primary classrooms since 1990 called *Different Ways of Knowing*. Marilyn Hohmann's reaction is presented in chapter 13. Cur-rently a senior consultant with the Center for Leadership in School Reform, she served from 1986 to 1996 as the principal a low-wealth high school at the fore-front of secondary school reform nationally. Dick Corbett is a veteran education researcher and author of numerous articles and books dealing with reform. The contributor of chapter 14, he is most concerned with looking inside schools and classrooms to determine the effects of reform on students.

The book concludes with another essay by the editors. In chapter 15, we recap some of the positive and negative effects we have observed to date with

Kentucky's reforms and, drawing on the cases, proposals, and reactions presented in the book, we propose an approach to accountability that we believe has promise for Kentucky and elsewhere.

Two additional introductory comments are in order. The first concerns confusion that has existed in Kentucky—and elsewhere—regarding significant distinctions between *KERA*—the comprehensive education reform legislation passed in 1990—and *KIRIS*—the assessment and accountability system devised in response to KERA that, in the words of state education leaders, was to "drive" reform of teaching in the state. A hallmark of KERA was a new vision of teaching and learning: they were to be performance-oriented. Curriculum was to be determined largely by school councils, those closest to the students, with advice from curriculum experts at the state level. Teachers and their students were to focus on how students might demonstrate what they could do with their knowledge—eventually defined broadly as a list of 57 "academic expectations." They would do this through various performances that were to be incorporated into the daily teaching and learning in Kentucky classrooms. They were to focus on a full range of thinking—recall, application, and problem solving as well as evaluation, integration, and synthesis of knowledge. It would follow that student assessment in the classroom should be performance-based.

Consistent with this approach to teaching and learning, KERA mandated that student assessment for the state accountability test was to be primarily performance-based. In the early stages of KIRIS, there was an emphasis on performance assessment. Parts of the test that were less performance-oriented were labeled "transition" items—the transition would eventually be totally to a "portfolio environment." The individual student assessments were aggregated to determine a school score, which in turn became part of an accountability index. The index was then used to determine how much gain the school was to make during the next cycle to gain cash rewards and avoid state sanctions.

This complex process is explained more fully both in chapter 1 and in chapter 7. The point here is that the emphasis placed on the accountability index and its rewards and sanctions for teachers and administrators led many in the state to equate *accountability* with KIRIS *assessment*. The emphasis in KERA on performance assessment easily became intermeshed with the emphasis in KIRIS on accountability and assessment that, over time, became less and less performance-oriented. This in turn led many in Kentucky to use interchangeably the terms accountability and assessment well as the terms KIRIS and KERA, blurring the distinctions that were clear in the early 1990s. This blurring of meanings is sometimes reflected in the cases presented here.

The second introductory comment that is significant to this book is that since these chapters were drafted, the state legislature has responded to the considerable dissatisfaction with KIRIS by passing a bill in the spring of 1998 mandating a new testing and accountability system. Although many decisions have yet to be made, the direction of the coming changes has been set. KIRIS has been discontinued and will be replaced with the Commonwealth Accountability Testing System (CATS). While the high-stakes nature of KIRIS has been retained, there will be even less emphasis on performance assessment in CATS—fewer entries in the writing portfolio will be required, the math portfolio has been dropped, and a standardized multiple-choice test has been incorporated into the testing system. The reader is cautioned to keep in mind, however, that the research presented in this book deals with conditions as they existed during KIRIS and its various iterations between 1990 and 1998. The lessons from Kentucky about using performance assessment for high-stakes accountability remain and can provide guidance to policymakers in Kentucky and other states as they struggle with balancing the state's need for accountability with the context-laden decisions teachers and administrators must make to improve teaching and learning for all children. Readers interested in current information about the state's testing program are encouraged to visit the web site for the Kentucky Department of Education at http://www.kde.state.ky.us.

Part I

Overview

1

Kentucky Lesson

How High Stakes School Accountability Undermines a Performance-Based Curriculum Vision

BETTY LOU WHITFORD AND KEN JONES

Kentucky has made a name for itself in the recent standards-based school reform movement. In 1990, the state legislature passed the Kentucky Education Reform Act (KERA), which established a sweeping set of reforms and called for performance-based state testing to be used to hold schools accountable. As this approach to school improvement has become more and more commonplace around the United States, Kentucky is often cited as a model that the rest of the country can learn from. After eight years, an important question is: what lessons can be learned from Kentucky's experiences?

Indeed, KERA broke new ground in terms of putting together a whole package of reform initiatives, an approach commonly called systemic reform. The premise of systemic reform is that school improvement is a complex undertaking and that a multitude of interconnected facets of schooling need to be addressed in concert. As enacted in 1990, KERA included an appointed, rather than elected education commissioner, an ungraded primary program replacing grades K–3, school-based decision-making councils, a new financing formula designed to improve equity of resources, preschools, technology, extended school services, regional service centers, family resource and youth service centers in schools with economically disadvantaged students, and a new approach toward assessment and accountability.

Predictably, implementation of this ambitious agenda has not occurred without problems. Some can be attributed to the lack of precedent for such a reform agenda. Other problems arose because little piloting was done, development of common understandings of the rationales behind the reforms was lagging, while the timelines were unforgiving.

Most stressful of all, schools were held accountable almost immediately through a new form of testing intended to measure the improvement of student performance according to new goals and expectations. This testing system, called the Kentucky Instructional Results Information System (KIRIS) quickly became a source of great misunderstanding and controversy. It became so high profile that it is has often been virtually identified by many people—teachers, parents, and community members alike—as KERA itself. Asking someone about KERA invariably draws a response about KIRIS.

And no wonder. The high stakes has commanded everyone's attention. KIRIS was designed to turn the results of student performance assessment into a school score for the state to use to determine rewards or sanctions for teachers and school administrators. If the score exceeded the state's expectation for a school, those teachers received substantial salary bonuses. If the score was not high enough or did not *continually* improve in each two-year measurement cycle, the teachers and administrators were placed on probation and the school taken over by the state.

Kentucky, through KIRIS, has been testing the combination of two distinct education reform approaches: performance-based instruction and assessment of students, a strategy embraced enthusiastically by many reform-minded educators, and a high-stakes accountability system thought by many to be necessary to persuade teachers to try new instructional practices. It is becoming increasingly clear that this linkage undermines the instructional benefits of student performance assessment, forcing teachers to focus on whatever is thought to raise test scores rather than on instruction aimed at addressing individual student needs.

The Evolution of KIRIS

The central and clearly stated belief underlying KERA is that all students can learn at high levels. This view of the school's mission is a dramatic shift from the factory model of teaching, testing, arraying students across the A-B-C-D-F grading scale, and moving on to the next section of curriculum. Rather, under KERA, schools are now to ensure learning, not just teaching.

The student learning goals of KERA emphasize new instructional approaches that require problem solving, reasoning, and communication in real-life situations, what is often called *authentic* teaching and learning. This approach, in turn, requires an assessment system designed to go beyond traditional standardized testing which does little to address such authentic skills. Thus, to evaluate the degree of progress toward the goal of success for all students, KERA mandated the development of a new testing system that would be "primarily performance based."

The law also specified that this performance-based approach to assessment would be coupled with a high-stakes school accountability system, intended to compel teachers to embrace the use of performance assessment and compatible instructional strategies and materials in order to enable all students to learn at high levels. How has this reform strategy played out over time?

At best, the evolution of KIRIS in the past six years reveals how initial plans, especially those developed in a complex, systemic reform effort, need revision when tested in the real world. At worst, the story is a powerful lesson about how such a high-stakes accountability system can distort and undermine original assumptions and visions for effective curriculum, instruction, and assessment practices. Changes in the state's KIRIS policy and practices have been influenced by six connected elements: outcome definition, student assessment, local control of curriculum, accountability index, expected rate of improvement, and rewards and sanctions.

Outcome Definition

The state-defined outcomes originally focused on six "learning goals." These stated that students should be able to:

1. Use basic communication and mathematics skills for purposes and situations they will encounter throughout their lives;
2. Apply core concepts and principles from mathematics, the sciences, the arts, the humanities, social studies, practical living studies, and vocational studies to situations they will encounter throughout their lives;
3. Become self-sufficient individuals;
4. Become responsible members of a family, work group, or community;
5. Think and solve problems in school situations and in a variety of situations they will encounter in life;
6. Connect and integrate experiences and new knowledge from all subject matter fields with what they have previously learned and build on past learning experiences to acquire new information through various media sources.

These six goals were then elaborated into 75 "valued outcomes" which were meant to serve as the basis of KIRIS. After KIRIS testing was developed and implemented in the first two-year cycle, the "valued outcomes" came under intense scrutiny from various public factions. To make them more acceptable, the State Board of Education decided that Goals 3 and 4 and corresponding outcomes—concerning self sufficiency and responsible group membership—were not "academic" enough and would not be assessed. Many others were rephrased, and the remaining 57 outcomes were rechristened "academic expectations."

It also became clear that the broadly-stated outcomes did little to reveal what content would be tested. Indeed, even in the state curriculum framework published in 1993, the state deliberately left unstated what exactly would be tested in order to honor the local role for curriculum development given by the KERA statute. Not surprisingly, a high-stakes assessment addressing content knowledge created increasing demands for a more precise state document that would identify not only what content would be tested (content standards) but also how well students would be expected to demonstrate command of that content (performance standards). By June 1996, the state responded with a draft of content standards in a document titled *Core Content for KIRIS Assessment*.

Student Assessment

As noted, KERA specified that the new assessment system should be "primarily performance-based." Work on creating such an assessment proceeded before much attention was given to defining content beyond the broadly stated outcomes. Prior even to the development of the state curriculum framework, a battery of state committees with strong teacher representation began composing test items in various formats: multiple-choice (later dropped); performance events (group problem-solving tasks); and open-response questions requiring short, on-demand written responses, given and scored under controlled circumstances. Guidelines for a writing portfolio, and later a mathematics portfolio, were constructed with specific scoring criteria. Both portfolios were to contain a student's best work rather than show progress over time.

As the system has evolved, certain effects have become visible. Given the high-stakes accountability involved, scoring reliability has become an overriding consideration. Open-response questions have clearly become the most reliable of the formats. Performance events, which were largely untried, have proven to be quite difficult to score reliably. Portfolios have yet to achieve a level of scoring reliability deemed acceptable for a high-stakes system, although there is evidence that the writing portfolio has resulted in more students writing more often (Appalachia Educational Laboratory, 1996).

Open-response questions, the most reliable format to score, have been given the greatest weight in the accountability index—the score each school receives. As a result, they have become a primary focus for most schools. Professional development activities across the state have focused on this format, and checklists for students to follow in answering these questions have become a standard fixture in classrooms.

Over the course of KIRIS testing, the increasing pressure for higher reliability and tighter alignment with a specified body of content, brought on by the high-stakes purpose of the state testing, has translated into a shift away from "open-endedness" and performance in the assessments. The logic is clear. The more open and performance-based an assessment is, the more variety in responses; the more variety there is, the more judgment is involved in scoring. The more judgment involved, the lower the reliability. Hence, less open-endedness and less performance.

During the 1996-98 biennium, multiple choice items were reintroduced, performance events discontinued, and the mathematics portfolio removed from the accountability index. According to many teachers, the open-response items themselves appeared to be more centered on "correct" answers, making them less and less "open."

Local Control of Curriculum

The KERA mandate for school-based decision-making councils (SBDM) was intended to change the balance of power between schools, their district authorities, and the state. An often-heard rationale was that those closest to the work should be empowered to make decisions about the best way to conduct that work. In particular, one of the most important functions given to councils was the right to determine the school's curriculum. In 1994, the state Supreme Court upheld this right.

By making schools as a whole accountable for student performance with KIRIS, the state created a need for school councils to overcome the common history of isolated teacher decision-making and to articulate a schoolwide approach to curriculum. Many state education leaders hoped that councils would be a powerful vehicle to focus schoolwide instruction on the state outcomes and on performance-based assessment.

However, school councils were not mandated for immediate implementation and have only been required for most schools since 1996. Those councils that have been in operation for a few years are only beginning to address matters of curriculum. For the most part, they are enacting policies intended to ensure that the school teaches the content and format of KIRIS. With the recent state publication of the *Core Content for KIRIS Assessment*, it is likely that more and more councils will simply decide that this document should be the basis of school curricula.

A further constraint to local curriculum development has been added by the growing state and district requirement for each school to have an improvement plan, once called the School Transformation Plan (STP), since 1997 part of a district process called Consolidated Planning. Required of schools that do not meet their target scores and for any school or district applying for state grant funds, this plan focuses curriculum, instruction, and funding tightly on the KIRIS assessment. Virtually all schools and districts are developing Consolidated Plans.

Thus, there has been a rebound effect. Pressure generated by the state test for high-stakes accountability has led school-based educators to pressure the state to be more explicit about content that will be tested. This in turn has constrained local school decision-making about curriculum. This dialectic has worked to increase the state control of local curriculum.

Accountability Index

Kentucky's accountability system is noted for translating student performance assessment results into school scores to determine a school's degree of improvement. Essentially, school quality is judged by how well students do on the state test.[1]

KERA required that the state department of education create an accountability index that would indicate student success rate. The state department, in cooperation with its testing contractor, developed a formula that aggregates the scores of students on the various components of KIRIS. Each year, a school receives a numerical score figured to the tenth of a decimal place.

It is important to note that KIRIS is designed to provide information for school accountability, not *student* accountability. This is primarily because there are not enough test items in any given subject area to assess individuals. (Despite this, individual scores on portfolios and open-response items are sent to parents.) State officials and the testing contractor have argued that open-response questions are valid at the school level because of matrix sampling, a technique that aggregates a larger number of subject-specific questions from multiple test forms. The lack of *student validity* means that the testing program also lacks student accountability, another source of frustration among teachers and administrators trying to convince students to take the test seriously when there is nothing at stake for them as individuals.

Perhaps the most significant controversy has arisen from the fact that, in determining whether or not a school is making progress, different cohorts of students have been tested each year. That means, for example, that one group of fourth graders gets compared with another group of fourth graders. This results in a circumstance where schools are judged—and rewarded or sanctioned—not by the improvement that individual students show over time but by how one group in the school compares with another. This practice is particularly problematic in small schools where differences in cohorts of fourth graders, for example, are likely to be greater than in large schools, thus affecting test scores more dramatically.

State officials have made some adjustments to address these problems. For example, testing has been spread over more grades, ensuring a larger sample size. And, to improve validity at the student level, more open-response questions have been counted in the student scores. The 1998 legislative session called for a new longitudinal component that compares test results for the same students over time, a process to be developed by the state board of education within the next year.

Expected Rate of Improvement

Creating the formula for establishing school threshold scores—the score each school must meet or exceed every two years to be rewarded and avoid sanctions—was an especially thorny problem. The outcomes were new, the assessments were new, the accountability system was new. Thus, there were no empirical data to suggest what might be reasonable to expect in terms of improvement. As a result, the formula had to be based on something other than empirical evidence.

State education leaders decided, based on the "all students can learn at high levels" premise, that in twenty years, schools must register a score of at least proficient, defined numerically as 100 out of 140 possible points. By that time, the argument went, all students would have experienced a KERA-based school system from beginning to end.

This reasoning then led to the following method for determining a school's threshold score. Since there are 10 two-year cycles in a 20-year span, in each cycle schools must gain one tenth of the difference between its first baseline score and the target of 100. Thus, if a school originally scored 30 in 1992, its baseline was 30 and its target for 1994 was 37 (i.e., 70 remaining to get to 100, divided by 10 cycles, yields an expected growth of 7). Each school is expected to reach or exceed its target during each two-year cycle. (Current discussions in state policy circles indicate that this biennial reckoning will be replaced by establishing a straight line from the present to the goal of 100 so that the numerical performance target for every two-year cycle is known well in advance.)

To say that teachers and school administrators feel that this projection to a score of 100 is an arbitrary expectation is an enormous understatement. The assumption of a linear rate of growth, cycle after cycle, towards total "proficiency" in 20 years has not been well accepted, to say the least. Along with the testing of different cohorts, this approach to determining target scores accounts for much of the lack of credibility in the system voiced by many educators.

Rewards and Sanctions

The use of external rewards and sanctions has been basic to KIRIS. Many in the state legislature and the public apparently believe that rewards and sanctions will work to improve schools in one of two ways. Teachers will teach better knowing they can receive a cash bonus (which can exceed $2,000 per teacher) for higher student test scores. Or, teachers will teach better knowing that if student performance does not improve, they will be sanctioned in various ways. Schools not meeting their target scores receive "assistance" in the form of a state-mandated improvement plan and the services of a "distinguished educator" or, as the position was renamed by the 1998 legislature, a "highly skilled certified educator." For the first time, in 1996, nine schools were declared "in crisis" for insufficient improvement in test scores. In these cases, the "distinguished educators" assumed control of the schools. Significantly, five of these schools were "in rewards" two years prior to this because they had exceeded their target scores. Several of the schools are small, with 120–200 students.

In such a context, schools are intensely involved in the pursuit of higher test scores. Everywhere, teachers are using KIRIS-style open-response questions in their classrooms. Some are targeting small groups of students for extra practice on the test formats in efforts to gain greater leverage on the school's score. Test-taking strategies such as restating the question, giving at least three examples, and writing longer rather than shorter responses are commonly viewed as ways to increase scores. There is also considerable push to "align curriculum" by concentrating on covering the state's *Core Content for KIRIS Assessment*. One regional resource teacher describes how teaching test-taking skills has loomed larger in the curriculum:

> The focus teachers have developed is on what can we do—what kind of tricks can we play—to fix this quick. What can we do in a quick and efficient manner to get our kids to do well on this test? They want me to show them how to "do" open response questions, not how to develop instructional strategies. . . . Teachers show the students a technique for answering these questions, usually the four-column method,[2] and they practice that method over and over and over again. They think teaching test-taking skills is what will work. And, the thing is, they've seen that it has worked in some schools. . . . One time, after spending two days practicing open response questions, a student asked me, "Could you just tell me why this is all we do? This is the third one of these I've done today. All our teachers practice this with us all the time. They do it on every unit test, they do it two or three times a week. I don't understand why we do this all the time. I don't understand why this is what school is all about. I want to know when we're going to learn something." . . . I see it in every school I go into.

Effects of KIRIS

Based on these developments, what can we say about the effects of linking performance assessment with high-stakes accountability? It is not yet possible to determine if KIRIS has improved student learning. Differences in a school's score could be attributable to many factors other than changes in student learning—for example, better test taking skills, school size, whether the content tested has actually been taught, the degree to which teachers have changed their practice, changes in cohorts tested. However, some trends bear mentioning. Extensive classroom-based research is needed to discover how widespread these trends may be.

Teacher-Student Relationship

Many consider the quality of the teacher-student interaction to be the heart of the matter concerning how well students learn. A good deal of theory, research, and documented practice suggest that thinking and learning are enhanced in constructivist classrooms where teachers know their students well and have the expertise to diversify instruction to meet varying student needs, include student interests and appropriate student choice in curricular decisions, promote social interaction and collaboration, and foster problem-solving and inquiry. In order to develop such learning environments, teachers must have the professional knowledge and power to make decisions and judgments regarding curriculum and instruction for particular groups of students.

Yet, as we have argued, Kentucky's accountability system has undermined such decision making at the school level, a condition the KERA-mandated school councils were meant to nurture. Instead of giving local schools and teachers a greater say in curriculum, the accountability system is inexorably driving the creation of a de facto state curriculum. While many educators do not trust the tests, they will continue to pressure the state to be more and more precise about what will be tested, given the high-stakes accountability.

While some welcome the development of such standardization, others recognize that the more the curriculum is specified and defined externally, the more the role of the teacher becomes that of the technician, expected to put into play decisions made by others outside the school. This is true whether the external source is the state, a textbook company, or a standardized test. In each case, professional judgment is curtailed. Teachers are to deliver knowledge and skills determined by others, not decide what is best for individual students. This inhibits the need for productive teacher-student relationships by creating a model that is counterproductive to constructivist learning. How can we expect students to be problem-solvers, thinkers, and decision makers when we do not expect the same from teachers?

Teacher-student relationships have been compromised in another way because of the accountability system. By making teachers, not students, accountable for student test results, teachers are assumed to be fully in control of their students' learning. This posture further assumes that the solutions to bringing about higher quality for all students are already known; they only have to be *implemented*, not *invented*. This view, in turn, promotes relationships based on control and manipulation rather than joint learning endeavors among teachers and between teachers and students.

Hence, there is a trickle-down effect. As teachers are subjected to rewards and sanctions, so do they treat their students. Great pressure is put on students to do well on the KIRIS test. Many schools have developed systems of external rewards for students who take the test seriously. It has become the norm rather than the exception that students, just like their teachers, resent the test, treating it as an unwelcome but required ordeal. How ironic and unfortunate that a form of assessment meant to engage students in more meaningful work is so dreaded.

Instructional Practices

A second effect is that the emerging state curriculum increasingly stresses learning that can be measured reliably and validly. What can be measured reliably and validly becomes what is important to know. It literally becomes "what counts" in determining whether or not a school is performing as the state thinks it should. While perhaps not the direction intended when state officials expressed the point of view that assessment should "drive" curriculum, this measurement orientation is nonetheless becoming the reality as psychometric concerns increasingly restrict assessments to what can be easily measured and scored rather than more open-ended demonstrations of what students can do with their knowledge. Some, in fact, argue that KIRIS has essentially evolved into a system that is not "primarily performance-based" as KERA mandated. In the 1998 legislative session, that mandate was, in fact, deleted.

As the test relies more on items with higher scoring reliability, it is less likely that KIRIS will "drive" teaching and learning toward constructivist, performance-based classrooms. The mandated portfolios have been considered powerful levers for instructional change, yet even with them, it is common practice for teachers to simply "add-on" portfolio prompts, without significantly changing routine classroom practice, by declaring "portfolio days" or giving prompts as homework. Such an adding-on strategy is even easier and more commonplace with the short open-response items.

With the possible exception of the writing portfolio, there is little evidence to suggest that teachers have incorporated the principles of performance assessment into their ongoing practice (Kentucky Insitute for Education Research, 1995). Thus, while the accountability system has gotten teachers' attention, there is little evidence to show that it has substantially altered either classroom practice or the relationships between and among students and teachers toward a more performance-oriented environment. A recent study of KIRIS suggests that there is a good chance the test score gains observed to date are the result of students getting better at taking the test rather than actually demonstrating improved learning (Hambleton et al., 1995).

It is doubtful that these instructional issues can be resolved with better psychometric techniques alone. A more fundamental problem is that using performance assessment as the primary basis for high-stakes accountability compromises the very nature of performance assessment. Performance assessment, based as it is on context and judgment, is well suited for improving student learning in the classroom, but at least in a high-stakes environment, they are not so well suited for producing scores to be used in external evaluations of schools.

Performance assessments that improve learning are focused on individual children as they demonstrate what they are learning through their writing, reading, speaking, facility with numbers, group skills, individual initiative and so on. The assessment is of a single child's work, assumed to be a demonstration of what he or she knows and is able to do. It often involves the learner in self-assessment, and it is done to help the child, the teacher, and parents understand what a child is doing and what the child might do to improve. Such assessments are not intended to be aggregated since they are directed toward individuals.

Because the emphasis is on the quality of unique, student-generated responses, performance assessment depends upon the exercise of professional judgment, both in design of tasks and evaluation of student responses. As a child's work is evaluated against a set of explicit criteria, often called rubrics, the evaluator—most often a teacher or coach—is making a judgment. Judgments by their very nature vary depending on who is judging. An office worker's performance might be judged differently by different bosses; surgeons make different recommendations based on the same diagnostic evidence; likewise, what a student might do to improve performance can vary across teachers.

For example, a teacher might listen to a child read and make suggestions about what the child should read next. The recommendation might be based on interest expressed by the child and also skills the child needs to develop. Teachers who are experts in children's literature will know some books to recommend, but the specific recommendation might vary by teacher. Further, the particular judgments and recommendations are responsive to specific learning contexts and dependent on knowing individual students and their experiences well. They are not necessarily generalizable for all students. What is important is that individual teachers need to be informed and capable enough to make wise professional judgments on behalf of their students.

To use performance assessment to improve learning, Wiggins argues that a number of principles must be followed: assessment must flow from the immediate curriculum; students must know what the standards for performance are; and feedback must be immediate and specific (Wiggins, 1993). A state system devoted to aggregating student results in order to produce an annual accountability score for schools does little to address such principles.

Thus, the Kentucky linkage of high-stakes accountability to performance assessment is an ill-fated marriage. As policy makers have emphasized accountability, the performance-oriented nature of KIRIS has receded. The two approaches—high-stakes accountability and performance assessment—are based on conflicting principles. One encourages conformity to externally imposed standards while the other grows out of emergent interactions among teachers and students in dynamic local classrooms.

Teacher Morale

One final trend is important to note based on our experience with Kentucky teachers and principals. The morale of school-based educators is on the downswing. Conversations tend to focus on what is lacking in students rather than on their strengths. Attention is on what the state demands more than on what the student needs. More and more teachers talk about the enormous pressure they are living with. They look and act tired. The sense of efficacy is on the wane as teachers struggle with the insecurity of not knowing how to keep getting higher and higher test scores, especially as their students come to them with increasing social and personal problems.

State policymakers subscribe to the theory that rewards and sanctions are necessary incentives to bring out the best work in people. One might question if that is what is happening in Kentucky. People talk little about the rewards. One central office assessment coordinator, in fact, noted recently that rewards seem to have a negative effect, saying that even the teachers in his "reward schools" did not feel a sense of joy or accomplishment.

Sanctions have had much more of an effect. The fear of being labeled negatively is heavy in the air. Now that the state has followed through with Distinguished Educators (DEs) taking over schools, there are real examples of impact that feed these fears. One principal spoke recently about the effect of the state sanctions on his school. Notably, his school has been at both ends of the spectrum, once categorized in "rewards" then later placed in "crisis."

> The system itself needs to be called into question. Once we got the label of "crisis," people really treated us differently. Some stayed away from you or came to you almost like there was a death in the family or something. Their perception was that your place was falling apart and you were doing a terrible job and gosh, I hope things get better for you. . . . I believe there was a fishing expedition from the Department of Education going on to find out what major flaw existed in our school to justify the crisis label that the test gave us. That's a part of the problem with the DE program. It's kind of a shame because instead of the support program that it might be, it wasn't that way. It was, "We've got to find a problem here so we can fix it." . . . No one wants their school or their work to be viewed by the public as inadequate. And you get that

from the community, by your colleagues in other schools, by the State Department, by visitors. My folks felt the cold shoulder from the Department, just like I did. They felt relationships change between people. They knew that they weren't perceived as being good teachers anymore, even though two years ago, when we were in rewards, the Department was sending us visitors to see what we were doing that was so great. That's painful. The system affected their hearts. It hurt their belief in themselves, no doubt about it. . . . And it changed the work they did with the kids, not for the better. Because the system is all about improving test scores, they stopped doing things for kids that they wanted to do. We lost a lot of great integrated curriculum stuff that was really turning kids on when the DEs took over, because that was all seen as not necessary. The DEs told us not to do that stuff, to concentrate instead on the content areas for the assessment. . . . You know, if you're doing work that you want to do, it almost doesn't seem like work. But when you've got the Department telling you what you have to do, it seems like twice the amount of work than it really is. We are pushing more papers, and there is definitely more work because of the need that the DEs have for documentation. But it also seems a lot heavier, because it's someone else's work, you know?

Alternative Approaches

Kentucky's accountability approach has undermined the very changes in teaching and learning that it was intended to promote, calling into question the use of performance assessment for high-stakes accountability. These conditions require that the state take some corrective action, replacing what is an arbitrary, punitive, control-oriented system with one that is more collaborative, professional, and improvement-oriented.

At present, Kentucky policymakers are choosing high-stakes accountability over performance assessment. While some education leaders privately acknowledge that the high-stakes system has unintended, dysfunctional consequences, they quickly add that the political environment will not permit backing away from it.

Improving the existing system is the approach taken by the legislature in the 1998 session. We believe, however, that the current accountability approach is fundamentally flawed and that school reform will not progress without major changes in it. Accountability that reduces school quality to a numeric formula is oversimplified and ill-suited to evaluating many important aspects of schooling. In fact, it contradicts the very premise behind systemic reform that school improvement is complex and requires multiple, interlocking components. What is true about systemic reform in general is also true about accountability systems in particular. A simple scoring mechanism just will not do. What is needed is a "next generation" of thinking about what school accountability means.

We agree that schools should be accountable, in fact, more accountable than they have been with KIRIS. Specifically, what schools are asked to account for should be broadened beyond student outcome measures to include professional practices and equity issues such as opportunities to learn. A school quality review process including school self-evaluations and periodic site visits is an appropriate means for developing and reporting such components of a school's practice. Efforts in this regard, based to some extent on the British inspectorate model, are being tried or considered in various places, including southern Maine, New York, Rhode Island, Illinois, and Oregon. Also, the National Study for School Evaluation, an organization of regional school accreditation associations, is currently enlisting its members to develop new indicators of school quality beyond simply counting inputs or aggregating outcomes.

Moving to such an accountability model would necessitate de-emphasizing high-stakes since no school visitation would reveal realities or foster improvement if it were perceived as a police action. Indeed, this model depends upon the repositioning of the state away from bureaucratic control toward providing support, an intended direction for the state Department of Education just after KERA was enacted. The posture that many reform strategies describe for teachers and administrators—facilitation and shared leadership—should be adopted by the government itself since mandates and coercion will undermine school quality review processes just as surely as they undermine performance assessment. As McLaughlin and others have argued, "You can't mandate what matters" (McLaaughlin, 1990).

A longer-range strategy needed to support additional school improvement is the shift away from bureaucratic control to professional accountability—that which guides and improves responsible practice (Darling-Hammond et al., 1993). For both student learning and professional practice to improve, bureaucratic control and teacher compliance are not enough and alone are wrong-headed. Rather, educators must be supported for working together to continuously invent new approaches to ensuring learning for all students. For this to occur, policymakers and education leaders must inspire commitment, not just compliance.

Inspiring commitment rather than compliance means that teacher preparation and continuing professional development must also improve. There is some evidence that school-university collaboration can improve teacher preparation, and teacher networks can provide much needed assistance for improving professional development. Other forms of ongoing professional support are needed as well that are explicitly designed to address the goal of ensuring learning for all students. In Kentucky, steps in that direction may have started with the state's commitment to implement the recommendations of the National Commission on Teaching and America's Future, which include strong support for professional practice (National Commission on Teaching and America's Future, 1996).

As such support increases in the state, professional accountability must also increase. Such an approach would include honoring the principles of performance-based assessment, reflection, and self-improvement, and the informed use of professional judgment to decide on matters of curriculum and instruction to best suit the learning needs of individual students.

If the purpose of accountability is to improve teaching and learning, then the methods of accountability must suit that purpose. In Kentucky, this means that the school accountability index, together with the rewards and sanctions, should give way to a more inclusive and collaborative accountability system that would include qualitative as well as quantitative information. In effect, it means that high-stakes accountability must be transformed into *high-resolution* accountability, where the level of detail provided matches the degree of complexity inherent in schools and the learning of individual children.

High-stakes accountability in Kentucky has focused attention on important questions about teaching and learning. But it has not and cannot supply the answers to those questions. Those must come from the responses of teaching professionals, released from the narrow constraints of a bureaucratically controlled, high-stakes testing system. In order to allow that, those who hold power over schools must move from a controlling role into a collaborative one.

Notes

1. "Noncognitive" factors—attendance, retention, dropout rates, and transition to postsecondary life-are also factored into the formula but about 85% of the score comes from student test scores.

2. The "four column method" is a prewriting technique developed by state Distinguished Educators as an approach to answering KIRIS open-response questions.

References

Appalachia Educational Laboratory. (1996). Five years of reform in rural Kentucky. *Notes from the Field: Educational Reform in Rural Kentucky, 5*(1). Charleston, WV: Appalachia Educational Laboratory.

Darling-Hammond, L. et al. (1993) *Creating learner-centered accountability.* New York: National Center for Restructuring Education, Schools, and Teaching.

Hambleton, R. et al. (1995). *Review of the measurement quality of the Kentucky Instructional Results Information System 1991–1994.* Frankfort, KY: Office of Educational Accountability.

Kentucky Institute for Education Research. (1995, August). *The implementation of performance assessment in Kentucky classrooms*. Frankfort, KY: Kentucky Institute for Education Research.

McLaughlin, M. (1990, December). The Rand Change Agent Study revisited: Macro perspectives, micro realities. *Educational Researcher 19*(9), 11–16.

National Commission on Teaching and America's Future. (1996). *What matters most: Teaching for America's future*. New York: National Commission on Teaching and America's Future.

Wiggins, G. (1993). *Assessing student performance: Exploring the purpose and limits of testing*. San Francisco: Jossey-Bass.

Part II

Inside Schools and Classrooms

2

Constructs from the Classroom

A Perspective on Reform

TERRY I. BROOKS

Scenes from the Northtop Elementary School

Vignette I

I, a visitor, enter the faculty restroom of the Northtop Elementary and am taken aback. The smell of cigarettes is pungent. This is a district that has rejected the federal ban about tobacco on school premises. After all, the district, according to the head of the local Farm Bureau, is "not about to hurt the farmers whose tobacco paid for those buildings just to make Washington happy." There are the trappings of every faculty restroom—a faded floral arrangement, a crocheted Kleenex box which looks like an artifact from a long-ago Fall Festival craft booth, and the omni-present government issued military green garbage can. However, there is a distinctive wall in this cramped little room—what the school's professional development committee chair calls "our professional development learning center." A bright piece of bulletin board backing is festooned with an array of yellow "post-its." A small table sits next to the sink. It holds a stack of professional journals, an "artist-in-residence" grant application, the minutes from the school's last site council meeting, and a small "honey-roasted" nuts can filled with pens and markers. A sign wrapped around the can cajoles, "Keep our restroom current!" Some of the posted "stick 'ems" are in answer to printed question tags—"How are you scrimmaging for performance tests?" Others are in response to hand-written queries—"What is something new to do for the 101st day of school?"; "B.J. and Sarah are still going too fast for me to keep up with. Help—does anybody have stations prepared on different number systems?" The backing paper holds notices about an upcoming Professional Development School session with another school as well as congratulatory notes to two teachers at the school for an award. Another post-it declares, "We're going for that University of Louisville action research grant. Is anybody else 'up' for joining?" I ask the professional development chair about all of this interior decorating. She laughs, "That's where women teachers read too. Can you think of a better spot to capture a captive audience?"

Vignette II

The school and the classroom in particular have been staggered by the flu. In a school where attendance routinely exceeds 96%, attendance is barely running at 80%. In Demi and Jodie's classroom, the remaining remnant of healthy students are going about their tasks with the stylistic norms of quiet chatter, informality of movement, and an attitude of purpose. Suddenly, a student becomes ill—very ill. The teachers have on their hands what Jodie describes as "one of those primary classroom throw-ups." The ill student hears a couple of cat-calls about the incident, and then he is pelted with a crescendo of verbal jabs. The student moves from physical to emotional distress and melts into sobs and tears.

The entire incident takes but a moment. The classroom is transformed from a place filled with a busy hum to one of total silence as Jodie and Demi quietly but assertively state with seemingly one voice, "To the carpet." The students move with speed and in total silence. They "circle up" of their own accord. The two teachers move into the circle. In measured tones, they begin to ask questions. They probe. "What happened?" "How could this happen in our classroom?" "And, now, what are we going to do about it?" The focus of the conversation moves to the classroom's looming dominant sign stating "The Golden Rule." The discussion is carried forth with neither rancor nor raised tones. Students move seemingly on a spontaneous basis to surround their ill classmate who is now obviously *everyone's* very best friend as he heads for home.

And without further direction from the teachers, the students drift back to their activities. The crisis is over, but it is not forgotten. Throughout the rest of the day and for the remainder of the week, students approach me to talk about it. It continues to be the grist of class talks, informal conversations, and the glue binding student journal entries. It would have been considered a common-place interruption in some classes. It would have been considered a discipline incident to be attended to in other classes. In this classroom, it was seen as a serious threat to group morality. Such a break from the standard of moral decency is so rare in this classroom that students, parents, and other school personnel as well as Demi and Jodie still speak of it as a referent point. It personifies the hard part of this classroom's culture which protects its inhabitants from even the most minimal or routine of moral dysfunctions. It becomes part of the classroom's lore. It is a story told time and time again. Whenever someone hurts another, the answer to the question, "What is the opposite of the Golden Rule?" has become, "The Throw-Up Incident."

In themselves, the preceding vignettes are not noteworthy. Beyond the events themselves, however, they loom large in significance. They symbolize the elements that make this story of two teachers—Demi Kidd and Jodie McKnight— a tale of real education reform.

This chapter is a result of fieldwork covering one year at Northtop Elementary School. Its development is based upon that formal qualitative study. As author, I must add, however, that its content is no doubt flavored by my own autobiography. My own experience had been in a large, urban setting. The study was in a small rural one. I had spent most of my career as a middle school principal or as deputy superintendent for the 100,000 student Jefferson County (KY) Public Schools. This is a reflection on two teachers in a primary classroom. I am a male with over a quarter-century experience in schools; the teachers in the study are females in their late twenties. And yet as Marshall and Rossman (1989) acknowledge, much of my work focused on meshing academic research with personal experience. Drawing inferences, analyses, and conclusions from such work is a "messy, ambiguous, time-consuming, creative and fascinating process; it is not neat" (p. 132). Furthermore, the study takes up the challenge of Glaser and Strauss (1967) for the researcher to go beyond objective data and draw conclusions and informing nuances because he "believes in his own knowledgeability . . . and has taken special pains to discover what he thinks he may know" (pp. 224–225).

The preceding vignettes reflect both my research and my own knowledgeability as symbols to contrast what many of the nation's restructuring gurus contend make a classroom and a school work and what actually is making this one classroom—and school—work. These vignettes—and this classroom—give visitors a glimmer as to what lies beyond "the smoke and mirrors of restructuring" (Hargreaves, 1994, p. 244). Indeed, the import of this classroom is to defrock much of the nation's and the Commonwealth of Kentucky's reform agenda and to confirm Bennett's (1992, p. 71) contention that, "Educational reform is not an arcane business; it is not a matter of great complexity but one of will."

Constructs of the Classroom

In watching Demi and Jodie throughout the year; in talking with them in formal and informal settings; in garnering impressions and stories about this teaching tandem from their colleagues, their superordinates, their students, and the parents; and, in looking at harder quantitative data, I found a number of "sensitizing constructs" (Whitford, 1994) that defined these teachers' professionalism and engagement in reform. This chapter will detail three. These are the constructs that underscore who Demi and Jodie are on a personal and professional basis; they define them individually and as a team.

The First Construct: A Personalized Set of Ideas to Govern the Enterprise

The process of crafting mission and vision statements has become a nonnegotiable component of many reform efforts. In Kentucky, mission statements are to be closely aligned with the KERA academic expectations, assessment results, and emanate from a Consolidated Planning process in which a school answers over 150 questions to discover its vision, beliefs, and strategies. That approach to defining the business of the school is not unusual. In fact, the reform establishment consistently pushes mechanistic and formalized approaches to promote efficiency, effectiveness and focus. A year spent observing Demi and Jodie makes two lessons eminently clear. First of all, there is a clear set of beliefs that "govern the enterprise" (Senge, 1990, pp. 223–225). This belief framework meets corporate expectations to "capture imagination and command attention" (Deal & Kennedy, 1982, p. 21). Secondly, there is a deliberate informality about this vision and an intentional focus on personalization.

Neither a single administrator nor colleague nor parent nor Demi or Jodie themselves acknowledge a formal mission statement as having any impact upon daily life at the school or within this classroom itself. Referring to the Kentucky Department of Education, one teacher suggests that, "Mission talk is something we have to do because of Frankfort." Another Northtop teacher describes Jodie and Demi:

> They're together. We all know it. Do you know anyone actually in a classroom who goes around calling for mission statements? That's what people who don't know what's going on need so they think they know something.

Jodie and Demi's perspectives on governing ideas are themselves divergent. Demi dismissed much of such talk as "all that mumbo-jumbo of all the words that people who aren't at a school try to make us do because they read Covey's last book." It's not that she can't verbalize what their classroom is about. She reflects:

My vision is a simple bottom-line. The kids need to learn how to be happy. I want this room to be their own Disneyland. My background in acting and dancing means that imagination is important—that's Disneyland.

Jodie, on the other hand, talks with insight about strategic planning processes. "I understand mission and vision and all. Why I could even critique the Department of Education's own process. They always talk mission without vision. Shows what they know!" She ponders the world that she and Demi have built noting, "We are not going to be governed by words. We're inventing Utopia for a bit of time for our kids. That business is too urgent to get caught up in politically correct notions of vision leading to mission which leads to beliefs which leads to goals and 'yaddy dah dah'. We've got important work to be about."

Both teachers are insistent that "the real world" of their classroom is of their own making. In many ways, their sentiments confirm the recognized need for teachers to own the locus of control for reform in their classroom (Rotter, 1966; Miller, 1994). A student put it this way—"We know that our class is just ours. What we study and do and everything is up to Ms. Kidd and Ms. McKnight." Parents have picked up on the issue of locus of control as well. "With these teachers, I never get an excuse that 'So and so says we have to do it.' In fact, I have no doubt that they'd take on anybody if they thought it was the right thing to do. In my other son's class, you'd think that the teacher was Boysen (then the State Commissioner of Education). Everything is defined and defended because of KERA. Not with Jodie and Demi. They say up front, 'We do it this way because that's the way we think it needs to be done.'"

Jodie reflected both teachers' sentiments in predicting, "Demi and I many times have said that after KERA is a distant memory, we're still going to be teaching the way we're teaching now." She explained, "KERA has not touched upon my philosophy one iota. Now in many ways, we personify KERA. Don't get me wrong. I'm into that stuff, but no, I don't teach KERA. I teach what is best for kids. I'm never going to get caught making my classroom a certain way for anybody else."

A colleague's wry summary may best illustrate the recognized passion Demi and Jodie have for controlling their own classroom agenda. She says:

Those girls both have guts. They are quick to say, "No" when the rest of us lower our heads and fill out the latest KERA required form. Demi and Jodie . . . well everything they do says, "It's our room. They're our kids. So just stay out." Now I don't mean it negatively at all. No, I mean it positively. They are so committed to what they believe, they will go to the wall. They make me know that I cop-out on some things that they would just never give in on.

Along with the purposeful lack of formalization of vision and the intentionality on locus of control, a third nuance of this construct emerges—autobiography. Stanislavsky (1936) argues that a major belief that serves as a barrier to greatness on stage is the notion that acting is mainly external. The Russian director unconventionally argues that one cannot act grief-stricken or joyous without ever having experienced grief or joy. Actors, he asserts, must be autobiographical to be authentic. Ayers (1993) contends that greatness in teaching requires a serious encounter with autobiography. Rilke's (1934, p. 134) conversation with a young poet could be advising a teacher when he counsels, "Search for the reasons that bid you . . . find out whether they (the reasons) are spreading out roots in the deepest places of your heart (1934, p. 134). Demi and Jodie resonate with autobiography when they speak of their professional lives. Illustrative of this tenet is Jodie talking about her father and how he shaped her as a teacher:

> It's really weird, I guess. But my dad is who taught me what I stand for as a teacher. He is an engineer and learned through models and pictures in understanding things. When I got in middle school, he and I would get in fights—huge fights because he was always wanting me to draw a picture of what this concept or that idea meant. I'd say, "Dad, that's not how they're teaching us. I memorized this fact. I know what it means." "Well, if that's what it means, draw it for me then," he'd say. "That's not what they want me to do. I'll get an 'F' on my test doing it that way. All I have to do is to memorize it," I'd yell back. He taught me about different ways of knowing before *Different Ways of Knowing* (A multi-modality curriculum used by Demi and Jodie). He also taught me to question, question, question. I was in science class, and we were learning the transition from Fahrenheit and Celsius, and the number '32' was in the formula. I just didn't understand the whole notion of it so I asked my teacher about it. I raised my hand and said, "Mrs. So and So, why is that '32' in the formula?" She said, "Jodie, it's just in there." I said, "No, no, no. My dad told me that there is always a reason for things so there has to be a reason for that '32' in this problem. She just stared at me and said, "Well, it's there because somebody was smart enough to figure it out. Now get back to work." I remember that conversation so vividly and contrast it to my dad as a teacher. He made questioning something like a sacred obligation.

Demi as well speaks of family in terms of her teaching. She, like Jodie, also references childhood experiences as profound impacts upon her professional decisions. In fact, she references a specific experience as the catalyst for entering teaching:

> I was a senior in high school, and we had a service requirement to graduate. My service was at St. Joseph's Orphanage. I got turned on being

around these kids who were so much rougher and more worldly as ten year olds than I was as a high school senior. Simultaneously, I began teaching swimming to the upper crust of Louisville, and I found a voice of neglect for those kids too. At the time, I was going into medicine, but those two experiences with such divergent kids came together and pulled me into teaching.

Listening and watching Demi and Jodie, a visitor sees neither framed statements of mission nor ongoing mechanistic processes to originate and validate visioning. Instead, informality, internal locus of control, and autobiography influence the ideas that drive these teachers. Perhaps, they personify what Scully (cited in Peters, 1992, p. 220) contends—"a spirit and excitement that lifts the mundane to a state of exhilaration."

The Second Construct: Collegiality and Collaboration

Thinking of each other as colleagues is important because thought is participative. The simple act of thinking of others as colleagues contributes toward interacting as colleagues. This may sound simple but it makes a profound difference. . . . Treating each other as colleagues acknowledges the mutual risk and establishes the sense of safety in facing the risk. (Senge, 1990, p. 245)

Considerable research documents the impact of collaboration and collegiality in organizational life (Harris, 1981; Schumacher, 1982; Naisbitt, 1989) and in the broader society (Etzioni, 1988). Van Maanen & Barley (1984) note the impact these relationships have in the schoolhouse as they find, "A collegial environment enhances both the level of opportunity and the level of capacity for teachers because it serves as a critical, essential source of stimulation and motivation. "Commitment to high levels of performance is more easily promoted through shared professional norms than through bureaucratic sanctions and controls," Sergiovanni (1994, p. 334)—drawing from the work of Little (1981, 1982, 1987, 1990); Lieberman and Miller (1984); and, Rosenholtz (1989)—asserts. He writes of the compelling support "for the importance of collegiality in building a professional culture of teaching on one hand and in enhancing commitment and performance on the other" (p. 119). Little (1987) perceptively notes that "collegial relations and structures have proven relatively fragile . . . cooperative work among teachers is scarce, fruitless, and hard to maintain" (p. 507).

Demi and Jodie exemplify collaboration. Interestingly, they also defy this precept. In fact, both teachers are quite conscious of a parallelism that balances collaboration and individualism. "We wrap our individuality into group when it makes sense," Jodie simply states. Part of that parallelism is the complementary rather than duplicatory nature of this teaching pair. Two Northtop colleagues who are identified by both Jodie and Demi as their mentors had the following exchange:

> *Sheila*: They are alike so much. And they are different so much.
>
> *Nicole*: And the key is that they embrace both the likenesses and differences. It's like Jodie is the emotional side and Demi is the objective side.
>
> *Sheila*: Jodie will read or hear about something and then say, "Let's try it out," and then she'd want to think about it after it had happened. Demi is the opposite. Once she has analyzed and reflected and studied— it really goes on and on you know—then it's, "We can now try this."
>
> *Nicole*: They are like us in that way. Both teams have a "Go do it! And, oh, were you ready?" person and a "Ready, get set, think, get set again, and then go ahead" person.

A parent speculates about the two partners. "Demi is more introspective. I would be willing to bet that she spends a lot of time thinking about the meaning of life and her place in all of it. Demi, I think, enjoys dialogue and discussion and study for the sake of dialogue and discussion and study. Jodie, I bet, thinks about the "Who?" rather than the "Why?" For her, I'd predict reflection is valuable only if it leads to action. See how that would flow together?" Another parent observes:

> Well, you know, Demi used to be an old first grade teacher, and she is very nurturing. The little girls just flock around her. I think Jodie is more like me. She talks to children as if they were adults. She's not cold . . . she's a great kid hugger . . . but she is not as physically close to the students as Demi. When you think about your little first grader, you want to have somebody like Demi around to nurture, but when you want someone to just lay it out . . . to say to my own son, "Sam, this is how we build a topic sentence," I want a Jodie right there telling him exactly what to do. She doesn't "coddle talk" . . . she uses the vocabulary with Sam that she would use with me.

Another parent contends, "It has gotten to the point where I can tell who wrote the newsletter just by the choice of words or focus." A colleague amplifies this theme of parallelism adding, "Demi is the organization one. She keeps it running like clockwork. Jodie defers to her on that. Kidwise, I think Jodie takes the lead, and Demi is more in the background."

The nuances of this team's complementary quality aren't lost on external observers. For instance, one parent remarks, "I think an interesting difference is how they view cooperation and competition. I don't see Demi emphasizing competition as much as Jodie does." Another parent in discussing the same framework adds, "From what I know, cooperation is big part of KERA. I think Demi is like that. I also think—and my husband is empathic on this—that kids need to know how to compete. I sense Jodie takes care of that dimension." Yet a third parent raised this same strand of collaboration. Her perception is, "It is a quite conscious thing on their part to feed into that sort of yin and yang. Jodie is making a purposeful effort to teach competitive strategies. On the other hand, Demi's entire methodology is built on cooperation. They both know how to get into the guys' heads about this stuff."

If differences enhance collaborative strength, so do similarities. "It may be intelligence that binds them together," observes a senior central office administrator who has worked closely with both teachers. "They are both so sharp, they build an intellectual synergy about their work." The Northtop principal notes, "You can just tell that's what drives them. They stay late; they plan thoroughly; they seek help when they need it; they ask questions, lots of questions. That raises two other elements that hold them together so well—work ethic and intellectual curiosity."

Jodie captures the internal view of this connection. She states, "Being with Demi has allowed me to throw an idea off someone. When I taught by myself, I could try something out but essentially no one cared whether it worked or not. Nobody else even knew. It was just between me and the kids. With Demi, I have to dig deeper. Why, why am I doing this? She demands proof. That relationship makes me learn. Plus, I feel responsible toward Demi. We're partners, each filling in the others' gaps. Working with Demi has made me a more responsible teacher and has given me the courage to push limits more than I would have ever done alone."

Successful teachers must also wrestle with interpersonal dynamics. As Darling-Hammond (1994) notes, "Appreciation of what individuals can contribute to each other's education is an important aspect of a joint relationship. But appreciation doesn't happen until there is openness and trust" (pp. 210–211). The interpersonal dimension in Jodie and Demi's collaboration is clear. It is well exemplified in the following exchange:

> *Demi:* It's very important to us to face each other openly and honestly. Whether it's a good day or a bad one; whether it involves a problem or a dilemma or an idea, I have revealed myself to Jodie as openly and honestly as I can. She knows my good side and my bad side. The first six months or so, I was spending all my time and energy on impressions. What she's thinking? That was so much baggage, and communication, openness, and trust eliminated that baggage. That respect didn't just happen.
>
> *Jodie:* We have intentionally kept our relationship raw—raw in the good sense; raw in the sense that it is neither layered nor coated. Hey, this is our profession. I have had to go through some of the toughest, hardest days of my life with Demi. I mean we have gone through it—

some very, very, very scary moments. Critical times. If I really thought
about some of those times. I could start crying.

Demi: The one piece of advice I'd give to anyone trying to work
together is respect. Respect is our glue. It holds us together.

Jodie: You have to know, we were just thrown together. Neither of us
sought this team arrangement. Our respect has been grown-up and nur-
tured from ground zero. Growing within collaborative relationships is an
imperative strategy for fostering such a workplace arrangement.

A major failure in collaborative relationships is the failure to distinguish
between congeniality and collegiality. Barth (1988) notes that an acceptance of
congeniality as a collaborative strategy may, in fact, be counterproductive (p.
230). Sergiovanni (1990) states:

Congeniality and collegiality are very different. Congeniality refers to
friendly human relationships and the development of strong supporting
social norms that are independent from the standards of the teaching
profession and the purposes and work of the school. Collegiality, by
contrast, refers to sharing, helping, learning and working together in
response to supporting strong school norms that emerge from professional standards and school purposes. (p. 118)

Demi and Jodie explicitly separate the two referencing collegiality as a professional practice and congeniality as a social feature. Demi, for instance, states:

Working together frequently puts me in bed all weekend. We are so
intense professionally that we can't rely on each other socially. That
would cause stress now and ulcers someday.

Jodie concurs:

We purposefully avoid using this relationship as a social one. It's kinda
interesting. The people I talk with around school about non-school
stuff are an entirely different set than who I talk school issues with.

Other colleagues agree. One notes:

There are some social clubs around Northtop so to speak, but I don't see
Demi or Jodie belonging. It's not an "in your face" thing. The social
milieu just isn't them.

Jodie distills the distinction:

Our professional status is what counts here. I believe that mixing social
and weekend and telephone chats—all that, "Let's be best friends,
too"—diminish professional focus. We just don't do that. It's not that
there aren't people around here—and especially Demi—who couldn't

be my friends. It's just that given a choice between being "buds" and colleagues, I choose colleagues.

Networks form another perspective on the professional nature of these two teachers. Both teachers' external networks are well recognized by observers and valued by Demi and Jodie alike. Their principal observes:

> I think they are both of the opinion that they can influence the inside of their classroom by going outside of it. They talk "kids," and that's why they are such leaders outside this building. They have a lot of clout in the district and even on state committees because people listen to what they say because they back their words.

A senior district administrator confirms that observation. "The higher-level, the higher stakes committee it is, the more Jodie shines. It has reaffirmed that she has her leadership and communication tool kit together. I have remarked to several other administrators, 'She is thinking all the time.' She is the one to bring up an item all of us experienced bigshots miss. Her involvement has raised her own and her school's credibility. Demi's the same way. She came in cold as the school's professional development chair and immediately blows you away with her reflective capacity and obsession with detail. She is not afraid to pick up the phone and say, 'I'm thinking of doing this. Will you critique it?' Both of those two welcome interaction with us locally and at the state and, I guess, they're just thriving on the U of L initiative as well."

Demi and Jodie see external networking as a pragmatic resource for their classroom. For instance, Jodie recalls:

> Our entire disciplinary system is because of Ralph (the U of L professor assigned to Northtop as its Professional Development School liaison). He gave us a copy of Charney's *Just Teaching Children to Care* and boom!—I found myself reading this book going, "Yeah, yes, yes, here it is. Just what I've been looking for!" The U of L connection has been a consciousness raiser for both of us.

Demi concurs adding:

> Maybe it's a timing thing. We're both kind of young and going to grad school and beginning our careers and it all came together as a learning network. Like me and the site council's professional development committee. It's right up my alley. It has given me wings within the school and the district.

Networking becomes even more complex internally. On one hand, every colleague interviewed mentioned multiple linkages both teachers had formed within the faculty. Typical comments included:

- "They've got their feet on the ground. They will work with anyone on a kid issue."
- "Both are seen as our resident experts on KERA. They do a lot of on-the-spot consulting."
- "I see both teachers as reaching out to people very consciously. Their reach within the school and at the Board is actually pretty amazing."
- "Demi and Jodie are real door-openers for the rest of us. If there's a Ralph or a new program or a district resource or whatever, invariably they're the ones who made it happen."
- Both ask my opinion frequently. I'm seen as an "old head." Pretty stodgy. But I see them plowing the ground for all of us. They are not out to impress. They are out to perform.

Both Jodie and Demi are quite conscious of internal networking. Demi, for instance, consciously makes style accommodations to expand and enhance internal networking. She states, "I do a lot of backing off to build relationships. I purposefully am trying not to play quarterback around here."

Jodie talks of building formality into the internal networks. She explains, "Demi and I met with two of our Northtop mentors on a regular basis throughout last year. It was a business meeting in tone. We didn't go for food and fun or even fellowship. We'd have an agenda of topics and questions and just share back and forth. We even expanded that into field trips. We'd go observe a school, get a hotel, go away and think as a foursome. Quite honestly, we didn't see good classrooms, but those trips changed the way we thought about good classrooms."

The principal in talking about Jodie and Demi internally remarks:

They are not hung up on pleasing people. Now, they're not snobbish or standoffish. But they are hung on teaching kids. They are willing to pay the price whether that's extra work, more training or social isolation to be classroom leaders. They basically come to issues with a, "Paint or get off the ladder" attitude, and that is going to offend some people.

A colleague adds, "There is some incestuous jealousy." Another suggests:

You hear they're showboating. If they are, I'm glad because I know who is profiting—the kids. Now there have been situations in this building where that was not the case. It was hotshotting for hotshotting. But not with Demi and Jodie. They just outwork everyone.

Demi and Jodie are insightful about the range of perceptions. Jodie postulates, "Some of the negativism is insecurity. That would have been there before but KERA rather uncorked those feelings. It has introduced more unopenness and uptightness because suddenly there is a state-sanctioned way to do everything." Demi concludes saying, "There's a range of views about us. You'll get, "They're awesome. They're as good as we have at this school." And you'll get, "They're young little hotshots who think they're too cool."

For Jodie, two antithetical events symbolize the internal networks' positives and negatives. The symbol of negativism was her involvement in the school's initial Primary Program Committee, which was formed in response to the initial adoption of KERA. A colleague recalls:

> That was bad. It was bad for me, and I was a wizened old bird. For Jodie, as a rookie, Whoa! Well, three of us—Jodie, a teacher no longer at this school, and me—we pushed the three-year multi-aged primary concept. It was hell. We got—and they (the rest of the faculty) got—down and dirty. We fought. We name-called. We were not exactly professional. It was a gut fight which, by the way, we won!

Jodie—somewhat incredulously, somewhat sadly—commented:

> We won? We won and we lost. We never reached consensus or anything close to it. It was just decided by the site council. But we—and I felt like I got most of it—got the blame. The Three Apologists of the Primary School. The Department of Education's Girls. Made me feel real team-like. I still think that when anything goes wrong around here, like in grouping, that cloud hangs over me.

In contrast, she remembers her "Teacher of the Year" Award:

> I do worry and wonder what other people think about me. And I was so worried over that selection. I didn't want them feeling like, "Oh, here comes Ms. Hotshot. She just told them the right things and was all be-boppy and that's why she's on stage and I'm not." But it turned out that the majority of the faculty here—and some whom I didn't think would be—were very supportive and even happy for me. I was glad because some of those teachers mean more to me than they could ever know. I do love a lot of the people here and that's why some of that unfair or unknowledgeable or personal innuendo hurts so much.

The Third Construct: Teaching as a Moral Matter

A third construct that drives Jodie and Demi is their persistent focus upon teaching as a moral matter. Fenstermacher (1990) reflects on that construct when he writes:

> What makes teaching a moral endeavor is, quite centrally human interaction undertaken in regard to other human beings. Thus, matters of what is fair, just, and virtuous are always present. Whenever a teacher

asks a student to share something with another student, decides between combatants in a schoolyard dispute, sets procedures for those who will go first or second or third, or discusses the welfare of a student with another teacher, moral considerations are present. . . . Teaching is a profoundly moral activity. (p. 133)

Jodie and Demi disconfirm Bernstein's (1985) that, "It is not easy to talk of 'moral imperatives' in today's schools. In swimming counter to the tides of moral relativism, one has to be prepared for an occasional dunking" (p. 231). They choose to swim those countertides with purpose and intentionality. While parents —in interview after interview—displayed an acuity of and appreciation for the tandem's instructional expertise, every parent gave the moral leadership provided by Demi and Jodie precedence. That parental perspective is exemplified by the illustrative comments that follow:

- The most important thing to me is manner. They always hold the child in respect.
- My son is hearing impaired. They have created a place where he is accepted, where he likes himself. Need I say more?
- Their thing is leading and guiding children in moral development. I want that for my child.
- They make kids glow because of the moral structure of their classroom. Everything else will take care of itself.
- They share the way they live and what they believe with the children. They are models. They embrace that as an ideal for teachers and so do I.
- They define the kids' character growth as damn important, and that is so clear in everything they say or do or send home.
- It is obvious their classroom is borne of religious beliefs. They have a very strong faith. It's not overt. They don't have to talk about it. It's inherent in their interactions and behaviors.
- They integrate ethics into everything from writing portfolios to math.
- Family values are not as hard as people want to make them. Do they go around saying, "Jesus?" No. Do they go around helping my kid and other parents' kids think about right and wrong? Yeah, and that's fine with me.

In asking students to define what makes their classroom special, invariably they reference moral issues and themes. To one it is that, "I've learned not to cuss so much anymore." Another points out, "When you're down in the dump, the teachers undump you." "If your classmate is in trouble, it is our job to get them out even if we don't like them," adds a third. A fourth student notes that, "We know that loving each other isn't for sissies." Several picked up a moral thread when the class performed "Silent Night" in sign language as something of a homage to their hearing-impaired classmates.

The moral climate of the classroom is revealed in a variety of ways. For instance, as referenced in one of the opening vignettes, a seminal moment in this classroom is referenced by school insiders of all ages as, "The Throw-Up Incident." If that appellation is a bit inelegant, its impact is unquestioned. Two students reflected on that event:

- It meant the Golden Rule was serious business to Ms. Kidd and Ms. McKnight. That's the most serious thing we can learn I think.
- Well, "The Throw-up Incident" showed we were like this giant pyramid and if any of us pulled away from the pyramid, we would all fall down. And it made me know how I would have felt if I would have been puking and everybody let me fall down.

A parent who is a management consultant remarks, "I use that incident when I give examples of value-added elements to an organization. We have no right to expect it, but it's a bonus." That value-added feature is evidenced in a variety of ways. It is the frequent grist for children's writing. It is felt in how weekly jobs are assigned, which books are read, how the most critical situations and the most trivial of details are handled. Students talk of a classmate who moved away and is lonely. They speak freely of moral dilemmas they are facing ("I cuss too much;" "Why is my daddy dying?" "I get into too many fights;" "Why do I sass my mama?"). Such a pervasive element is neither accidental nor spontaneous.

The tone of and emphasis upon morality is purposeful. Both Jodie and Demi are clear about that. Demi quite comfortably deals with her classroom and morals stating, "It is real powerful for me to tie the God thing or morals or whatever you want to term it into schooling. I find it hard—no, unconscionable—to be quiet about value-based issues. And I can't—or won't—won't teach outside of an ethical framework."

Jodie interjects the notion of moral pedagogy. "I work to turn classroom moments into moral lessons." She explains:

Somebody pokes someone else in the arm with a pencil. We don't just discipline. We talk. How'd that make them feel? How could you do that? You make them dig deeper than the incident itself into issues of right and wrong. Kids can be bubbly and funny, but I demand the serious side be explored too. If the whole classroom routine has to stop cold dead in its feet during a moral teachable moment, then it stops. You've got to seize that moment. Like the "Throw-Up Incident," you see?

Demi adds, "Moral moments—they have to be authentic. That's when it sticks."

Both teachers—and this view is validated by students, parents, and colleagues—contend that their classroom's moral fiber is defined by their discipline policy—the Golden Rule. The partners suggest that the Charney book—as Jodie says—"gave us the courage to just lay it out there. We linked ethics and classroom management." She continues, "We just came right out and said, 'Our only rule is the Golden Rule. We told the kids. We told the parents. That is our rule. It is our only rule.'"

The concept struck a chord in other members of the Northtop school community. A parent says, "We see it on two levels. At one, it's for classroom behavior. Like last year, we used to have ten or twelve rules . . . you know, 'Don't run in the halls' stuff. And sure, one rule simplifies all that. But more than that, it's what Jodie and Demi are all about as teachers and as persons." Another parent notes, "We've tried to raise the boy, you see, but this year that 'Golden Rule' thing just clicked with him. Whether it's at Burger King or his ballgame, he's always working it in. Amazing stuff to me."

In a classroom in which hearing-impaired students are valued members, it is not an accident that a prominent poster of Heather Whitestone, the then-reigning Miss America who is deaf, hung. It is no accident that quotes from the theologian Charles Swindoll hang alongside Shel Silverstein's "I Will Not Play at Tug-o-War." It is no accident that the banner that festoons and seemingly encompasses the physical space of the classroom states simply, "Do unto others as you would have them do unto you."

Both Jodie and Demi stress the "principle in action" notion. It is another method of pushing ethics into the fiber of the classroom, they contend. "We are constantly dealing with issues I would term ethical," Demi states. Jodie agrees, adding, "It is ingrained into our daily teaching rhythms and classroom routines. It doesn't have to be big. We take dailyness—how to store bookbags—and make it moral in nature." Demi continues, "We would be considered on the edge—over the edge?—by some, but it's those daily things that give you the authenticity I mentioned. I mean something like Monday job assignments are lengthy moral moments. Sometimes by accident and sometimes on purpose." Jodie confirms that perception. "Moral behaviors have to be taught. We create an expectation of morality on little things. It's putting coats in plastic bags to avoid lice contamination. It's cleaning up the centers. It's those things. I mean, I know if I went home and told Jack (her husband) that today's big moral issue was head lice, he'd say, 'Huh?' Unfortunately, too many teachers take that same 'Huh?' attitude. We're conditioned to think that way, but you win ethical battles by chipping away at the little, daily things these kids encounter as a community in this classroom. Yeah, we're fanatics about wet paper towels in the boys' restrooms as a moral issue. And we're fanatical on purpose and with reason."

The Northtop principal reflects, "We can't go back and rebuild kids' lives. If we could, that would be just fine. But Jodie and Demi have an extra sense about potholes in kids' lives morally speaking. They're always patching up kids' potholes."

A parent perhaps crystallizes the construct's impact when she observes, "They do amazing things for all of our kids' spiritual development. The ethical side of what those two do makes you shiver."

Closing Reflections

This study was a catalyst to reflect upon my own public school experience and future work canvass. Demi, Jodie, and the wonderful inhabitants of their classroom left me with three lingering reflections. I would assert that these reflections could push reform beyond its current parameters in Kentucky. On the other hand, these reflections are heretical since they promulgate "not believing what everyone else believes or what one ought to believe" to be accepted in conventional circles of wisdom (Szasz, 1976, p. 1). I fear that these styled reflections—in both the increasingly "politically correct" strictures of national reform and especially in the high-stakes, prescriptive, and punitive reform arena of Kentucky—become labeled as "beyond the walls of reason, the boundaries of belief . . . and unspeakable. (Where) to utter them is not merely to disagree, but to be wicked" (Hargreaves, 1993, p. 51). It is my hope, however, that the following reflections could be catalysts to help shape colleagues' answers to the hanging query posed by Fullan and Hargreaves (1991), "What's worth fighting for?" (book title).

Genuine reform is not systemic. Personalization and context always take precedence.

Successful politicians have long known the fact—all politics are local. Educational reformers would do well to accept the same premise. Education is reformed neither at the national nor state nor district level; it changes in local schoolhouses and classrooms.

Many will dismiss this as simplistic or even fatalistic. It certainly threatens the lucrative employment of national experts who dispense prescriptions with clarity for those engaged in the actual enterprise of schooling. Invariably, advocates of systemic reform are not—and frequently have never been—in the flow and flux of a local school.

Reform must, ultimately, take the cumbersome and unwieldy pathway of individual by individual, schoolhouse by schoolhouse. My own career sensitized me to this premise. "Principal-ing" in a poverty-impacted urban setting versus an affluent suburban community versus a rural environment teaches me that the most critical and fractious issues affecting reform are those of context rather than generalized theory. For schools to be successful, the elements dominating decisions must be the "Who?" and the "Where?" of a schoolhouse rather than the generic solutions so frequently bantered about by those who are outside the particular contextual frame.

This field study reaffirms the power in this belief. It convinced me that context—of place and of autobiography—is far more important than many practitioners understand and of far more significance than members of the innovation establishment dare admit. Without the context of people and place, lessons are not learned and understandings are lost.

School reform initiatives may be superimposed from above or from "outside in." Invariably however, external reform becomes a mere issue of compliance for those inside schools. In contrast, commitment to reform is invariably generated from within. This means that national standards and courts and well-paid educational gurus may invite or even command change, but that change will always play out in local expressions. To suggest otherwise is to rewind failed change strategies of the past. One can no more transplant the hopes and dreams, the norms and taboos of the educational enterprise of a Cedar Rapids, Iowa, to a Louisville, Kentucky, than one can assume that Demi and Jodie's classroom—regardless of its inspiration and magnificence—could or even should be replicated . . . even within their own school. To do so denigrates the senses of both place and personage inherent in a school. Educational reformers must go beyond their well-rehearsed universals; they must come instead to respect that the "who" and the "where" of restructuring are its most salient and significant elements.

Collegiality and collaboration are too essential to be left to chance. They are also too natural to be "mystified."

Observation and experience paint a compelling and consistent portrait of collegiality and collaboration as imperative dimensions for school success and teacher efficacy. Yet research and action policy tend to either minimize their importance treating them on the periphery of reform or they are made to be so complex and so complicated that they are posited as nearly impossible working realities to be achieved.

I am not suggesting the rather frequently prescribed—but oxymoronic—cures of mandated collegiality or forced collaboration. I am suggesting that those elements be publicly and privately treated as imperatives. Partnering practices will have less to do with macro-policy statements than with space utilization, the master schedule, performance assessment, reward systems, and patterns for professional development. Collaboration and collegiality must become ingrained in the regularities of daily schooling. The question must become, "How can we do it?" rather than "Should (or will) we do it?" for every teacher in every schoolhouse. Failure to operationalize this premise is to continue to sentence teachers to the "poisoned chalice" (Hargreaves, 1994, p. 186) of isolation.

Perhaps, I am too colored by my own experience. Perhaps Demi and Jodie are too atypical to illuminate the issue. However, I do not believe that teachers by individual proclivity or through group norms reject the collegial and collaborative elements of their profession. One needs only to sit in on a team meeting of engaged teachers to sense collaboration in action. In fact, I believe that the vast majority of teachers see these processes as the "cup of comfort" Hargreaves describes (1994, p. 186).

Yes, the processes inherent in collegiality and collaboration must be worked at overtly and persistently. Yes, they may evidence themselves in a myriad of manners. The expressions of this construct are simply too evident and too real— as a "lunch bunch" member for one teacher, as a member of the Coalition of Essential Schools National Faculty for another, as a union activist for a third, as a member of an interdisciplinary team for still another—to be seen as antithetical to the profession or so complicated as to be virtually impossible to foster within existing structures. Collegiality and collaboration will not be invented from behind the keynoter's podium or from the think tank's latest monograph. Rather, collegiality and collaboration must be pounded into reality in the hallways, the lounges, and the classrooms of local schools.

Academics are, of course, necessary, but they are insufficient. The real imperative for the profession, for the schoolhouse, and for the classroom must be that of moral fiber.

Under Kentucky's reform act, two of the initial six overarching goals deal explicitly with moral matters. Yet the current landscape of state accountability totally ignores this arena of schooling, a condition reflecting the lack of national conversation around the issue. In stark contrast, there was no more striking feature in this field study than the pervasive professional priority placed on moral matters. The matter of public schools and moral fiber is an uncomfortable fit for many. Yes, we do live in a diverse society. No, the classroom is neither church nor synagogue nor mosque. Does that mean that we as a people—and as school communities—cannot define a common ground for moral matters? I would hope and furthermore suggest that this is not the case.

I am not offering answers. I do not know how to engender that common ground-styled formulation. Is a national conversation called for? Or is such moral consensus best hewn out in New England–style town meetings in this state's hills and hollows and the nation's cities and neighborhoods? I do not claim the answer. I do believe that the moral fiber of schools must be restored to primacy. We can no longer endorse, afford, or condone classrooms that have the bland neutrality of "moral Switzerlands."

Beyond the larger issues of legality, policy and governance that such an assertion generates, there lies a more immediate—and perhaps more significant— element. Demi and Jodie's professional skills have created a distinct moral pedagogy in their classroom. Disciplinary scenarios, daily patterns of interaction, the rhythms and regularities of schooling—be they job assignments or holiday events, the classroom's physical dimensions, and instructional foci are all tools used in the consistent and persistent application of this moral pedagogy. That pedagogy is driven by instinct and courage and experience. I wonder . . . can— and should—that styled methodology be honed into a more formalized and public "best practice"?

What does the "decency" advocated by Sizer (1984) have to do with Lipsitz's (1984) "essential goodness"? Are they congruent with Charney's (1993) advocacy of teaching children to care? Does moral pedagogy play a more prominent role in a primary classroom than in a senior chemistry lab? If so, should it? How can moral pedagogy become part of the teaching craft? As we begin to answer these questions, then, perhaps, other parents can join those in this classroom marveling at how the teachers' moral craft "makes you shiver."

A Final Note

Many aspects of this study confuse, trouble, and threaten me. If this study has merit, its implications point toward a pathway to reform that is far more complex, far more tedious, and far more demanding of ingenuity and persistence than is commonly thought. By the same token, this study reaffirmed and reawakened in me a sense of awe and respect for what a classroom—and what a schoolhouse—can be. And finally, I have once again relearned that, "Education change depends on what teachers think and do. It's as simple and as complicated as that" (Sarason, 1971, p. 193).

References

Ayers, W. (1993). *To Teach: The journey of a teacher*. New York: Teachers College Press.

Barth, R. S. (1988). Schools: A community of leaders. In A. Lieberman (Ed.), *Building a professional culture in schools*. New York: Teachers College Press.

Bennett, W. J. (1992). *The de-valuing of America*. New York: Simon & Schuster.

Bernstein, R. J. (1985). *Beyond objectivism and relativisim*. Philadelphia: University of Philadelphia Press.

Charney, R. S. (1993). *Teaching children to care: Management in the responsive classroom*. Greenfield, MA: Northeast Foundation for Children.

Darling-Hammond, L. (1994). *Professional development schools: Schools for developing a profession*. New York: Teachers College Press.

Deal, T. E. & Kennedy, A. (1982). *Corporate cultures*. Reading, MA: Addison-Wesley.

Etzioni, A. (1988). *The moral dimension toward a new economics*. New York: The Free Press.

Fenstermacher, G. D. (1990). Some moral considerations on teaching as a profession. In J. I. Goodlad, R. Soda & K. A. Sirotnik (Eds.), *The moral dimensions of teaching*. San Francisco: Jossey-Bass.

Fullan, M. & Hargreaves, A. (1991). *What's worth fighting for? Working together for your school*. Toronto, Ontario: Ontario Public Schools' Teacher Federation.

Glaser, B., & Strauss, A. (1987). *The discovery of grounded theory*. Chicago: Aldine.

Hargreaves, A. (1994). *Changing teachers, changing times: Teachers' work and culture in the postmodern era*. New York: Teachers College Press.

Harris, M. (1981). *America now*. New York: Simon & Schuster.

Lipsitz, J. (1984). *Successful schools for early adolescents*. New Brunswick, NJ: Transaction.

Little, J. W. (1987). Teachers as Colleagues. In V. Richardson-Koehler (Ed.), *Educator's handbook: A research perspective*. White Plains, NY: Longman.

Marshall, C., & Rossman, G. B. (1989). *Designing qualitative research*. Newbury Park: CA: Sage.

Miller, S. K. (1994). *The nature of managerial work*. New York: Harper & Row.

Naisbitt, J. (1982). *Megatrends: Ten new directions transforming our lives*. New York: Warner Books.

Peters, T. (1992). *Liberation management: Necessary disorganization for the nano second nineties*. New York: Alfred A. Knopf.

Rilke, R. M. (1934). *Letters to a young poet*. New York: Norton.

Rotter, J. B. (1966). Generalized expectancies for internal versus external control of reinforcement. *Psychological Monographs, 80*(1).

Sarason, S. (1971). *The culture of the school and the problem of change*. Boston: Allyn and Bacon.

Schumacher, E. F. (1982). *Small is beautiful: A study of economics as if people mattered*. London: Blond and Briggs.

Senge, P. (1990). *The fifth dimension*. New York: Doubleday.

Sergiovanni, T. J. (1992). *Moral leadership: Getting to the heart of school improvement*. San Francisco: Jossey-Bass.

Sergiovanni, T. J. (1990). *Value-added leadership*. Orlando, FL: Harcourt Brace Jovanovich.

Szasz, T. (1976). *Heresies*. New York: Anchor-Doubleday.

Sizer, T. *Horace's compromise*. Boston: Houghton Mifflin.

Stanislavsky, K. (1936). *An actor prepares*. London: Routledge and Kegan Paul.

Van Maanen, J, & Barley, S. R. (1984). Occupational communities: Culture and control in organizations. *Research in Organizational Behavior, 6*.

Whitford, B. L. (1994). Personal communication.

3

A Multi-Age/Multi-Ability
Primary Classroom in Action

CHRISTY D. MCGEE

Katherine Alexander Futrell doesn't take the easy way. Over and over, she has made decisions about her classroom practice that meant more work, more time, more creative soul-searching. That's because her eye is on trying to do what's best for kids, sometimes despite how it complicates her own life. Professional commitment is the name of her game.

Katherine was teaching fourth grade when the Kentucky Education Reform Act (KERA) was established in 1990, but was so intrigued by the mandated primary program that she requested to be allowed to develop a classroom that embraced this philosophy. The "critical attributes" that defined the primary made sense to her: developmentally appropriate practices, multi-age/multi-ability classrooms, continuous progress, authentic assessment, qualitative reporting methods, professional teamwork, and positive parental involvement. She wanted to put them into practice for the benefit of kids.

Katherine established her primary classroom in 1991. This chapter chronicles how one strong teacher embraced the initial teaching philosophy of the KERA primary program, used it and adapted it to make sense in her own classroom, continuously seeking to improve student learning. The first section presents a brief overview of the classroom and its structure. The next section discusses the teacher, Katherine Futrell, and how she came to develop her own approach to the primary program. The section entitled "Workshops" gives the reader a glimpse of a typical day. Next, the role that individualizing instruction and assessment plays within the classroom is discussed. Finally, there is a reflection about teacher accountability and commitment.

The Classroom and Its Structure

Katherine's classroom in 1992 was self-contained and composed of nearly equal numbers of 6-, 7-, and 8-year-olds. In 1994, Katherine included 5-year-olds, and because of numbers in the school, dropped the 8-year-olds. During the 1997–98 school year, Katherine moved to a new school and her classroom reverted back to containing 6-, 7-, and 8-year-olds. Katherine has taught art and special education classes, as well as first, second, and fourth grades. She was the first teacher in her building to implement the primary program with more than two age groups of children.

It is important to note that Katherine adapted her already well-developed classroom structure to younger children. She did not significantly change the way she taught or thought about teaching because of KERA—quite the opposite. The reform confirmed that the ways in which Katherine approached teaching were "best practice." She was no longer just "that odd teacher in room 102."

The structure of Katherine's classroom is based on a holistic approach to learning and on the teacher's belief that each child has the right to learn at his or her own pace. Instruction is based on a series of workshops (reading, writing, and math) and an in-depth study of social studies and science concepts referred to as Unit Study.

Regardless of the age composition of the classroom, the 24 children of this classroom are arranged in six multi-age/multi-ability "offices." Offices are four desks grouped together. The students work together in these offices in most curricular areas. This method of grouping encourages responsible group membership and self-sufficiency, two of the goals of KERA.

The Teacher

Katherine has taught for nineteen years. During those years, she has gone through a series of transformations, as most good teachers do. Her first year of teaching, she says, was spent "imitating what I had seen as a student myself—reading groups, the need to get the 'right' answer, and teaching straight from the textbook." The need to move toward a "more child-centered" approach to learning became apparent to her during her first year in the classroom. She read professional journals in search of ways to expand her teaching style, but she admits, "Mostly I just watched the children." Katherine feels strongly that the art of teaching is demonstrated in a teacher's ability to observe children and be aware of what each child needs in order to understand concepts being introduced to them. She believes "the science of teaching is applied when the teacher uses the training received at the university to properly develop teaching techniques to help children understand concepts." She explains:

> In my first year of teaching, I could see that using the approach of following the teacher's manual was not reaching all the students in my

classroom. It's sort of like the park signs that read "You Are Here" and then give specific directions as to how to get somewhere else. By using that old approach we are saying that all children start at the same place and that by imparting the correct instruction to them, they will all end up learning the same things to the same degree. If a child happens to come at a concept from a different angle, he or she is lost, just like the person in the park who doesn't follow or understand the "You Are Here" signs.

The primary program developed by Katherine was an outgrowth of this understanding of children and how teaching groups of children should be approached.

During her second year of teaching, Katherine was a special education teacher in a Learning/Behavior Disorders (LBD) classroom where she piloted the Success Program (a highly structured approach to teaching reading and writing using a whole language approach). She found that her children moved up four or five levels on the Levels Test that was administered in the school system at the time, when in the previous four or five years, those same students had not progressed nearly as rapidly.

She moved to teaching in a first-grade classroom and continued to use the Success Program, modifying it as a result of reading that she was doing in professional journals. She moved back to teaching fourth grade using a modified version of Success with her students. After her first year of teaching fourth grade, she became involved in the Louisville Writing Project, the local affiliate of the National Writing Project, which has continued to influence how she teaches children to read and write. By that time, she had increased her classroom library sufficiently that she no longer had to use the basal readers as a supplement. Rather, the children in her classroom learned to read using good children's literature, supplemented by "levelized readers" such as the Sunshine series for emergent and early readers.

When Katherine began her multi-age/multi-ability primary classroom, she realized that she could teach reading and writing in the same way that she had with older children. She believed that "unit study" could also remain the same because, "if the activities are open-ended and challenging, all children can take something away from them," but that designing a mathematics curriculum for the younger children was going to be far more challenging.

As a fourth-grade teacher, she taught math to the whole class with "lots of remediation after school." When she thought about the wide developmental range of children aged six to nine years, she realized she would have to make drastic changes in order to address every child's needs. She thought about having three groups and teaching math three times a day, but she knew that would foul the multi-age/multi-ability concept that was so critical to her vision of a student-centered primary program. She decided that the only way she could possibly handle math and meet all the children's needs was to individualize a portion of math time. Over the seven years she has been working in a primary program, she has refined a math workshop approach, which will be discussed more fully in the next section of this chapter.

The Workshops

Using a workshop approach to teach reading, writing and math is intended to allow each child to achieve at his or her individual level. The approach attempts to create a classroom environment where children can learn to work cooperatively within a group and still meet their individual educational needs. In the following sections, Katherine's workshop in each curricular area is portrayed using vignettes which illustrate student/teacher interactions.

Writing Workshop

In the writing workshop, the influence of Katherine's involvement with the Louisville Writing Project is evident in a variety of ways. For example, children are encouraged to write freely about many topics, conferencing and revision are normal activities, and writing for real audiences is cultivated. There is an excitement in the class during this workshop. The children love to write, as can be observed by their enthusiasm for their work. In the *Parent Handbook* that Katherine prepares for parents, she comments that the "students generally pick this time as their favorite."

Katherine has adjusted her writing workshop program since 1991. Instead of allowing all writers to work independently, seeking their own partners for the editing process and participating in a whole group writing talk, she now organizes the children into three flexible groups: Early Writers, Writers Associates, and Writers Express. During the early years of *Katherine*'s primary program, children were not grouped in any way during their writing workshop. All the children in the classroom were exposed to the same writing talks, explored the same genre, and were involved in editing their own and each other's work. Clearly, children of different abilities and readiness took away different understandings and demonstrated varying strengths in writing, but the classroom agenda was one of continuous progress

In the more recent configuration of writing workshop, children are grouped by their understanding and experiences in writing and move freely in and out of these groups as their abilities and needs change. In these groups, the students learn to plan their writing, revise their pieces and edit each other's work. Most of the time, the children are able to choose which genre they would like to use to express themselves; however, occasionally, Katherine makes assignments to encourage exploration of unfamiliar styles. Whatever the choice, they write, confer with other authors, and publish (produce finished books) during this time.

Why did Katherine choose to change the configuration of her writing workshop? She states:

> I realized that students could get more help working with children in groups that were purposely formed to support their writing development. With this arrangement the students seem to work more closely with their peers in the editing process and they can assist each other because they are working from the same perspective. I also am mindful of the need of older writers to be prepared to write in a greater variety of genres so they can develop well-rounded portfolios to take with them as they enter fourth grade.

Katherine also allows that this adjustment is related to the fact that the state-mandated writing portfolio, used for school accountability at fourth grade, requires certain prescribed types of work and defines explicit performance standards that all students are expected to meet. This "standards-based" orientation at fourth grade has created a tension with the "continuous progress" norm of the primary program, where students are allowed to improve according to their own developmental clock.

The following excerpt is an example of a typical activity in Katherine's writing workshop. It is a "writing talk" which introduces the children to the importance of lead sentences. This vignette shows the comprehension and excitement that can be generated with writing in a particular genre when that genre is given a real life connection to the class. Ages of the children are indicated in parentheses.[1]

The students want to write a letter to every teacher in the building urging them to read the book *The Hobbit* by J. R. Tolkien to their students. Katherine uses this desire to help the students see the importance of strong lead sentences.

> *Katherine*: Remember yesterday when we talked about the importance of paying attention to your audience when writing a persuasive speech? Today, we are going to continue that discussion by working on lead sentences. Who can tell me what a line leader is?
>
> *Megan* (9): A person who leads the line.
>
> *Katherine*: Right. So what might a lead sentence be?
>
> *Jenna* (7): The beginning sentence.
>
> *Katherine*: Okay, what else?
>
> *Stephen* (8): The sentence that makes the person want to read the paragraph.
>
> *Katherine*: Good. The lead sentence makes the person want to read on.
>
> *Tyler* (7): It's hard to write the second sentence without the lead sentence because it tells you what the rest of the paragraph is going to say.
>
> *Katherine*: That's a good point. Today we are going to develop ideas for lead sentences. (She is using the overhead.) What are your ideas?

(She begins to call on students randomly. They do not seem intimidated by this practice. If they don't know the answer, it is acceptable to get help from another classmate.)

Katherine: Do you think we should tell what the paragraph is about right away? Megan?

Megan: You could say once there was a story about some kind of animal.

Katherine: Amanda?

Amanda (7): I'd like to tell you about a story. . . . (Katherine continues to write the student responses.)

Katherine: If I got this in my mailbox I would definitely want to read on.

After continued discussion, the students decided upon using "Say goodbye to *Ramona* and hello to *The Hobbit*," an interesting and catchy lead sentence for their persuasive letter to teachers.

Following writing talk, the second activity is devoted to silent writing time. During this time, no conversation is allowed and no one (except under the direst of circumstances) is allowed to leave the room to use the restroom. After observing children work over the years, Katherine has decided that some students need absolute silence to collect their thoughts and get them on paper. This attention to the needs of others assists students in understanding what it means to be a responsible group member.

All of the children's work during a term is placed into a folder. At the end of each term, Katherine conferences with each child to select four pieces from the folder to be placed in the writing portfolio. Each child has a say in what he or she considers to be the best writing pieces. Along with the children's work, Katherine files anecdotal notes taken throughout the term during writing workshop and a written analysis of each child's writing development.

Reading Workshop

This workshop has evolved considerably since 1991 as well. Originally, Katherine started all students reading alone and choosing their own books. In order to teach reading strategies, she held individual reading conferences with each child every week. During the 1997–98 school year, Katherine decided to try beginning the year by working with a small group of emergent readers to assist them in developing appropriate reading strategies. While she assists the small group, the rest of the class participates in practice reading time that involves self-selection of books and independent reading. After she feels comfortable that an early reader has a repertoire of strategies to use when reading, that student is allowed to participate in the independent reading with the rest of the class. This is not a skills-based reading group, but rather a group of students learning strategies to improve their reading.

Throughout the school year, Katherine conferences with each child independently at least once a week to share a private reading time and to discuss the strategies that he or she is choosing to use during reading. The following excerpt is from a reading conference with Lisa (7) that Katherine begins with a discussion of Lisa's reading log.

> *Katherine*: Lisa, you did a really nice job of filling out your reading log last week. (Lisa hasn't always been diligent in completing her reading logs.) Why did you choose this book?
> *Lisa*: Because it is funny.
> *Katherine*: What made you think it was funny?
> *Lisa*: The pictures on the front.
> *Katherine*: It's good to get clues from pictures. Let me hear you read some of the book to me. (Lisa reads with a great deal of expression, and as she reads, Katherine laughs and makes comments on the text and about the pictures. She is positive and supportive of the reading.) How did you know that big word?
> *Lisa*: Sometimes big words are made up of a lot of little words.
> *Katherine*: So you used that strategy to figure it out.
> (Lisa continues reading.)
> *Katherine* (stopping Lisa's reading to comment): Do you think that's going to be a big lie?
> (Lisa laughs and nods her head in affirmation.)
> *Katherine*: That's an exaggeration. How many is that so far? (Lisa shrugs) Do you think this book is going to have a lot of exaggeration?
> *Lisa*: Yes.
> *Katherine*: I think so, too, Lisa. I really have enjoyed your reading today. Keep up the good work.

Lisa returns to her seat smiling and continues to read her book. Katherine gets out her clipboard that contains the anecdotal notes she keeps about student reading conferences. She writes down today's observations on a large address label. At the end of the year, she puts each child's observational notes in chronological order and adds them to his or her reading file.

In 1991, only one type of reading log was used to assist students in their reading comprehension. The students recorded what they read in the log and added a comment on what they gleaned from their reading on that particular day. Katherine collected the logs and then commented on their reading selections and insights. During the 1993–94 school year, she expanded the types of logs the children could use. Having a choice in recording their reading experiences now gives students a variety of ways to express themselves.

Literature circles have always been a part of Katherine's reading workshop. On Thursdays and Fridays, students have the opportunity to discuss a book and participate in projects and activities that focus on some story element by sharing books that are connected through their author, subject matter, theme, or genre. Katherine has developed a three-year cycle that covers authors and a variety of subjects and genres.

Each day, reading workshop ends with a celebration of authors. Students have an opportunity to read aloud their own work, or they may choose to read another author's work. At this time, Katherine also reads aloud to the class. It is a favorite time of day because Katherine is an excellent reader, using many voices for the characters in the literature she and the class choose to read.

Unit Study

The time spent on unit study is a time of exploration and hands-on experiences with science and social studies. Since children typically stay in her classroom for three years, Katherine has arranged a three-year cycle of thematic units to explore science and social studies concepts. The thematic unit studies last from one to two months.

Unit One: Home Sweet Home	Unit Two: Beyond the Doorstep
Year 1: Our Bodies	Year 1: Neighborhoods
Year 2: Our Families	Year 2: Kentucky
Year 3: Our Homes	Year 3: Louisville
Unit Three: Our Physical World	Unit Four: Exploring Our World
Year 1: Matter	Year 1: Immigrating to America
Year 2: Sound and Light	Year 2: Moving West
Year 3: Motion and Machines	Year 3: Exploring Space
Unit Five: Cycles in Our World	Unit Six: Regions of Our World
Year 1: Rock Cycle	Year 1: Oceans
Year 2: Water Cycle	Year 2: Forests
Year 3: Food Change	Year 3: Deserts

As the *Parent Handbook* (a comprehensive guide to the classroom) states, "Students are encouraged and expected to ask questions and be curious. They will apply their reading, writing and math skills as they search for the answers (or possible answers) to their questions."

In the following vignette, from the unit Sound and Light, the students have been exploring the concepts of objects being transparent, translucent, or opaque. The students have already classified objects into categories of artificial and natural light, and they have studied how light travels. On this day, they are reviewing what they already know about light and preparing to start the concepts of reflection and refraction.

Katherine: Let's summarize what I think you are telling me. Last week we ended up with three groups. One [group] was objects that block light. They are opaque. The second [group] was objects that do not block the pathway. They are transparent. The third group was objects that make things look blurry. What are they called, Kenneth?

Kenneth (6): Translucent.

Katherine: (Places a sign with the word translucent on the board.) What do we say happens to the light?

Amanda (7): It scatters the light.

Katherine now uses a real-life situation of a builder's need to choose the proper building material for each of his tasks in order for the children to apply what they learned about material that is transparent, translucent, and opaque.

Katherine: Okay, now we are going to do some problem solving. We are going to use these symbols (she writes O, Tp, and Tl on the board under the appropriate sign) to represent those three groups. We got a little confused last week. Let's see if we can decide what type of material we need to use when we help some people plan their buildings.

(The students have their own small chalkboards and chalk. They are to write the correct symbol when Katherine asks for an answer and then hold it up so Katherine can see them.)

Katherine: You are a builder and you have clients that come to you to help them decide what kind of windows to put in their new house. (She switches to her Southern voice.) My bathroom window faces the street. I like a lot of light in my room, but I don't want to be seen naked on the street. What kind of window do you recommend? (She switches back to her normal voice.) You must decide if it is going to be transparent, translucent, or opaque.

(The children write on their boards. Most students had Tl. Anthony [9] has Tp, Joshua [6] is lost.)

Katherine: You should have chosen translucent because it lets light in but you can't see through it. The next situation is that I own a warehouse. Workers in my building slack off and don't do their job. I need a wall so that I can see what the workers are doing. What kind of wall would your recommend?

(Megan [9] has O and Joshua [6] has Tl. The rest have Tp.)

Katherine: If the owner of the warehouse wanted to be able to see the workers, they would need a transparent wall. Megan, if they had opaque wall, would the owners be able to see anything?

Megan: No. (She smiles and quickly changes her board.)

Katherine: The next client who comes in is a teacher (uses a high-pitched teacher voice). I have very distractible children and I have one student that drives me batty. I want to have a partition to put this student behind. What type of material shall I use?

(Most of the children write O. Joshua [6] has Op written on his board.)

Katherine: Let's do one more. A little boy wants to build a box for his gerbil. (She uses a little boy voice.) My name is Raymond. I have a gerbil and his name is Snowpuff. He likes to see out, and I have to see him. What can you build for me?

(Zachary [6] copied the correct answer after looking at Evan's board. The rest of the boards said Tp.)

The rest of science time is spent on exploring the concepts of refraction and reflection. The children use a variety of materials to experiment with these concepts.

The next vignette depicts the students working on the unit entitled "Moving West." On this particular day, the students are developing their mapping skills and using what they know about math to discover the length of their trips. This unit is designed to have the students experience a trip west during the 1800s. Before the unit is completed, the students will have formed families (their office mates), and given each other new family names and birthdays, as well as developed a family history. They will do research to discover why the westward movement took place and then decide why their particular family is making the trip west. The "families" will have packed their wagons with the necessary supplies, made the trip west, and built their new homes. Katherine will give them trip packets that describe events that occur during the trip resulting in problems for the travelers that must be solved before they can continue their trip. They will chronicle their trip through diaries written from the point of view of the family member they are portraying.

Katherine: Welcome, everybody, to our trip west. (The children are noisy and excited about their adventure so there is extra talking.) Listen, we have a job to do. You must decide what state your family is starting from, its destination, why it is going, how many miles it is to the destination, and how long it will take your family to get there. Then, we must take time to prepare for the trip by packing our wagons.

Katherine: Office captains need to get an atlas and two rulers for each office. (The captains retrieve the needed supplies. She has a transparency of a U.S. map on the overhead.) Is this map larger or smaller than the U.S.?

Chorus: Smaller.

Katherine: Why is it smaller, James?

James (6): Because it is too big?

Katherine: What's too big?

James: Can't show how big it is on the map.

Katherine: Right, I could make the water bottle on your desk the same size on the overhead, but I can't make the United States map the same size as the real United States. So I must make my map smaller. How do you go about using this small picture to find out how big the U.S. really is? (She stops to wait for quiet.) We do this by making maps to scale. Scale means they have reduced the states on the map in proportion to the real states. Texas will be bigger in proportion than Rhode Island. (She points to each state as she talks.) Is there a scale on this map?

Chorus: (They look at the map.) No.

Katherine: We can't do it on this map. The other day we wanted to know how far away Somalia was. (She pulls down a map of the world.) We found Somalia. It was pretty far away. On this map we have a key. (She points to the key.) On the key is a scale. For every inch on this map, you would travel 400 miles. Shows them on the ruler how small an inch is. So if you measure 2 inches you would have (pause)—Amanda?

Amanda (7): 200 miles

Chorus: Nooo.

(Kevin [7] and Tyler [7] and a few others say 800 miles. Amanda shrugs her shoulders and nods yes.)

Katherine: What if I wanted to go somewhere that was 1½ inches apart on this map. So if 1 inch is 400 hundred miles how much is a one-half of an inch? Evan?

Evan (6): 200.

Katherine: Right, let's look at Africa. It is almost 12 inches across. How could we find out how many miles that is? We could add twelve 400s or what else could we do?

Matthew (8): Multiply.

Katherine: So what is 12 × 400. I'll tell you, because you don't have your calculators. 4,800.

(The children are amazed. They look back and forth at each other with wide eyes. They then compare the United States, which is 9 inches or 3,600 miles, and Asia, which is 14 inches across.)

Katherine: Let's practice working with this scale of miles. In our class atlas on pages 22 and 23 is a big map of the U.S. First see if you can find the scale of miles information on the page.

(They work with their partners, and everyone finds the key.)

Katherine: The scale doesn't tell how many inches equal the scale. How can you figure out how long that line that equals 500 miles is?

Jessica (7): Measure it.

Katherine: That's right.

(They measure it and find out it is about two inches.)

Katherine: We are just estimating how many miles from one place to another because we are measuring straight lines and the roads might be curved. (She uses the overhead and writes 2″ is about 500 miles.) Find the state of Kansas on your map. Was Kansas one of our western states?

Chorus: Yesss.

Katherine: So look west of the Mississippi. Raise your hand when you find Kansas. (Waits for them to find it and helps some who can't.) Measure how big Kansas is in inches and be ready to tell me. (They begin to raise their hands.) Is Kansas more than two inches or less?

Chorus: Lesss.

Katherine: It's about 1¼ inches. So, we can say that Kansas is a little less than 500 miles across.

(Several in the class disagree. They think it is more like 1½ inches. She looks and sees they are right.) So we know it is less than 500 miles across. If 2 inches is 500 miles, what is 1 inch?

Aaron (7): 250 miles.

Katherine: 250 miles, but we only need half of that. Go get my calculator please, Matthew.

Stephen (8): 125 miles (He doesn't use a calculator.)

Katherine: We don't need a calculator, we have one in *Stephen's* brain. Suppose Kansas was 6 inches. How would we find out how many miles across it would be? We would need to add 250 six times or what else could we do . . . .

Tyler: Multiply

Katherine writes on the overhead

$$\begin{array}{r} 250 \\ 250 \\ 250 \\ 250 \\ 250 \\ 250 = 250 \\ \times\ 6 \\ \hline 1{,}500 \end{array}$$

Katherine: Let's do that same thing with each family's destination.

They pass out their sheets that give the family names and other information and go to work. The purple office figured out that with their destination being 2,075 miles away it would take 138 days to make the trip. They worked out that if they divided 138 by 30 they could discover how many months it would take. They discovered 4.6, which is almost 5 months.

This unit was designed to target all six KERA goals. Students used basic communication and math skills (Goal 1) in their journals by calculating the trip length and map scale and in measuring and packing their wagons. They applied the core concepts (Goal 2) of social studies through their exploration of the western movement. Self-sufficiency (Goal 3) was continuously demonstrated in the structure of classroom management. Responsible group membership (Goal 4) was required in order to accomplish the "family" setting for their pretend trip. Thinking and problem-solving (Goal 5) was also a core prerequisite to accomplish the trip because the children had to overcome various obstacles incurred on the trip. And finally, integration (Goal 6) is evident in the inclusion of math skills, reading, and writing to produce the final product of the unit—a successful trip.

Assessment in this unit took many forms. Students kept a learning log that required them to record what they learned after each activity. These logs allowed Katherine to assess each child's understanding of the KERA goals focused on in this unit. The logs were also used to assess each child's understanding of grammar and punctuation rules discussed in the writing talks. Parents were kept informed of their child's progress through the use of weekly progress reports. Katherine also kept anecdotal records of each student's progress.

Another method of assessment was analysis of the student's diary of the trip. Because the family configurations were heterogeneous, each child brought something different to the development of the project. The six-year-olds' diaries were not nearly as comprehensive as the eight-year-olds' work; however, at the end of the unit even the six-year-olds had begun to write in a voice that was different from their normal writings. They were attempting to imitate the authentic diary entries from people moving west during the 1800s that Katherine had shared with the class each day.

Because students remain with Katherine for three years, these multiple assessment techniques allow her to keep track of and build the continuous progress of her students. This is a rich data collection system.

Each of the families had chosen a different area of the west to begin a new life. In researching the reason families move west, the students learned much about how this country grew. They became so involved in their families that they even adopted the family names they had chosen and used them during the other parts of the day. When their trip west finally ended, all of the families wanted to continue the unit by building an appropriate home in which their family could dwell. This wasn't a part of the planned unit, but Katherine realized the necessity of completing the trip for the children and allowed the extension.

The students' final task was to share with each other what they had learned about their family's motivation to move west, the conditions they faced on their trip, and the type of dwelling they would inhabit once they arrived at their destination. Parents were invited to a special evening viewing of the children's work on this unit and were kept apprised of activities through weekly progress reports. This activity is an example of authentic instruction with assessment that was performance-based, applied to the children's work and the "real-world" that they had created in their families.

Math Workshop

In many mathematics classes, teachers group children according to skill development or ability. In Katherine's workshop there is no ability grouping. At times, the children may group themselves if they want to work together on similar concepts, but it is important to remember that these groups are self-selected. Students work at their own pace, which means they are working at a continuous progress level. The real advantage to this system is that children may move on to other math concepts when they need to and are not detained by the slower progress of others. In other words, students continue to move at a pace that is individual to them and not to other members of the class.

Math workshop is divided into three time periods: daily practice and application, working with partners or in a small group during game time, and a whole class activity entitled Math Exploration that emphasizes problem solving. The workshop begins with a time for students to work on concepts and their applications using textbook assignments. Until the children reach the third-grade book, they may choose what unit to work on in their consumable math books. They do not have to follow a sequential order. If they choose a unit that is too difficult, they place it back in their book and choose a new unit.

During this first period of time, every student is working in an area that is appropriate for his or her development. Evan (6) has an excellent understanding of math concepts. He quickly worked through the first-year book and moved to the middle of the second-year book by January. By the end of the year, he was ready to begin the third-year book. Robert (7), who has progressed more slowly in reading, is "above grade level" in math and working with concepts appropriate to his needs. Megan (9) and Cari (8), who came into this classroom afraid of math, are beginning to feel more at ease with math and are now progressing at an appropriate pace, according to Katherine.

During the time in which the students work individually, Katherine is busy moving from one student to another answering questions, reassuring them about concerns, and taking anecdotal notes. She talks often with students to check on their conceptualizations of the math theories. Here is an example of what happens during individual math time in Katherine's classroom.

- James (6) is working on subtraction. He is using counters and an addition-subtraction board to assist him with his workbook pages. He is talking to himself:

  If I have six things. Let's see one, two, three, four, five, six, and I take away four things (again he counts four objects), how many do I have left? (Pause as he contemplates.) I have two things left. Two goes right here. (He writes down the correct answer on his sheet. The board and counters have helped him sort his answer and begin to understand subtraction.)

- At the office next to James, Kevin (7) is working on regrouping and trading. He uses a place value board. He quickly makes the "trades" necessary to regroup and puts the correct answer on his paper. He no longer needs the board, but he likes to check his answers with it.
- Cari (8) is also working on place value. She isn't using any manipulatives, and she is having difficulty with this concept. Her hand is up in the air while she waits for Katherine to come and help her. Katherine has been working with Stephen and Matthew on a problem-solving technique. They nod as they listen and go back to work. Katherine moves to Cari. They are talking quietly, and Cari smiles and nods her head yes. She too goes back to work, and Katherine moves to the next student to observe and help if necessary.

After the workshop, Katherine takes a minute to record some of her observations about the students' work. She will check each day's work for each child when she collects the math logs on Thursday.

Students may play a math game after they have finished their individual work. For some students, the individual work time might be as long as 30 minutes, for others it might only be 10 minutes. During the game-playing portion of math workshop, the students are free to play any of the many math games Katherine has assembled. These games are designed to take the math skills the children are learning from their texts and apply them to the games. A visitor might find Cari (8) and Julie (6) playing "Shake Those Beans" or Brian (6) and Kevin (7) playing "Doubles." The children are responsible for making sure they play a variety of games. This is a time that the students really enjoy, and yet each game reinforces a math skill or concept. The children often choose partners of different ages and gender without hesitation or complaint.

After the children finish their individual work and play a math game, they are required to write down their activities in their math log. At the end of the week, they attach all their work to their completed log and give it to Katherine. She reviews each log and writes comments concerning the children's work on each log. These logs are then sent home to parents for review. Parents are encouraged to take time to sit down with their children and discuss their math work.

Katherine is careful to make sure each child is progressing in his or her understanding of math concepts. One week, Cari's math log had a worksheet involving sets. Cari had missed every answer. Katherine told me that Cari's past work indicated she understood the concept of sets, but she wanted to check her understanding again. She took Cari over to the floor and had her show several different arrangements of sets using unifix cubes. Cari was able to display every arrangement. Katherine said, "Obviously she understands sets; she just didn't understand the directions." Smiling, Cari joined her friends to play a math game knowing she just made a mistake in directions.

Math workshop also includes a time for a whole class activity. It may be a game played in teams using Papy's minicomputers, Venn diagrams, or a cooperative learning game that emphasizes the development of a variety of math concepts. Again, this time allows for children to use logic, problem-solving, and their understanding of math skills to work through these activities.

Math Workshop is a time built for student success. Each student is challenged to reach his or her own potential. Cari, featured in the vignette above, was one of the children afraid of math mentioned earlier. She was able to work through her difficulties and walk away feeling successful.

Individualizing Instruction and Assessment

Since Katherine's classroom is multi-age/multi-ability, it is necessary to accommodate children at different developmental stages by establishing curricular goals that will keep older children in this age span motivated and excited about learning without, at the same time, overwhelming the younger children. Regarding this, Katherine observed:

> Children of varying age levels are going to take different understandings away from reading and writing workshops, unit studies, and math workshop. It is important to develop learning activities that will engage the children in active learning so that each child can take something away from that activity and feel successful.

For example, during the light and color unit, Joshua (6) understood categorizing objects as clear or opaque. He was able to do that during a classroom activity; however, he could not put that knowledge into practical use, as was obvious from his answers in the vignette about the builder mentioned earlier. Had he been in a traditional first-grade setting, it is unlikely he would have been exposed to these concepts at his age. In contrast, most of the third-year students were able to answer all the questions in the builder vignette.

Three of the "critical attributes" that describe the primary program are particularly relevant with respect to individualizing instruction and assessment. These are continuous progress, authentic assessment, and narrative reporting.

Continuous Progress

A continuous progress approach allows students to proceed through curricular areas at their own rate, while not comparing their achievement with the progress of other children. Katherine believes that continuous progress is the key to a successful primary program. She comments:

> Once you group children you stop somebody's progress. You almost automatically start teaching to the middle or the top or the bottom.

Somebody is going to lose out. You can try homogeneous grouping, but you can't homogenize people.

Children have to be allowed to move at their own speed. There is no sense in holding children back, or for that matter, pushing them forward, just to keep up with a group. That's why I have developed the workshop approach to reading, writing, and math. That approach allows each child to progress at his or her own pace. Look at Brian, he is already in a third year book in math and he is only 7 years old. Because he is only 7 years old, does that mean I should make him do second grade work? I don't think that is what the primary program is all about.

Observations in this classroom over a three-year period confirmed that this classroom is individualized in reading, writing, and math, which encouraged students to make continuous progress in their development as learners. Those who quickly caught on to a particular math concept as Katherine mentioned, did not have to wait for other students to reach an understanding before they could move on. Brian was able to skip over many pages containing the concepts "count forward, count back, and skip count," as well as classifying objects by sets, because he had either already demonstrated his ability to perform those concepts, or was able to perform them after one page of work. He then moved directly into grouping and place value, concepts normally associated with older children.

In order for Katherine to encourage continuous progress for each child, she must carefully record each child's progress in each curricular area. Thus, anecdotal records, learning logs from unit studies, reading and math logs, writing portfolios and reading conference records are essential to this classroom. These authentic assessment tools enable Katherine to select curricular content that is suitable for each child. This selection process is a critical part of maintaining a classroom environment supportive of continuous progress.

Authentic Assessment

Authentic assessment was defined within the definition of Kentucky's critical attributes for the primary as assessment that occurs within the context of the learning environment and reflects actual learning experiences that can be documented through anecdotal records, observation, journals, conferences, and so on. (Kentucky Department of Education, 1993). While this definition of authentic assessment varies from the more common usage that refers to real life tasks, the ongoing and informal assessment techniques are much the same.

Katherine is adamant about using such assessment strategies in her classroom. She commented:

By making anecdotal records, having the students keep learning logs, and using reading and writing conferences, I am much more aware of what my students actually know than when I was giving tests. When I tested the children, I knew they knew the test material, but that is so limiting. With journals and conferences, I can actually see and hear what the children know—in their own words.

The vignettes describing the activities in unit study and the production of student-authored books reveal that authentic learning and assessment are a way of life in this classroom. Students "traveled" west in the Moving West unit. In this unit they had to apply what they knew about math to determine how long their trip would take. They had to plan what supplies the families would need to make the trip and then had to use problem-solving techniques as families ran into difficulties. During the light and color unit, the children applied what they knew about light and reflection of light to assist a builder with a variety of projects. In another unit when the class built their own rainforest, they again had to use what they knew about math to measure the plastic for the huge bubble that they were going to build. In order to be guides to other students in the building, they had to research the tropical rainforest and its inhabitants. When they planned and planted their own garden, they again had to apply math skills in measurement so the plants would be properly placed and have enough room to grow. During Sibling Day, the kids had to remember what they had learned in each unit so they could explain the learning centers to the younger children visiting the classroom.

Just as instruction is individualized in Katherine's classroom, so is assessment. A good example of this is the way in which spelling tests are approached. In many classrooms, spelling words are parts of lists that are generated by their common "spelling rule"—rules that may mean little or nothing to the young student. In Katherine's classroom, spelling words are generated from each student's own writing, which means that every child has a group of words that are important to him or her. In order to assess the student's ability to spell these words correctly the words are written on a spelling list that is specific to each student. It is the student's responsibility to study these words throughout the week. On Wednesdays, the children give each other their spelling tests based on their individual word lists. Katherine records the results of the tests to report to parents. Any word not spelled correctly automatically goes on the next week's list. Correctly spelled words are entered by the child in a personal dictionary that can be used as a reference by the child and that also provides an excellent record of all the words the child learned to spell during the year.

The writing process and being an author are considered extremely important by the students in this classroom, so learning to spell words that they are using in their own piece takes on a greater significance. Spelling is easily incorporated into the children's daily work. There are no traumatic days when someone misses many words on a test and feels incompetent. Children learn to spell a variety of words during their three years in this primary program and are generally considered good spellers by their fourth-grade teacher.

In general, when Katherine assesses the children she is looking for conceptual understanding in each area as well as the ability to apply new knowledge in other situations. Are their spelling words spelled correctly in their writing in all curricular areas? Are the skills they are working on in math applied when appropriate in unit study? Do they take conceptual understandings gained in one unit and apply them to their next area of study? Katherine keeps written records of student progress as they complete activities designed to support the KERA goals she is focusing on during each particular unit. Their writing and in-class activities reveal whether they have attained these goals, or are progressing toward attaining these goals. Her anecdotal notes concentrate on these areas as well. With all of this information she has a variety of sources to assist her in describing each child's progress when she completes each child's nine-week report.

Qualitative Reporting

Qualitative reporting methods deal with the way in which student progress is communicated to the children's families. Katherine is a strong supporter of qualitative reporting and uses several methods.

> I feel it is important to keep in close contact with each child's family. That's why I send home weekly progress reports, the math and reading logs, and the newsletter. Parents have the right to know what their child is working on while they are at school. Teachers need to be accountable to them because we are, after all, dealing with someone they love very much and whom they want to see succeed.
>
> I have always kept in close touch with my parents. It seems to me that we need to be a team working together in order to provide the best education for each child. You can't be a member of a team unless you are informed about what is happening. Since parents can't be at school every day to see their child's progress it is up to me to devise ways to keep them informed.

Katherine's classroom is filled with examples of qualitative reporting of the assessment of student work. As mentioned, the students keep reading and math logs. These logs are sent home each week to be reviewed and signed by parents. The students plan individual writing strategies with Katherine that cover a certain period of time and set up parameters within which the child will work. Katherine sends home weekly progress reports to parents in order to keep them abreast of their child's progress, and she dutifully adds written comments that are individual to each child on the nine-week report cards.

Accountability and Commitment

KERA is now in its eighth year and has evolved over this time. Issues of accountability are growing as the pressure to move all children to proficient status on the
KIRIS tests pushes educators to strive for ways to satisfy the state's requirements.
Katherine's views concerning accountability seem to be different from many educators who are so deeply concerned about the rewards and sanctions tied to
KIRIS. Katherine feels she is primarily accountable to "the children in her classroom, their parents, the principal, and professional standards." When asked to
describe her feelings in more detail she states:

> Accountability in Kentucky is a hot topic. The goal is that all children
> should reach the proficient level on the KIRIS tests. How can that pos-
> sibly occur? The "givens" for children are not being taken into account.
> I mean, it's a given that all children do not come from homes that have
> a print rich environment, or have parents that know how to support
> their schooling, or for that matter, are well-fed. How can we expect all
> of these children to reach the proficient status? It is certainly our oblig-
> ation as teachers to take each student as far as we possibly can during
> the time we have them in class, but to make us accountable to seeing
> that each child reaches the proficient stage is pretty unrealistic.

Katherine is relatively unfazed by the high stakes of sanctions and rewards
that are attached to the KIRIS assessments. She explains:

> Whatever sanctions and rewards the state decides to attach to the test-
> ing procedure should not affect what I know to be good teaching strate-
> gies. All of the research I have read indicates that teaching reading and
> writing holistically is the best way for children to learn. I do not think I
> should be asked to change the way I teach because someone is nervous
> about whether or not students do well on standardized tests. My belief
> is that children should leave school prepared to be good citizens. In
> order for them to be able to make the kinds of decisions good citizens
> make they must be able to think and solve problems and they certainly
> must be able to learn how to work with other people. The goals of
> KERA demand that I give children these skills and by structuring my
> classroom the way I do, I feel I am doing my part in helping students
> become responsible citizens.

As she mentions, Katherine does feel an obligation to be accountable for the
children in her classroom's progress. She is diligent about keeping parents well-
informed about their child's education. The fact that she sends home weekly
progress reports along with reading, learning and math logs and has devised the
Parent Handbook and a *Learning at Home* booklet (a guide to practical ways they

can encourage their child's education) reveals her interest in being accountable to parents and to engage them as co-educators of their own children. Parents are encouraged to participate in classroom activities in many ways. She has a parent meeting once a grading period to allow parents to come and see for themselves what is happening in the classroom. There are often parent volunteers in her room publishing student books, reading to the children, sharing a special skill or just observing.

It is also important to note that Katherine is a strong proponent of the continued implementation of the primary program component of KERA. She asked to be allowed to create the first multi-age/multi-ability classroom in her building a year before the program was mandated. She has woven the "critical attributes" throughout her ongoing approach. What the implementation of the KERA primary program did for Katherine was to legitimize her already effective practice. Katherine reports:

> I believe that multi-age/multi-ability classrooms that reflect the attributes of the primary program are good for kids. It is a shame that many teachers are retreating from implementing primary classrooms as they were envisioned by the creators of KERA, but it is pretty obvious that you can't mandate programs like this. From the very beginning teachers who did not want to teach using the philosophy upon which the primary program was based found ways to circumvent teaching in a multi-age classroom.

Further evidence of Katherine's commitment to the primary program is her support of colleagues in her building. After Katherine's first year as a primary teacher she was approached by two other teachers in the building who wanted to create a similar multi-age/multi-ability approach to teaching in their own classrooms. Katherine teamed up with these teachers to provide encouragement and assistance. Of course, she also gained support and assistance from them.

One area of concern for many teachers is the need to ensure that students entering fourth grade are prepared for the fourth-grade curriculum, which includes the KIRIS tests and the assessment of student writing portfolios. To address this situation Katherine, the two other primary teachers she is working with, and a fourth-grade teacher have formed a new team. Working with the building principal, these teachers have arranged for the three primary teachers' third-year students to enter the fourth-grade teacher's classroom the following year. The team meets every month to work to align the primary curriculum to meet the criteria necessary for fourth-grade work. To accommodate students who have been working under the continuous progress philosophy, the fourth-grade teacher has begun implementing an individualized math program along with using the reading/writing workshop approach to her language arts curriculum in these areas. The fourth-grade teacher expresses amazement that so many of the children are working well above grade level in math and are such prolific readers and writers.

Katherine Alexander Futrell is committed to developing an environment that nurtures the whole child. She incorporates authentic learning and assessment that entices the child's natural curiosity and eagerness to learn. And, from all the present evidence, she has been quite successful at making the KERA primary program work to enhance student learning in an innovative and rigorous way.

Note

1. Names of all students are changed to protect anonymity.

References

Kentucky Department of Education. (1993). *State regulations and recommended best practices for Kentucky's primary program.* Frankfort, KY: Kentucky Department of Education.

4

"The More Mathematics You Know, the Better Your Life Is Going to Be"

KEN JONES AND BETTY LOU WHITFORD

Mary Jo Foster is working from an overhead, showing the Algebra I class transparencies of some student responses to a geometry problem.[1] Each student has a handout of the same page. They are working as a whole class to analyze two student portfolio entries. One has been chosen by a state committee as a benchmark paper illustrating "apprentice" level work; the other has been chosen as a "proficient" benchmark paper. Portfolio pieces in Kentucky are scored as novice, apprentice, proficient, or distinguished.

"What's good about this entry?" Mary Jo asks about the apprentice piece. "Look at the scoring guide and tell me what you can see that this student does." There is a brief exchange about correct computation.

"How could this piece be improved?" she asks. Several students offer possibilities that have to do with clarity. Mary Jo affirms what they say and asks for more. "What about math representations? Could this student include some tables or graphs?"

This give and take continues for another 15 minutes until the students' enthusiasm begins to wane. Mary Jo begins to prowl the room, speaking more pointedly, making connections from the sample entries to mathematics that the students have already done. She gets students to talk about the scatter plots they have just finished that are displayed around the room. She asks them to explain how the data being discussed have anything to do with the functions that they've been investigating in their texts and with their graphing calculators. The students remain less than enthusiastic.

Frustrated, Mary Jo suddenly jumps onto a chair, balancing her tall, athletic frame first on one leg, then the other, holding her arms at various angles to model the shapes of different functions. Now she has their attention, and laughter rolls through the room. She gets the whole class on its feet to follow her in these mathematical calisthenics. High school students having fun role-playing mathematical functions: it is a sight to see.

As an experienced mathematics teacher, now in her twenty-seventh year of teaching, she might be expected to rely upon tried and true routines for navigating through the complexities of instruction and classroom management. And, in this era of fast-paced school reform, one might assume that changing those routines would be very difficult indeed. Old dogs, new tricks, and all that.

In fact, says Mary Jo, during her first eighteen or so years of teaching, she had been a fairly traditional teacher, running a tightly ordered classroom, using the textbook as the sole source of her curriculum, giving only objective tests that measured straightforward computation and the use of procedures and formulas. But about nine years ago, she began changing her approach, finding new life in many of the changes brought on by technology, by the redefinition of school mathematics in the National Council of Teachers of Mathematics (NCTM) *Curriculum and Evaluation Standards* of 1989, and by the massive school reform mandated through the Kentucky Education Reform Act (KERA) of 1990. Reflecting on these, she comments:

> I used to have students sit in straight rows—no talking. They had to raise their hands and wait on me. That's awful! . . . I hate routines. I didn't used to hate them. I didn't know any better. But now teaching has to stay exciting for me, so I can help make it that way for the kids. . . . I think my philosophy of teaching probably changes about every year now. I'm figuring out that all students can learn at a higher level than they have been learning. I truly believe that. It's just that all students don't learn at the same rate or in the same way. . . . I'm becoming more flexible.

Mary Jo Foster now uses a variety of entertainment, texts, technology, and her own considerable wit to try to get her students engaged in mathematics. She continually adapts her instruction to the performance of her students, mixing up whole class instruction with small group work and with individualized work, always looking for what will get students involved in their own learning. She reflects on her approach:

> I continually try to "read" my students. Their attention span often dictates more small group or individual work. I like some whole class opening and closure. I also like variety. . . . I don't spend more than fifteen minutes or so lecturing in a class, because they don't listen anyway! They've got to be active. A whole lot of kids need the hands-on, seeing it, making it work. They learn by doing easier than they learn by getting

preached at or trying to read it out of a book. . . . I think you have to learn to explain things different ways to different students. And I can't always do that. You know, often, kids can help kids better than I can.

Moreover, Mary Jo is learning to modify her instructional approach as she goes, often through trial and error, but also with remarkably good humor despite the many frustrations. "Mostly, I'm learning from the mistakes I make," she laughs. On one occasion, after patiently but unsuccessfully trying to prod students into remembering some understandings about the concept of slope they had been working on for a couple of weeks, she dropped to a squat on the floor, making a sound through her lips like a tire deflating. Then she got up and had students hold both their arms out horizontal to the floor, modeling a line with zero slope. In a radio announcer voice, she boomed, "If you went skiing on a flat slope, you'd have zero fun!" Next she had students hold one arm straight up and the other straight down to model a line with undefined slope. The announcer voice warned, "If you went skiing on a vertical slope, you'd be undefined at the bottom!" Then, she gave a quick, step-by-step demonstration on the board of how to find slope and assigned some exercises so that students could learn, once again, by doing. Later, she commented on her frustration:

> In mathematics, it sometimes takes us a long time to get anywhere. These kids can do this. They just take time making connections. With them it just seems to take more repetition than I'm used to. Ah, they can be such blockheads! You've got to love 'em. They're all so precious in their own frustrating ways.

In addition to trying new approaches, Mary Jo has grown more reflective about her work, evaluating particular strategies and deciding what to keep doing, what to modify, and what to stop doing. As she observes, "When you see something finally connect, it makes your . . . minute!" Along with this new-found flexibility and the cycle of action and reflection, she is also developing a vision of "good mathematics," as she calls it. She explains:

> Students can get correct answers and it doesn't mean anything. Maybe they can't explain how they got it or can't transfer it to a real life problem, can't *use* it. If we give them more open-ended questions or tasks, where they use basic skills *and* higher-level thinking to help solve a problem, they can make the connections within mathematics and beyond mathematics. Mathematics is different now in that we expect students to investigate and explore rather than just give back some correct answers that the teacher already knows. . . . We expect them to use technology because it's so available and efficient. Computers can crunch numbers a whole lot better than we can. Basic skills in arithmetic are still important so we you can do estimation and mental arithmetic and

tell if you have a reasonable answer. And there are even more basic skills than that. In secondary mathematics, basic skills include being able to solve an equation, analyze data, use a calculator, use computers as tools, use formulas. . . . Mathematics is not just dealing with the world of certainties. We don't know what the correct answers are in all situations. We come out with what we think might be a best solution, but we might continue to revise it and get a better one.

Background

For 20 years now, Mary Jo Foster has taught in a small, rural public school system about 30 miles from Louisville, Kentucky. Two school buildings house the system's approximately 1,750 students, a K–6 elementary and a 7–12 high school. To accommodate recent growth, a new building is on the drawing boards and a new middle school is being organized. For now, however, the high school is still very crowded with 767 students.

The population of the county is mostly white and many are poor. Nearly 43% of the students in the district receive a free or reduced-price lunch. Tobacco, corn, grain, hogs, and welfare are the primary sources of income for residents, although that is now shifting as farmland is turned into subdivisions for a growing number of urban commuters. Many students, says Mary Jo, come from homes where parents do not have high school diplomas, "which is a constant battle." Last year's dropout rate was 3%, about the same as the state average, while the rate of students going on to college was only 43.3%. Mary Jo worries about her students:

> We have kids that are chemically dependent, kids that don't know how to control their anger, some pregnant kids. More and more are working. They don't have time to do their homework. And there are some good kids that are trying to save their money for a car, or car insurance, or college. That's a challenge because, you know, you want them to learn a lot, do what they can, so they don't have to do what they're doing right now their whole lives, flipping hamburgers or whatever.

While Mary Jo feels that community pride in the school might be greater ("We don't have football or soccer teams yet"), she does see that there is a fair measure of community support, as seen in the well-attended fund-raisers and PTA-organized events. Many of the teachers in the school grew up or go to church in the community, so community ties are deep rooted.

According to the school counselor, Mary Jo is well liked and respected in the school. She observes, "I've always marveled at her. She's polite, firm, and fair with students, is a good disciplinarian, works on helping kids feel good about themselves. She's a real lady." Mary Jo is also the mother of two children, active in her church, and an avid University of Louisville football fan. She has served on the school council and has been the chair of the six-person mathematics department for the past 10 years. A couple of years ago, she was selected as a state semifinalist for the prestigious Presidential Award for Mathematics and Science Teaching.

The Classroom and Day

Mary Jo's classroom is full. It's small in the first place, 25 by 25 feet in dimension. Eight rectangular tables recently replaced the individual student desks, providing a bit more walking space and flat surfaces on which students can work with materials. "Now we have a level playing surface," Mary Jo jokes.

Around the edges of the room are five computers ("They're antiques! Boy if I could just have some of those Windows machines"). File cabinets, shelves, and boxes—all brimming—line the walls. Her desk is in a corner, covered with baskets, texts, rulers, and other assorted stuff of the trade. To the side of her desk, against the wall, is a small technology outpost with computer, printer, TV, and VCR. An overhead projector sits on a cart in front of the desk. The walls are filled with colorful posters, scoring guides for student work, called "rubrics," and chart paper displaying student-generated scatter plots. On top of a filing cabinet sits the remnants of a large, 3-D tetrahedron fractal model.

During the 1997–98 school year, the school has used a seven-period day, which translates to Mary Jo having six classes and three preparations. She teaches three Algebra II classes, two Pre-Calculus classes, and Integrated III, a class for seniors who have had Algebra II and Geometry but do not want to take Pre-Calculus. Many of the students in Integrated III need to complete an apprentice-level mathematics portfolio, a district graduation requirement. The district has maintained this requirement even while the state withdrew the math portfolio from KIRIS for more research and development, aiming for higher reliability and validity. Over the course of the day, Mary Jo sees 95 students, an enrollment considerably down from her usual load. "It just happened this year with kids changing their schedules and what not."

The normal day in this school is fast-paced, punctuated with starts and stops signaled by a schoolwide buzzer to mark the beginning and end of the classes that change every 45 minutes. Mary Jo is frustrated by the schedule. She would prefer having a four-period block schedule, as many high schools in the state now use. She believes that seeing fewer students in a day for longer periods of time would provide more effective opportunities for the kind of in-depth work and follow-through necessary for students to develop real understandings in mathematics. Further, she believes larger chunks of instructional time are necessary in order to give students the kinds of learning opportunities needed to fully cover and understand the mathematics content specified by the state and to do well on KIRIS.

The Core Content

What mathematics should students be taught? Should all students learn the same mathematics? How much time and depth should be devoted to particular topics? These are questions Mary Jo has wrestled with while transforming her practice. Before the recent publication of the state's *Core Content for KIRIS Assessment*, she made curricular decisions based on the NCTM standards and her own judgment about what students needed. She reflects on how her thinking has changed:

> I think I certainly need to know why I'm teaching a concept and what my outcomes or expectations are for the students. Before, I taught systems of equations because that's what I thought you were supposed to teach. You know, it was, well, "we're going to do this page and this page today," but not "what is it I want kids to know and be able to do when I finish this unit." And now, it's more like, "so why do we teach this?" If I can't come up with a good answer, I just might not teach it. . . . I can see in the NCTM *Standards* the lesser important things sometimes get so less important that we just might not get to them for awhile. Like factoring quadratics—I'm doing almost zero factoring. We'll talk about it for a day or two, use algebra tiles to do some factoring, and that might be enough. They need a little bit for the ACT, but after that, they're not going to use it again! They are not going to factor. You don't have pretty numbers in the real world.

Mary Jo has little patience with those who insist on preaching about "back to basics." She sees basic skills as necessary but not sufficient and rejects the notion that it is an either-or proposition as to whether teachers should focus on basics or higher-order thinking.

> Basic skills are important, but we have to go beyond basic skills. Lots of people are writing to the paper and stirring things up about, for example, kids not being able to do their multiplication tables. If they haven't learned those by the time I get them, I don't think I can magically help the kids learn those. They may not want to for some reason. But I can help them overcome that and still be able to solve an equation, still be able to analyze data, and know a little bit about probability and geometry. They can still do some of that higher level mathematics even if they have trouble in basic skills. . . . Basic skills are important. And the basic skills we learned when we were little aren't necessarily the same basic skills that kids need today. I think they need a whole lot more. Technology has changed things.

The state *Core Content for KIRIS Assessment* was published in June 1996, and state's description of high school courses, found in the *Program of Studies*, was approved by the state board of education in February 1998. These have now assumed a strong guiding role for Mary Jo. She likes the state content, noting that she was on the state advisory committee that helped to develop the core content document. At the same time, she feels pressure to adhere to the state content because of the high-stakes state test. She says:

> I like the core content because it supports me teaching what I'm teaching. Not all teachers in the state, I'm sure, feel the same way about it. I think that what's in those courses reflects change over time. A lot of what's [still] being taught around the state consists of mathematics that most of our students don't really need very much. A lot of teachers aren't doing very much with data analysis. . . . If you focus on the core content, which is where the KIRIS test questions are coming from, that's what we need to be doing—if we want to see the scores improve. If a department doesn't have its curriculum aligned [with the core content], they might be teaching some pretty good stuff, but it might not be what the kids will be tested on.

The pressure resulting from rewards and sanctions has created mixed feelings in Mary Jo. Her comments run both positive and negative:

> It puts a little more pressure on us to do what we should be doing. I really truly believe it's helpful. It makes the whole department strive harder to get the kids to a higher plane, but I haven't yet had a DE[2] telling me what I had to do. . . . I don't know what rewards would do to us. I'd just be happy if they bought me new computers. I don't really truly believe that our school would be any better if we had a DE in here than we are right now. . . . I think all of us would feel less stress if we knew we weren't gonna [be sanctioned]. . . if nothing happened, though, if our scores went down and nothing happened, I truly believe teachers would not continue to strive as hard as they are right now. I think there has to be something.

When asked what she would do if a student wanted to pursue a topic that was not in the core content, she responded, "I'd love to have that problem! I'd probably let the kid pursue it and then try to work the core content into it." At another point, she added, "I don't like the KIRIS test because it takes so much time out of school."

Time, in fact, seems to be in shorter and shorter supply for Mary Jo as the demands of the core content compete with the demands of the assessments used on the state test. The core content document could be seen, not as a guide indicating "core" knowledge in mathematics, but rather as a comprehensive and detailed description of what students are expected to know and be able to do. Thus, this document signals teachers that they should cover specific content, while the state test focuses on depth of understanding and communication ability. Breadth and depth seem to pull in opposite directions, creating dilemmas about how best to use classroom time. Mary Jo puzzles over these conditions:

> How are we going to have time to get through the curriculum? To do portfolios? To teach the kids all they need to know for KIRIS and the ACT (American College Test)? And everything else? How are we going to have time to do it?

There is increasing pressure on teachers from the state accountability approach to cover more content. Teachers generally approach the need for coverage by using teacher-directed strategies because they are more efficient than strategies which engage students more actively. Despite these pressures, Mary Jo believes that hands-on activities help students learn "good mathematics" more effectively. Here is an example of a strategy she used several years ago to engage students in data gathering and analysis. She does fewer of these types of activities now.

A Small Group Project

POP!! A balloon bursts. As students laugh and point, Mary Jo smiles and continues circulating around the room, asking questions, prodding activity, looking for proper documentation and graphing of the data. Teams of students are blowing up balloons, putting tape measures around them, holding two books on the outside of the balloons, and measuring the distances with meter sticks. Other groups have finished that part and are going into the hallway with stopwatches to release the balloons and time how long it takes them to run out of air. Others are recording and graphing the data. Each group does several trials using varying numbers of breaths to inflate the balloons, collects and graphs the data, looks for a line of best fit, and interprets the results. This work is part of a whole class portfolio project in the Algebra I class, an idea that Mary Jo found in the National Council of Teacher of Mathematic's (NCTM) monthly journal, *The Mathematics Teacher*.

As the work proceeds, the noise level rises and falls, mathematical conversations mix with teenage laughter and bantering. Students get up and move to and from the hallway. "We'll do this in an orderly fashion," says one girl to her group with a tongue-in-cheek, pseudo-authoritative voice. Mary Jo acts as instructor, traffic officer, resource manager, and cheerleader. One student needs help using the stopwatch, another is advised not to squeeze the balloon while measuring, while still another needs graph paper. It is a whirlwind of activity.

A boy in one group has proudly blown a balloon into huge proportions with just three breaths and is showing it off, prompting other boys to want to do the same.

Mary Jo: Since you've done this with only three breaths, you don't have much data to work with. Had you realized that, what might you have done differently?

Student (somewhat sheepishly): Taken smaller breaths?

Mary Jo: Just make sure each breath is consistent. Try to get different measures with up to five or six breaths. (Smiling) Maybe you need an Inflator with less breath.

Mary Jo notices that some of her students are recording inaccurate times, so she corrects them and remarks in an aside to a visitor:

I think many of their times are off. I watch them use their stopwatches. Some kids just want bigger numbers. If I catch them, I make them do it over. Some of their measurements will be so inaccurate that the actual graph may not be realistic. But, at this point, I don't really care. If they are actually collecting, organizing, and analyzing data, and giving reasons why, that's a big step.

As she moves through the room, Mary Jo is often as animated and personal as the students, laughing, putting her arm around a student's shoulders, teasing and cajoling. She obviously enjoys the action, and for the most part, she says she has come to terms with the noise and confusion such activities entail.

Sometimes, even to me, it seems like utter confusion because kids have to do this and this and this. I still have problems with noise, but it's a wonderful kind of noise when they're on-task. Still, I have to take a deep breath and hold my tongue because I don't like noise. Some people would say I've lost control. A sub once told me that she'd had a good day because even though the students hadn't worked very hard, they were quiet. How crushing! I would rather have the opposite.

With about 20 minutes left in the period, amidst a growing sense of disorder, Mary Jo calls time-out. "Many of you are ready to move on. What should you be doing?" No one responds. "Let's read the two pages I gave you." There is a flurry of paper shuffling. "Okay, let's have materials-getters return stuff to the table and everyone get busy graphing." There is still some commotion in the class. Mary Jo raises her voice. "I am trying to talk." Quiet now reigns. "Do you need some guidance or do you know what to do?" Still quiet. "Okay, let's get busy." In less than a minute, Mary Jo has skillfully redirected the energy in the room into purposeful action.

With about 10 minutes to go in the class period, Mary Jo once more commands attention. "I'm going to give you two more papers that will help you know how you will be graded. One is the checklist you came up with yesterday. I typed it up for you. The other is a self-assessment guide that should help you to revise your work if necessary." She moves through the room, passing out papers and answering questions as students continue their work.

As the period comes to a close, students start to relax, talk, and get ready to leave. Mary Jo quickly summarizes the class activity and assigns homework. "Any questions? No? Have a nice day!" she chirps with a big grin.

Projects like this require a great deal of planning time just to think through the sequence of activity and organize the tools and worksheets. Sometimes, Mary Jo also needs to study the mathematical concept behind the activity so that she understands it well enough herself before having the students tackle it.

> I probably spend 2–3 hours every night I'm home and at least 6–8 hours each weekend planning and studying, learning this material so I can teach it. That doesn't count all the time grading. I think it's fine to learn along with the students, too. It's exciting to all of us that way. But there is a comfort level in knowing the direction of where you want to be. If you don't have that direction because you just plain don't know what's going to happen, that's very uncomfortable. There's so much to know. One teacher can't know everything. You can build and build and build and never stop.

Professional Development

How does Mary Jo come up with the kinds of activities that will generate interest with her students and serve to enrich the curriculum? How does she sustain her drive to keep improving her work? Mostly the ideas and support so critical to her practice have come through her pursuit of meaningful professional development activities. In fact, she states that her professional experiences have been a greater force in her changing than any state mandate or national standard. It was, she says, a connection to summer weeklong Woodrow Wilson Institutes, pre-KERA, that provided the turning point in her career. There, she discovered some of the possibilities for using computers and graphing calculators in her teaching and got inspired. "I saw that with technology, you could do some good activities that would be fun!"

Since that time, Mary Jo has looked for and found professional development opportunities that fit her changing teaching approach. She has spent part of three summers with the Wilson Institute, a summer at the Fermi Lab studying fractals and chaos theory, and a summer as part of the Graphing Calculator Enhanced Algebra Project. She has participated in statewide initiatives, such as the NSF-sponsored PRISM project (Partnerships in Reform Initiatives in Science and Mathematics) and the Kentucky Mathematics Portfolio advisory committee. She continues to take part in teacher networks, including the Louisville-based LATTICE (Learning Algebra Through Technology, Investigations, and Cooperative Experiences), a regional Technology Alliance, and a regional Goals 2000 curriculum-oriented initiative called Project SCIMATCH. She also cites several courses at the University of Louisville as influences on her work.

> I just think professional development is extremely important to keep up with ideas coming in, to share with other people, keeping up with technology, and the new trends in math education. I think if you're going to be successful, there's no way around it.

Mary Jo also makes an effort to share with and learn from her fellow mathematics teachers in the building. Sometimes she shares materials, tools, or ideas that she has gathered in a workshop or at a conference. She will give quick lessons to other teachers on how to use a piece of equipment or software. And, she keeps her eye out for instructional materials for her department and makes recommendations.

Her professional development is not only influenced by mathematics specialists. She has also developed a friendship and a working relationship with an English teacher who used to teach across the hall and recently became the school's reading/writing specialist. She gives this teacher credit for helping her to stay focused on what she wants students to know and be able to do as a result of any lesson or unit and for seeing the importance of providing authentic audiences for student work as much as possible. They often chat about students and lessons.

As department chair, she meets regularly with her mathematics colleagues, who during 1997–98 have all had a common planning time. In addition, every Thursday, students are released an hour and 20 minutes early from school so that teachers may work together to plan and discuss lessons and plan the department's curriculum. While this time together is worthwhile, she expresses mixed feelings about taking the instruction time away from kids.

> I like the working time we have as a staff, department meetings, professional development, faculty meetings. That time is real valuable. I don't like that classes go by so fast that it's really hard to accomplish anything. I don't like taking the instruction time away. Overall, though, it's probably worth it.

In a profession known for its isolation, where teachers often simply go into their own rooms and do their own things, Mary Jo Foster stands out as someone who takes initiative to work collaboratively with others. Why? What motivates Mary Jo to add that extra effort? Part of the answer seems to lie in her sense of professionalism, another part of her commitment to prepare her students for the needs of a changing world.

> I guess because I just want to do the best I can. I feel that I have to be organized and prepared. If I'm not prepared, then I'm not being fair to the kids—to get them prepared for their next step. . . . I think the jobs

in this country and around the world will require people who understand technology, can service it, keep it going. We're going to have to
know a whole lot more. . . . I have lots of kids who don't like mathematics. In spite of that, I encourage them to try, to do the best they can
do, to learn all they can so that they don't end up having to suffer later
on because they didn't learn some math. That might keep them from
being a writer, or an artist, or whatever they want to be. The more
mathematics you know, the better your life is going to be.

These new ways of working are rooted in a belief about the importance of
moving each student to higher or "better" mathematics. This requires sustained
attention to individual student performance rather than merely teaching a topic,
averaging class grades that array students across an A–F grading scheme, and
moving lock-step on to the next topic in the curriculum. Mary Jo has made strides
toward this goal as well as the next vignette illustrates.

Individualizing Instruction

The students are seated in groups of three and four. Mary Jo gets the class started
with a quick directive, "Some of you need to work on the text activities, some on
tests, some on portfolio pieces. Try to figure out what you need to do. I'll be with
you in a minute."

Two students have their portfolios out and are trying to decide which of the
entries need revision. Looking at the entries, one student comments, "This one's
okay. At least it satisfies me. This one needs help. Hmm. . . she didn't like this
one?"

In another group, a student explains what a test question is asking. A couple
of students get up and move to other groups. One student goes up to talk with
Mary Jo about an idea for developing a portfolio piece.

Mary Jo is on the move, tugging on a box of color-coded working portfolios.
"Anyone else need their portfolio today?" She moves from group to group, check-
ing in, commenting on their work, posing questions. She frequently asks students
to make sense of their solutions with remarks like "So what?" or "So now what do
you know?" or "So now that you know that, what are you going to do about it? Be
happy?"

In the corner of the room, a student pops in a video that comes with the text
materials and watches the TV. None of the other students looks up or seems to be
distracted by it. Another two students are busy getting a computer printout. The
mix of activities in the room include some easy socializing as students joke, flirt,
and move around to work on their particular tasks.

This kind of "decentralized" learning environment has become a normal
part of Mary Jo's instructional repertoire. How does she keep track of it all and

keep everyone working? One key, she says, is the how she chooses text materials. Certain texts allow students to be more self-directed than others. Some provide modules that are not so tightly sequenced that one unit must precede another in the published order. Such materials allow Mary Jo to give students choices about what topic they will study individually or in small groups. Mary Jo keeps track of who is doing what, assigns deadlines, and poses tasks to serve as end-of-unit tests.

In all of her classes, Mary Jo tries to balance whole class direct instruction with small group activities and projects and individualized work with text materials. She explains:

> In mathematics, you've got to take kids from where they are and move them further up the scale. There are so many levels within a classroom. That's part of the reason I've gotten away from big lecturing and talking. In Algebra II and Pre-Calculus, I can still do that some, but in other classes, I find that even two to three minutes, trying to show kids something as a whole group, about fifty percent of them can't stay tuned, don't understand, or don't gain anything. Sometimes, I see I don't have their attention anymore, so I have to try something different. Most of these kids, they have to do something, write it, measure it, do an experiment, have something physical. They're at that model level where they need to see it or do it, maybe they're a visual or kinesthetic learner. It helps.

But Mary Jo is quick to add that she has not thrown away the textbook in her classes. "I still use textbooks a lot; it's just that the materials that I'm choosing are more activity-driven."

Student Assessment and Accountability

In such a learning environment that emphasizes a mix of direct instruction, group tasks, individualized learning, and portfolio projects, how does Mary Jo assess student work, develop report card grades, and hold students accountable?

Her response is that she uses different assessment formats for different purposes. Tests and quizzes give her information about individual student knowledge and problem-solving ability while daily participation grades serve to give her students a push. She observes, "If I don't give some of these kids grades every day, they won't do anything." Performance assessments give students the opportunity to show what they can do to apply mathematics. She gives out weekly grade slips based on completed homework and scores from the various assessments, using software to keep track of the calculations.

Occasionally, when students need a boost, Mary Jo uses a system of calculating individual bonus points based upon the combined improvement of their cooperative learning group. This is a strategy that she learned from a colleague in the district who had adapted one of the cooperative learning models of Robert Slavin to ensure group interdependence. Mary Jo finds that it helps to get students to do their best and to help each other and works especially well with the younger students.

> I'm not as structured with cooperative learning in some classes as much as I am in others. Seniors know how to work together, in most cases, better than freshmen and sophomores. So you don't have to teach them [how to work in a group].

When asked about the role of intrinsic versus extrinsic motivation strategies in her classroom, Mary Jo says that most of her strategies are extrinsic.

> I would like it all to be intrinsic, but I mostly use extrinsic rewards. Kids aren't mature enough. They don't see their real needs. I like to give kids some choices. . . . Kids always try to take the easy way out. We're trying to make that easy way [connected with] a little bit higher [mathematics].

In order to motivate students to keep trying, Mary Jo allows students to do work over if they want a better grade for a test or quiz. They can improve their grade up to a B in this manner. She explains:

> If a kid doesn't learn it today or tomorrow, all right, he learns it next week. That's wonderful! So if he can turn in some assigned work and it's late, I still take it and accept it. Years before, I'd say, you know, it's due today. You turn it in today or you get a zero. That's pretty stupid.

Mary Jo especially likes to use performance assessments in her grading scheme. Open-response questions are used as quizzes while portfolio entries are part of projects; she uses both assessment strategies as tests. These more open-ended assessments suit her developing vision of mathematics as a way for students to learn in more flexible and investigative ways. She explains:

> That's one thing I really like about the way I'm doing assessments. I use the portfolio, which should also help [students handle] open-response questions, because they're explaining, they're showing multiple ways to get to some kind of a solution. Sometimes, there's no one right answer. [On one test,] students chose their own sets of bivariate data. They were all different. So they can help somebody else understand the process. And isn't that neat? If students can learn something from a test? . . . A test I gave once was on using Hook's Law, putting a slinky with a cup of beans on the bottom and measuring the length of the spring, plotting the number of beans and the length of the spring. It's pretty linear, so they fit that line to the data, write the equation of the line, and then write a summary and introduction. Most of them did it. Most of them

mentioned, you know, this test was kind of fun. And it helped them to connect. . . . It was a cumulative test, actually, of what we've had before and before. And you can't always do that.

Reflection

For Mary Jo Foster, transforming her practice has meant focusing on a vision of mathematics based on modern standards and learning to become more flexible in her teaching methods. As she has grown comfortable with a different approach to teaching, she has made many more decisions affecting her classroom than she did when she "taught computation straight from the book." Now her decisions are more complex, related to curriculum planning, choice of materials, and day-to-day instruction and assessment of students exhibiting wide ranges of achievement.

Her motivation to change has been driven less by Kentucky's extrinsic reward-and-sanction accountability system than by her own developing sense of what her students need in order to be successful in a world that requires a higher level of mathematical competence. Professional development has been her wellspring. During the past nine years—predating KERA, she has sought out extended, meaningful professional development activities. Some focused on mathematics content while others on a mix of content and pedagogy to actively engage students. These have taken different forms, including summer institutes, graduate courses, and teacher networks. The passage of KERA in 1990 reinforced and extended her desire to work in new directions. The legislation legitimized a direction she was already heading and expanded her opportunities to work statewide with other mathematics teachers experiencing similar transformations. She became a state, regional, and local leader in the reforms embraced by KERA.

The curriculum guidance provided by the state in terms of core content and portfolio guidelines has given her support for implementing the kinds of changes that she already understood to be important and necessary. KIRIS has been a tool, especially in her work as chair of the department. The pressure to align the school's curriculum with the state's core content document has served to focus both her teaching and her leadership in the school. KIRIS math scores have steadily improved and are higher than the scores in most other content areas. She and her colleagues have not experienced any state sanctions; nor have they received rewards. Her work has been steadily focused on what the state has asked her to do while she has continued to expand her repertoire of ways to help all students achieve.

KIRIS has indeed gotten Mary Jo's attention. At the same time, she has a commitment to teaching that comes from her own sense of purpose, not from this external mandate. It is this purpose that gives her the energy to keep learning new content and methods in mathematics and to keep generating new lessons and units that appeal to students' interests. Simply stated, she does what she does because she believes in the importance of her work and cares about its effects on her students. It is more a matter of vision, caring, and hard work than a matter of state rewards and sanctions.

As Mary Jo has continued her professional evolution, she has come to appreciate a new stance as critical to her mission as a teacher. "You've got to deal with uncertainty by being flexible," she advises. Rather than operate as one who simply follows the prescriptions of authorities, she has taken it upon herself to understand the changing world of mathematics education; to stay informed about technology, resources, and what other teachers are doing; to "read" her students; and to rely upon her own judgment and creativity. She is not afraid of change but sees it as a fact of life, even fun:

> We've all got to change and grow. We just need to do things one step at a time. We can't do everything overnight. I used to teach the same way I was taught. But times have changed and we've got to change with them. Besides, it's more fun and exciting to me as a teacher. It's more interesting to students. They're not intimidated as much. We've got to get over the hurdle of "Oh, I can't do mathematics." All these kids can do mathematics. They can see that they can do it. There's always more to learn, so professionally I keep growing, which helps me help the kids keep growing. That's a big reward. It takes a lot of time, but for me it's almost a hobby. Instead of an outside hobby, this is it.

But Mary Jo is reluctant to hold herself up as a model. She recognizes that she makes mistakes and is dubious about the idea that one person can teach another so-called "best practices."

> There are no two teachers that are alike anyway. Everybody needs to modify things to her own style and to her students' styles. There's no algorithmic way of teaching mathematics because we're all human beings and every child is unique. There is no one right way.

As Mary Jo says about mathematics, so she also believes about easy or pat answers about how to teach mathematics. There is always uncertainty, often no one right answer, and as she said of her decision to drop factoring from the curriculum, "there are no pretty numbers in the real world."

Notes

1. We collected the data for this study over a six-month period in 1994 primarily through classroom observation and interviews. We observed in Mary Jo's classroom for six full days and interviewed her at lunch time and at the end of the day on four separate occasions at the school. We also interviewed the school's counselor, and talked informally with the principal and students during our visits.

The interviews were audiotaped and transcribed. Field notes taken during observations and interviews were also transcribed. Several follow-up conversations to clarify particular points were with Mary Jo via e-mail. We also examined documents related to the mathematics curriculum, various curriculum materials, samples of student work, and the school's KIRIS scores. We returned to Mary Jo's classroom for one afternoon during the winter of 1998 to interview her in order to bring the case up to date. We reviewed all of the data several times and prepared a draft of the study. Mary Jo read the draft for accuracy of information and logic of the explanations. As a result, one correction was made concerning the number of classes she taught during 1997–98. The case is written in the present tense to enhance the reader's sense of "being there" though it is a blending of events and comments from 1994 to 1998.

    2. State-appointed Distinguished Educators are sent as sanctions to schools who fail to produce sufficiently high test scores on KIRIS.

5

Teacher Community and Commitment

A Case Study of a High School Social Studies Department

LETITIA HOCHSTRASSER FICKEL

It is hot. The humidity in the un-air-conditioned library hangs in the air making it feel thick and heavy. In shorts and T-shirts, not their normal teacher attire, the nine members of the social studies department are planning for the new freshman social studies course they have created. They have already been there most of the morning and are beginning to think about breaking for lunch. But, before they do they want to get at least a framework for the class hammered out.

Sara, one of the three women members, leans back from the table and says, "I think we are on the right track except for the project. I think it is too big, too involved for us to do the first year." She turns to the department chair and says, "Teresa, you had some ideas you talked to me about."

Teresa begins by asking the group, "What are the skills, knowledge base we want?" She notes that as a group they have all expressed the desire for the class to focus not only on students' intellectual development but to include a citizenship component that would get students involved. She suggests that the final project could be a way to do both. "How about take our real community and have them explore problems here and have them make proposals."

That seems to spark some interest from the group. Various ones of them jump in with ideas about local community issues like employment, economic development and job creation, quality of life issues, the lack of activities for teens. Kevin points out there are other problems too. He asks if they had seen the local paper today. "They talked about development in the county," he tells them and then asks, "Can we do it this way, have the students take the role of various local political officials and different citizens like a single mother of three who works a manufacturing job?"

In fleshing out his idea to the group he proposes that each student could get a biography and could explore these community issues from that perspective. Teachers could develop chance cards that students would draw that might change their individual circumstances but real local events would be the focus for inquiry. For the final project he proposes the students could "present recommendations for how to improve the community or how to deal with a current issue."

Around the table there are tentative nods of agreement, yet their faces remain canvases of thought and consideration. "Would it not be better," Michael interjects, "and you might be saying this and I'm not hearing it, if kids are assigned roles it takes some of the reality out of it. But, what if we have them elect the mayor, the magistrates, and other officials from each area [of the county]?"

He points out that those that did not have an office could represent citizens from that community. They would work as a group to investigate the perspectives of people from that community and bring those to the class discussions of county issues. A number of the members agree that they like the idea of not assigning roles and allowing students to have some choice. Kevin reminds them, however, that they have to find a way to get a diversity of perspective in the mix. It can't be "just the perspective of all elected officials."

After some more talk about possibilities for the culminating project, Kevin turns to Donald, the respected senior department member with twenty-two years at the school, and asks, "Tell us from all your years of experience, is the vehicle good enough?" His impish grin in place, Donald assures them, "It will excite their little butts."

Contrary to the collegial and collaborative efforts displayed by the teachers in this vignette, most teachers practice their craft in isolation, behind their individual classroom doors, and away from colleagues. Because of their isolation in "egg-crate" schools (Lortie, 1975) most teachers have come to think of teaching as a private act, one not discussed or shared with colleagues. But what happens when a group of teachers "crack the walls of privatism" (Fullan, 1982) and develop a collaborative community (Little & McLaughlin, 1993) for the collective engagement with curriculum and pedagogical change? How do they go about doing it? What changes for the teachers and their students does it bring about? How does a state context of mandated reform and assessment affect such efforts? This chapter presents a case study of a high school social studies department that is working together to meet the challenges presented by Kentucky's reform agenda.

Methodology

During my doctoral internship with the Kentucky Department of Education Multicultural Education Branch, I served as a presenter at a professional development session for Wilson County High School.[1] One of the teachers in the social studies department had been my colleague during my teacher education program. For the lunch break, he invited me to join him and several colleagues from his department. Their apparent rapport and politically and intellectually lively conversations intrigued me. My own teaching experiences had not included such seemingly open and collegial relationships. They piqued my interest and I wanted to learn more about their relationship and how it affected their collective work.

Thus, in late September of 1995, I began an ethnographic case study to explore how they were constructing their departmental culture and the effects on their instructional practices. The study continued through the 1996–97 school year and, over the course of that time, I spent a total of 40 full school days on site. During these visits I observed in the classrooms of the department members, ate lunch with them, and attended their department and faculty meetings. On the days when there were no meetings scheduled after school, I frequently remained to talk and listen, or just "hang out" with whomever was around.

Throughout the school day I would listen to and engage in the informal conversations among the department members that emerged in the ebb and flow of the day. These conversations served as one form of informal interviews. I also initiated informal interviews with individuals or a group of the teachers in which I would question them about a past event or something I had observed. During my observations in classrooms and at formal meetings, I scripted notes and attempted to capture verbatim much of the dialogue. I did not take notes during lunch or the various informal conversations. Instead, I would go to the library or the teachers' lounge during class time to write notes about the conversations. At the end of the day, I would often sit in my car in the parking lot and expand these notes with observations and emerging questions. Eventually I began using a tape recorder to dictate notes that I later transcribed. I also conducted formal taped interviews with the department members and collected department documents such as course syllabi, meeting notes, and classroom instructional materials.

The data presented in this case represent only a slice of the larger research study (see Fickel, 1998). The case draws from all the multiple data sources but is focused on the development and implementation of a required freshman course that the department members collaboratively created and taught.

The School and Community Setting

Wilson County, and the county seat of Newtown, serve as a bedroom community to the adjacent metropolitan area for many professional families. The town has been experiencing a boom in development in the last five years. New subdivisions have been built on the east side of town along with a new shopping center. Nevertheless, a small and vibrant service-oriented business and financial sector still occupies the downtown area of Newtown. A number of light manufacturing companies have relocated to the community. However, the verdant, rolling hills of the county with their large and prosperous farms suggest that agriculture will remain the primary economic base for some time to come.

Wilson County High School is on Main Street just where the city limits of Newtown start. The architectural design of the two-story building makes obvious its 1960s construction. The school is a departmentalized, comprehensive (9–12) high school of about 1,100 students and a certified staff of approximately 70 teachers, administrators, and counselors. The school curriculum offers a wide range of required and elective courses in the core discipline areas as well as vocational, agricultural, business, and humanities courses. Students also have the opportunity to participate in school–work cooperative courses. Classes for preparation for the Advanced Placement (AP) national exam are offered in mathematics, English and foreign languages, history, and psychology.

The student body reflects the general population demographics of the community: predominately White, middle- to upper-middle-class students. Approximately 8% of the students in the school are African Americans. There is a growing population of Mexican families who are seasonal farmworkers in the community. However, most of the Mexican children are elementary age students. During 1996–97 the high school enrolled only 6–10 of these Spanish-speaking students.

During the 1996–97 school year the school instituted a "block" schedule with four 90-minute class periods per day. Students now take four classes each semester, and may therefore complete eight classes in a school year. Most teachers in the school, including the teachers in the social studies department, are responsible for three classes per term and receive a daily planning period of ninety minutes. The school began the block schedule with a 60-minute flextime in the middle of the day. This time was designed to serve as a lunch break and enrichment opportunity for students. However, due to faculty concerns with supervision and student use of this time, flex was canceled in October of 1996. This necessitated a reorganization of the class schedule including the return to a lunch schedule which "split" some third block classes into two segments of 45 minutes each.

The mathematics, science, and English and foreign language departments track students into advanced, honors, and regular level courses. Other than two AP courses, U.S. History and Psychology, the social studies department makes no "track" distinction in its course offerings; therefore their classes tend to be more heterogeneous. However, due to the tracking within the other departments, students often cluster together into certain sections of the social studies courses resulting in more homogeneity in these classes.

The department offers the largest number of electives in the school. Students may select from the A.P. courses in U.S. History and Psychology, as well as World Civilizations, Geography, Political Science, Sociology, Psychology, Law and Justice, Cultural Diversity in the U.S., Global Issues, and, new during the 1996–97 school year, Kentucky Studies, History of Armed Human Conflict, and the freshman introductory course, Social Studies I. When the study began, the only required course for all students was U.S. History.

The Social Studies Department: The Teachers and Their Relationship

The hallway that houses the social studies department serves as a main artery of the building running from the library at one end to the gym at the other. The banner and pictures above the lockers give the hallway the look of a wall of fame. Large block letters announce this is "The Social Studies Department." Below them hang large photographs of the department members with their names neatly aligned underneath. In the mornings the hallway is abuzz with students chatting, storing their belongings in lockers, heading to and from the gym or cafeteria, and popping in to ask one of the teachers a question or just say hello.

The teachers in the department are an eclectic lot, displaying a wide range of political views, personal interests, teaching experiences, and instructional repertoires. The two most senior members have been teaching in the department for 22 and 13 years respectively. The 13-year veteran serves as the department chair and was completing her third year in this leadership role during the study. The other seven members have been teaching for eight to two years and have all joined the department since 1991. A number of these new additions came to the teaching profession from a variety of other careers including a stint in the Army, real estate, childbirth education, and manufacturing sales.

The majority of the department members received their teacher preparation or advanced degrees at the same university in Kentucky and worked with the social studies educator there. However, two completed their teacher education at small private colleges in the state. Eight of the department members are residents of Wilson County. In fact, two of them describe themselves as "lifelong members of the community." The two other members commute daily from the nearby metropolitan area.

The teachers in the department describe themselves, as one put it, as having "either subtle or strong ideological positions" that are often not collectively shared. These differing positions and perspectives are quite evident in their conversations throughout the day, and for some, in the little personal flourishes of their room decor. One of the women in the department has a small cabinet in her room that is festooned with bumper stickers from locales exotic and domestic, and decals and stickers from a range of organizations from Amnesty International to National Geographic. Down the hall the strains of Jimmy Buffet or the Rolling Stones will welcome you into the day's activities in the classroom of another teacher. One of the men has his personal collection of John Dewey prominently displayed on the bookshelf behind his desk. Meanwhile, next door, Alexander the Great sits stoically watching over the classroom of his colleague.

To the careful observer, these personal artifacts speak clearly of their individual interests, values, and worldviews. Thus, it is no wonder that the political, historical, and social debates these teachers engage in with one another, especially at lunch, are always lively and not infrequently heated. Even so, department members express a deep respect for each other, and the individual teaching strengths and areas of expertise that they each have. As one explained, "We have a healthy respect for individuality." Among this group of teachers having a healthy respect for individuality means valuing each other for their differences, not in spite of them.

Because they value the individual strengths that each member brings, they expect that each will continue to expand those strengths, develop new areas, and above all will share their learning and knowledge with the others. One of the women explained, "We expect that we'll help each other" using and overseeing a simulation, or helping devise some "creative type of gimmicky thing" that will get students motivated. Further, they have been known to use each other as guest speakers in their classrooms. They will invite the former Army sergeant in and have him organize the students into a Roman legion formation and march them off to battle as he tells them about life as a centurion. Or, they will have the resident women's scholar teach a lesson on the suffragettes or other facet of women's history. As they have embraced their individual differences, they have come to see more clearly how this diversity strengthens and expands their individual and collective work with students.

The department members seem to define their teacher role broadly. While classroom teaching remains the primary role definition for them, they see teaching as more than just that. Within the department, teaching is also defined as service in extracurricular activities with students. Each of them has taken on the responsibility of sponsoring a club, or serving as an athletic or academic coach.

The teacher's role is also defined as colleague. They define the role, within and beyond their departmental relationship, as a collaborative one. They believe teachers should work with each other, question, debate and be leaders for change within the larger school context. To this end, individuals in the department have spearheaded the change to a block schedule, sought out grant opportunities, led professional development sessions locally and in other districts, as well as reached out to colleagues in other academic departments to develop interdisciplinary units or support.

While their membership on the various committees of the Site-based Decision Making Council reflects a schoolwide requirement, the teachers in the department view this service as an integrated part of their professional role. For them it is not just a part of their job description to be complied with. They take keen interest and put substantial time and effort into their respective committees. Because serving on the committees includes a significant time commitment, the members of the department identified which committees they wanted to be represented on and then each of them selected one they were interested in serving on. In this way they could lessen the time any one of them had to devote to meetings, while still having a colleague there to voice their individual and collective concerns, and keep them informed and "in the loop."

The teachers in the department talk a great deal about change, the need to grow and alter how and what they do with students. Every one of them in some way seeks feedback and input from students about content, activities, and ways to improve. In interviews they spoke of needing to reflect on what they do to improve and keep learning. One member talked about their valuing of change by saying, "None of us I think has ever taught the same from year to year. You have to change and be flexible. If you can't move ahead with each year, and change to reflect that, then you have really lost the point of teaching."

For them, change requires reflection and a willingness to share not only the "successes" but the "troubles." They bring their concerns to the group, or some number of their group, for collective reflection and grappling with the problems and tensions of the work. One of the men shared how after a particularly draining class on the Japanese internment camps during World War II, in which two students adamantly defended the practice using what he considered to be "racist ideology" to support their position, he sought out his colleagues. He wanted them to help him think through his dilemma. He asked them, "What do you do when something like that happens? How do you get them to see the other side or acknowledge that there is another side?" While they don't always walk away from these conversations with "right answers," they believe that sharing and grappling with these "troubles" helps them reflect on their work with students and grow as teachers.

Finally, change for this department also includes rotating the courses each person teaches. While that has generally been common practice in the department, it has now become an explicit, but not written, group norm. They believe the electives provide more teaching "space," more autonomy and creativity, than the required courses or the typical "core" courses of U.S. History and World Civilization. Therefore, everyone has a schedule including both electives and "core" each year as a way to keep them intellectually and creatively engaged.

Their valuing of change and critical reflection is further displayed in their collective vision of the purpose of education. For the school's 1995–96 community curriculum showcase, a schoolwide open house, the department jointly created a department brochure that included this statement: "We, the Social Studies Department, see social studies as applicable to the real world and a vital part of our students' lives. Our aim is not to provide all the answers, but to encourage students to raise the questions that will take us into the 21st century." They understand the future to be a process of change in which students will have to be critical thinkers and questioners. In order to prepare for that future and to ask the questions, the department members believe that students need to explore issues around local and global citizenship from multiple perspectives and with a critically thoughtful mind. The veteran member of the department summed up the group's shared belief in this goal saying, "I think there is a strong desire . . . to produce independent learners who are reflective, critical thinkers . . . [who engage in] reflection upon the social world in which they live."

The Growth of the Relationship

> I think the other teachers think we are just a bunch of people
> who got lucky, and that like each other. That is not necessarily
> true. I guess we do. But, we have our differences . . . we know
> we have a good thing and we want to keep it going.
>
> —Kevin

It would be easy to assume that the social studies department did just get lucky. However, the above quote points out that these are very different people who come to teaching with a variety of styles, personal beliefs and prior experiences that shape how they approach and practice their craft. So, how did this eclectic group of individuals develop a collegial relationship they all agree is a positive, supportive one? They worked at it.

During the interviews, and in our casual conversations, they shared that they had been explicit about their desire to develop their relationship. At the beginning of the 1993–94 school year, they set a goal of developing a stronger sense of collegiality by spending time together, "socially, outside the school setting, at least once a month or once every six weeks." For that year, one of them explained, "We worked at it at first to get there. That I think was the key. We almost worked at it like you'd work at a professional development activity at first. What we started doing at first was getting to know each other really well."

They would go out to dinner in the adjacent city 15 miles away, carpooling to get there. For them, the travel to and from was as important as the dinners themselves. There was no planned agenda for these gatherings, no purpose other than spending time with each other. Yet, as they pointed out, the talk always turned to school, the work, the stress, and the students. What happened during those dinners was that they talked about themselves, about their beliefs, and feelings about teaching, and about the world. Having personal knowledge of each other, getting to know each other as multifaceted, complex people was important for them. It helped them open up even more to trust in each other and confide their struggles and share their needs.

The Fruits of Collaboration: The Idea Unfolds

The change to a block schedule meant that the school had to increase the number of required classes since students would now be able to complete eight credits a year. The district and school board had approved changing the graduation requirements to ensure that students could not be done by the end of the first semester of their junior year. However, departments were going to have to expand the selection of courses they offered to provide the students with alternatives to select from. The principal encouraged departments to use the opportunity to address the learning needs of students and use the established state learner goals and academic expectations to help guide them:

Kentucky Academic Expectations for the Social Studies

- democratic principles
- forms of government
- social groupings and institutions
- ethnic and cultural groups
- economic decisions
- geographic interaction between people
- historical events, conditions, trends, and issues
- human relationships

At a meeting at the end of September 1995 the social studies department met to talk about the possibilities for new courses and to explore some ideas. The change in graduation requirements meant that students now had to complete two social studies courses, one of which had to be U.S. History. The department chair wanted the department to consider how any new classes would both address the learner goals and fit with the existing course offerings. Different department members suggested courses such as Kentucky Studies, Modern Social Problems, Anthropology, and Military History. One of them even suggested that perhaps they should change U.S. History to World War II to the Present. He was concerned that they never seem to get past the war and into any more recent history that students might connect with.

One thing they all agreed on was that the content and topics of any new courses had to connect with students. They wanted the classes to engage students and get them excited about social studies. One of the women pointed out that for many students, once they took a social studies class they got hooked, became "groupies" and ended up taking a number of the various elective courses. When they kept coming back they had more opportunities to learn both content and inquiry skills. It was those students who would speak up in class, express an opin-ion, challenge an opinion, actively participate, and engage with ideas. That was what they wanted to do for more students. So, what they needed was to use the new classes to get more students hooked.

Over the course of the next few months the department engaged in an ongoing dialogue about how best to address both the academic expectations and engage students. The dialogue was recursive and free flowing. They would talk at lunch or in the hallway between classes. It might be two or three of them or five or six. Ideas would get tossed out by one of them and others would add on or spin off other ideas and ask some "what ifs." A conversation might start one day and be picked back up days or weeks later. Woven throughout these conversations were three interrelated issues that continued to reemerge as they talked.

As a department, their goal had always been to engage students in experi-ences that involved them in the processes of social science inquiry, helped them learn to grapple with the complexity of social issues, and went beyond the text-book. In order to do that students needed a set of research and intellectual pro-cessing skills as well as social interaction skills. They had found that when the students got to the U.S. history class, far too many of them came with only rudi-mentary development in these skills. The same was true of the electives. In order for students to engage with the content in a complex and meaningful way in these classes, they needed some skills and process knowledge. Although each of the teachers had tried to attend to these skills in their individual courses they were not able to help students cultivate them in a developmental and systematic manner. This concern for the differential opportunities to acquire the social inquiry processes and skills was further compounded by the need to cover the content on the state exam.

When the exam was first being developed, the State Department of Edu-cation and the contracted developers had attempted to provide an exam that respected the local control of curriculum required by the broader KERA reforms. They had initially explained that the exam would include questions and perfor-mance events created to assess student knowledge regarding the broadly defined academic expectations for each of the discipline-based content areas. The teach-ers in the department understood this to mean that the exam would focus on the core concepts of the social studies, as presented in the academic expectations, and the application of the various social science processes and skills, as well as critical thinking within the content area. However, it quickly became apparent to the teachers that the exam was in fact laden with highly specified content. To try and get some handle on just what the exam covered, the department members ana-lyzed the released test items. In doing so, they noticed that the questions required students to know and recall specific and discrete information and facts, much of which came from historical epochs and eras they had not included, or only briefly touched on, in their course curricula.

Their analysis illuminated for them that the questions on the exam could in fact be drawn from the breadth of U.S. and world history, as well as the content and inquiry skills of all the social studies cognate areas. At the time they were involved in these curriculum decisions, the state had not yet released the *Core Content for KIRIS Assessment* documents. So, there appeared to be no way of knowing what specific factual information students would have to know or what skills they would be asked to use to demonstrate their knowledge.

If the students in the school took only one course in common, the required U.S. history class, the teachers in the department were faced with a dilemma. The test appeared to be prescribing a curriculum that covered thousands of years of history and civilizations, and all the social science disciplines, from which questions could be drawn. Therefore, they felt enormous pressure to cover content. Their response had been to make the history courses a "rush through time." Even so, they hardly put a dent in it and rarely dealt with recent history that students might have more interest in. Moreover, they felt a professional responsibility to help students cultivate the critical and questioning mind so crucial to democratic citizenship. They knew the development of the inquiry skills and critical thinking that supported these sensibilities required cultivation through in-depth and focused study with themes, problems, or historical eras. However, the press to cover content meant that very complex and multifaceted historical events often came across as one dimensional. Thus there was nothing for students to struggle with or to critically inquire about. Try as they might there was just not much to "think" about at that pace nor was there time to attend appropriately to the development of the skills needed to do it.

Finally, there was the timing of the state exam. Traditionally, U.S. history was required for juniors. The exam was moved that year, 1995–96, from twelfth to eleventh grade. With the block schedule being implemented the next year, the students who took the course in the spring would only have had a little over half of the course. Further, since students were not required to take any other social studies courses before that, many of them might not have taken any since eighth grade. Students could not demonstrate knowledge about which they had not even had the opportunity to learn.

At different times in their conversations, a couple of the department members had told the others about freshman social studies courses that this or that school was teaching. There was also a push by the school counselors and the school administration for departments to take the needs of freshman into account. So, as the department members talked more and more about how to address their concerns, they decided that perhaps they would not opt to have electives serve as the second required course. Instead they decided to develop a required course for freshman that would help students begin building a base of conceptual and factual knowledge and skills that would facilitate more complex learning in history and the other electives. By working together with all the freshman they could provide a similar set of learning experiences on which to build and to draw on in subsequent courses. This course would also allow them to help students cultivate a common set of social science inquiry skills and sensibilities. Most of all, the class would provide the department members with early contact with freshmen so they could get them excited and increase the likelihood that more of them would take multiple social studies courses. More classes meant the department had more opportunities to engage students with critical issues of active citizenship that the members saw as their primary goal. In sum, the Social Studies I class would expand the breadth of content and skills students engaged with and increase their opportunities to participate in social studies inquiry. It was their hook.

The Course Takes Shape: Social Studies I

The department members first considered having the course address all eight of the state's social studies academic expectations. However, using the disaggregated data from the KIRIS results, they identified the economic, geographic, and government expectations as those areas where students were the weakest on the exam. They agreed that these were areas that they tended to neglect in the electives and in the push to cover content in the history classes. They decided to structure the class so that in an 18-week semester, the students would rotate through each of the three content areas for a six-week unit that would culminate in completion of the class. Each six-week unit would be taught by one of the department members who had special expertise in that area. For each section of the course there would be three teachers and approximately 90 students. To accommodate all the freshmen, they were going to need two sections of the freshman course each term.

In order to plan for the teaching load, the department chair had outlined each person's certification areas. Due to state certification requirements one member was not eligible to teach the course because his only cognate area was sociology. Another one's certification was restricted to history so he couldn't teach in the class. Everyone else in the department at the time had social studies certification that made them eligible to teach in the freshman course. However, each of the teachers had content majors and minors that they felt most comfortable teaching. The chair and another teacher both wanted to teach the government sections. Another member had a major in economics and was excited to be able to focus in on that. The most recent addition to the department had a minor in economics but he really preferred taking on geography. One of the women thought she could do the government section but because she had been teaching the geography elective lately she would prefer to teach that section.

Teaching in Social Studies I meant a teacher would not be teaching some other elective class or classes. However, each of them had elective courses that they found intellectually stimulating and that they wanted to continue to teach. Also, there were the other new electives and the history courses that had to be covered. Nevertheless, they were all very excited about the course and wanted to be involved in it. Later, the department chair described the process of hashing out the teaching assignments as an interesting experience. She said it was "so fascinating to listen to each person talk about 'I'll give up one of this class, if you'll promise I can keep this other class.' It was so great how we made sure everyone both gave to and got from the group."

With the teaching load settled, they began work in June on the curriculum, both content and skills. That summer, two new teachers joined the department and quickly joined the collaborative efforts. Thus, all nine of the department members participated in fleshing out the curriculum or the course. Together, they developed a list of skills they wanted the students to learn along with the instructional activities that would help them develop the skills. They included skills such as: reading maps, interpreting graphs, reading and analyzing different sources of information, developing a social sciences vocabulary, conflict resolution, public speaking, and oral and written communication. Across the three units of the course, students would engage in simulations, "fish bowls," write a "defend a position" paper, write article abstracts, construct graphs and maps, make oral presentations, and have weekly vocabulary quizzes to help them develop these skills.

They also collectively brainstormed what content from these three areas would prepare students for future courses and lend themselves to the creation of a cohesive course and not three in one. They decided to use the local community as the overarching focus and to have the students engage in a culminating project that would require them to integrate the knowledge and skills of the different units. Each of the three units would have content themes to organize around. For geography they were map skills, physical and political geography, demographics, and the environment. In economics the students would focus on personal, macro- and micro-economic themes. The government unit would deal with citizenship by investigating issues of responsibility, authority, privacy, justice, and community.

Teaching in the Shadow of State Assessment

Social Studies I is a course designed to help students recognize and understand the relationship between people and geography and apply their knowledge in real-life situations, as well as to give students an understanding of and practice in the American political, social, and economic systems. The goal of the course is to provide students with a knowledge base strong enough to help them be successful in other social studies classes

and active participants in our community at large. All students
will be expected to actively participate in a variety of activities
designed to simulate our political, social, and economic systems.
Students will work collaboratively on a culminating project
that will utilize the thinking skills necessary to become contributing citizens.

—Course syllabus

At the threshold of the classroom stood a female student. She tentatively
glanced around, her eyes trying to survey the faces of those already in their seats.
With a deep breath she darted across the imaginary line and into the room.
Others in the room sat chatting and catching up on summer news. The last few
students trickled into the room with the morning bell and found a seat. With a
warm smile the teacher at the front of the room greeted them; "Welcome to
Social Studies I. I'm Ms. Morrison and I'm really looking forward to this class."

Thus began the first section of the Social Studies I class. In their rooms two
other department members were similarly helping the freshman get a sense of
how the class would work and what they could expect. One of them told the students, "A lot of what you will learn will be from your classmates. You'll also teach
me things. I figure if I can't learn things from you then I'm in the wrong business.
I always learn something from students. You all have lots to teach."

Through the early part of the fall semester things went well for the department. The Social Studies I class had hit the ground running and they were all
finding the new block schedule to their liking. The teachers in the department,
not just those teaching the course, maintained an ongoing conversation about
the curriculum, the selection and design of lessons, units and instructional activities, as well as what process and discipline-based skills, knowledge, and "habits of
mind" the students brought and were developing. They also shared their own
struggles with motivating students, classroom climate issues, and many of the
other facts of life in classrooms.

Late October brought cool weather and the results of the KIRIS exam. The
teachers in the social studies department had been relatively unconcerned. The
student scores on the social studies section had been rising steadily and had consistently been the highest of any academic section for the school, as well as the
surrounding counties. However, the state exam had been moved to the eleventh
grade from twelfth grade last year and thus the students had completed only about
two thirds of the U.S. history class before the exam in early April. Therefore, they
were expecting that the scores might be down a bit, or at least not show the same
consistent gain. Even so, when the principal got the test results a week before
they were released to the public he was concerned. The social studies scores were
down more than they had expected, especially in comparison to the school's
scores in science, mathematics, and reading. Knowing how much work the
department had been doing and the changes they had devised and implemented,

he was afraid what their reaction would be. Eventually, he shared the news, joking with them that he hadn't wanted to break the news because he feared they'd be suicidal.

Although they already knew about the drop in their scores, at their department meeting the week the scores were released to the public their disappointment was still palpable. That morning I found the department chair in her room pouring over the regional newspaper, which had posted the scores from across the state. By the afternoon she was ready to help the department take a look at what they were doing and make plans to "get a handle on this."

"We can make all kinds of rationales" about why the scores are low, she began. Nevertheless, "the community wants results." She explained that she had looked at the scores from the surrounding counties and they were doing better and that that is how the "community is going to judge" this. Then she informed them that the test would be changing yet again next year. A brief give and take ensued among the group about how this state metaphor of "flying the airplane as you build it" was getting old. Questions peppered the room: How are we supposed to keep up with it? And, how can we be accountable when we don't know what for?

She passed out a summary of the changes outlined at a recent state meeting on testing. It included core content for assessment in the social studies as well as the changes to the test. One of the group members commented on the revival of multiple-choice items and the suspension of the performance events. They agreed that seemed to be "moving away from the intent of the reform." Regardless, their chair reminded them, "we are accountable" and "need to take a look at what we are doing" to identify areas for improvement. She pointed out that the freshman course should be helpful, since that "helps us focus on the [content] areas we were neglecting." Others also noted that the class should help students develop their thinking and processing skills. Looking over the core content the state had released, they noted that their course curricula seemed to be aligned with it. But, they knew they were "going to have to make changes in strategies." After a week of informal talk with department members, her suggestion was the purchase and use of a nationally acclaimed, interactive history curriculum series.

One member shared with the group that one thing he was not doing enough of was open-response questions. He was having students do plenty of writing; in fact, more than ever. The students produced pieces for portfolio selection, essays, and research papers. However, while his students were writing more he was not having them do the "quick, response type" open-response pieces. The chair and others agreed that there were things, such as this, that they needed to do to help students be prepared for the format of the exam. One member suggested that the drop in scores might suggest that they were not meeting the needs of their "clients," that they weren't making the work relevant for the students. Again, the chair agreed that some of the problem with the lowered scores was probably a matter of motivating the students but, she told them, "We need to work on things, too."

The more traditionalist member of the group appeared to take the reference of the need to change strategies as a direct challenge of what his colleagues perceived as his predominately lecture-based teaching methods. He shot back, "You are also not dealing with the fact that we are not getting them ready" to take the test. He expressed his concern that although the students know a great deal, they are not prepared to deal with the extensive amount of content on the test. They do not seem able independently to organize and present what they do know on the test. Moreover, he also thought the students were not accustomed to maintaining focus on one task for long stretches of time as the test requires. He asked them, "I mean, where do you think they get some of those things?" referring to the organized note taking and more individually focused structure of his class.

Working in groups was a great way to learn for many students. He agreed with them about this and reminded them that he also had students do this, although not as much as they obviously did. However, he pointed out that on the test "it is just them." The students do not have a group with which to brainstorm or share ideas or responsibility. Thus, he told his fellow department members, he believed strongly that students need to feel confident in their ability to perform as individuals. He thought his instructional strategies offered the students such opportunities and rounded out their learning experiences in the department.

As the conversation bounced around the room the senior member, the self-described social educator, quietly asked, "Don't you feel that at some point you don't want to compromise or give up our goals; our beliefs about what makes good social studies; what we want for students? Do we agree with this [the test as the goal]?" The conversation stopped abruptly as they all looked at him. The near perfect unison of their gentle, affirming nods made it obvious he had struck a chord.

After this moment of silent, mutual reflection, the chair refueled the discussion by pointing out that using the new curriculum materials would let them do both because it was "good stuff" and fit with their ideas and beliefs about teaching. Members who were familiar with the materials pointed out to each other that the materials were focused on critical thinking, were interactive and engaging for students, and offered a well-articulated content strand. Besides, the chair summed up, many of the released test items seemed to be "taken straight from this stuff."

In December, four members of the department were sent as representatives to attend the professional development sessions for the curriculum materials that were offered in the nearby city. Their charge was to bring back the information to the rest of the members. At a subsequent department meeting they shared with their department colleagues the strategy of using an interactive notebook to offer creative ways of connecting kids to content, and a preview of the materials and the format of the curriculum. One of the four told them at the meeting that the training was "good stuff" but not that much different from what most of them got in their teacher education program. As he put it, "it is just good teaching." Out of that meeting they made plans to use the notebook in the Social Studies I classes the next semester and encouraged each other to try the strategies in all the required courses and electives. They hoped to have the complete set of U.S. history materials early in the spring semester of that year.

Another outgrowth of that meeting was that they also begin taking turns writing open-response questions to share with each other. They agreed to give students in each Social Studies I and U.S. History class an open-response question once a week. The consensus was that no one had to use the designated question, they could develop their own to better fit the context of their current unit of study. But, as one of them pointed out, getting the questions from each other helped them each build a resource file for future use.

The Local Effects of State-Level Reform

The teachers in the department have been able to effect changes in their instructional practices and, in doing so, expand students' opportunities to learn. However, these changes have not taken place in a vacuum. The multifaceted and extensive nature of the state reform initiatives, especially the state assessment system and its use for accountability purposes, has served as an important context of change.

For the teachers in this department, the state reform has been both professionally liberating and somewhat constraining. One way that it has been liberating for them is that the philosophical perspective promoted by KERA publicly validated and supported the educational goals for students that they individually and collectively embraced. With KERA's focus on critical thinking, engaging students in authentic learning situations and assessments, and the emphasis on lifelong learning rather than knowledge transmission, all the teachers in the department felt a renewed sense of purpose and legitimacy regarding their classroom practice, most especially those among them who had long embraced more "active" roles for students. In this climate of systemic change, these teachers felt more comfortable openly sharing with each other about their use of such student-centered instructional strategies. However, because of the diversity of teaching styles among the department members, they also sensed a need to have more open debate and dialogue about pedagogy. In turn, this openness provided all of them, regardless of their preferred instructional style and strategies, with expanded opportunities to learn from each other, and a safety net to try out new ideas, and ultimately make changes in their classroom practice.

The state reform was liberating for them in another sense. Little (1990) notes that opportunity for joint work and a collective sense of interdependence are the necessary conditions required for teachers to develop the "strong" relationships with colleagues that are characteristic of collaborative communities (Little & McLaughlin, 1993). The state's explicit expectation that schools and teachers were collectively accountable for student success and the increased state focus on providing time for school-based teacher professional development seems to have provided the fertile environment for this particular department to begin developing such a community.

As previously noted, within this state climate of reform these teachers initiated collegial dialogues about substantial teaching issues. They recognized that the state-level focus on reform provided a unique opportunity, as well as a pressing need, to talk honestly with each other about what happened behind the "closed doors" of their classrooms. Within this context, the teachers in the department were able to move successfully from their individually based sense of professional responsibility and commitment to one that is collectively shared, supported, and maintained. Furthermore, as the department members developed their collaborative community, they gained some sense of control over the reform process and thus became better able to respond pro-actively to state expectations.

The state reform has further supported their collective work by providing a set of clear and common academic expectations for all students. In keeping with the KERA goal of local control of the curriculum, the district and school administration allowed the teachers broad professional discretion in curriculum development and implementation. The charge to the teachers was to develop a social studies curriculum derived from the needs and interests of the students and yet clearly focused on meeting the state academic expectations. The teachers in the department have used the state's expectations and testing data as guidelines for assessing, fine-tuning, and altering the content and design of many of their classes. This is especially true of the elective courses that they offer, but less so of the required courses. Further, they have used the expectations as a framework for restructuring their course offerings, such as the addition of the Social Studies I course, in an attempt to create a more cohesive and interconnected set of learning experiences for their students.

Clearly, the state context of reform has provided these teachers a rich environment for collaboration and offered them direction in meeting the learning needs of their students in the form of the academic expectations. However, at the same time, at least one facet of the reform appears to serve as a potentially limiting factor. The high-stakes climate of the testing system places pressure on the teachers to "teach to the test" and the test is defined as the *Core Content for State Assessment*. The effect of this pressure, whether intentional or not, is that the core content is becoming a state curriculum that is quite prescriptive about what specific content students should know.

Even before the release of the core content document, the teachers in the department felt pressed to "cover content" because of the rather "institutionalized" way many parents and community members thought a history class ought to "look and be like." The increased emphasis by the state on specific content for the exam and the continued high-stakes environment will most likely only increase their sense of pressure to cover as much content as possible. This focus on coverage will hinder even more the department's goals of cultivating thoughtful classrooms that foster critical citizenship through inquiry and collective grappling with historic and modern ideas, issues, and problems. Further, as we saw in the department's reaction to the falling test scores, the high-stakes climate serves to focus instruction on test-taking strategies such as writing open-response prompts, rather than more real-life, authentic application of knowledge that is advocated in the broader KERA goals. At the least, the pressure to perform on the test serves to curtails the use of such authentic performances or activities. At its most detrimental, this pressure could threaten to make the use of such instructional strategies and forms of assessment for classroom learning questionable and suspect. After all, one might ask, "how will these activities help the student perform well on the state exam?" In sum, because of the high-stakes accountability regarding test scores, the content of the test is likely to increasingly limit the teachers' ability to make local, professional decisions about curriculum and instruction in response to student learning and needs.

Final Thoughts

As to what effects the cumulative efforts of their collaboration will have on the social studies scores, the department will have to wait and see. It will be two more years until the freshman in the first Social Studies I cohort take the exam. However, the effects of the collaboration on them as teachers is evident. Being a part of this collegial, collaborative community (Little & McLaughlin, 1993) is an important part of these teachers' personal and professional lives. It provides them a space in their working day and lives for peer interactions, support, and care. They have learned from themselves and each other as they questioned, reflected, and shared their "successes" and "troubles." They have in their own words become "better teachers." The hard work and commitment to quality instruction, as well as the willingness to share their expertise and practical knowledge, were easy for them because, as one of them explained, "at the heart of the reason we are here is the kids."

As noted, the teachers in this social studies department, and many like them, are highly committed professionals with clear educational aims and a vast and growing knowledge base about sound instructional practices. One of the original goals of the state reform was to unleash this wealth of knowledge to effect school change in pursuit of educational equity for all of Kentucky's students. However, we must be concerned that the "top-down" nature of the curriculum and "unreliability" of the testing system are likely to take their toll on these otherwise highly committed teachers. We run the risk that using the state assessment system for "carrot and stick" accountability will ultimately keep teachers focused on preparing kids for "test-taking" and not on the original state goal of providing educational experiences that prepare students for the complex and unknown "situations they will encounter throughout their lives."

Note

1. Pseudonyms have been used for all people and places.

References

Fickel, L. H. (1998). *Teacher culture and community: An ethnography of a high school social studies department*. Unpublished doctoral dissertation, University of Louisville, Louisville, Kentucky.

Fullan, M. (1982). *The meaning of educational change*. Toronto: OISE Press.

Lortie, D. C. (1975). *Schoolteacher: A sociological study*. Chicago: University of Chicago Press.

Little, J. W. (1990). The persistence of privacy: Autonomy and initiative in teachers' professional relations. *Teachers College Record, 91*, 509–536.

Little, J. W. & McLaughlin, M. W. (Eds.) (1993). *Teachers' work: Individuals, colleagues, and contexts*. New York: Teachers College Press.

6

The Tortuous Journey toward School Reform

A Middle School's Efforts within the Context of a State-Mandated, High-Stakes Accountability System

JAN CALVERT, DONNA GAUS, AND GORDON RUSCOE

Introduction

The following is the story of West Middle School's attempt to fashion school reform within the context of the Kentucky Educational Reform Act (KERA) and the Kentucky Instructional Results Information System (KIRIS). The story consists of the combined reflections of the school principal, who launched the school on its journey, and of the two evaluators of the school's federal school-to-work program, Future Connections, funded a year into the principal's journey.[1] These reflections are told in the first person to represent the combined voices of the principal, her staff, and the evaluators.

The case illustrates how implementing reform is made difficult when two rather different paradigms for change do not always reinforce each other. On the one hand, the curricular philosophy of KERA holds out the promise for higher performance for all students through authentic, systemic, school-based reform; while, on the other, the reality of KIRIS emphasizes a state-mandated, high-stakes accountability system. To be sure, the philosophy of KERA and the reality of KIRIS are cut from the same cloth. Both KERA and KIRIS hinge on the common assumption that reform is an ongoing process of continuous improvement and that this improvement must be examined school by school. And every two years KIRIS does in fact compare each school with its own previous performance. But in the implementation of KIRIS, the state's use of mandated, performance-based

109

assessment continues to hold on to conventional conceptions of reliability and validity and to reduce the assessment of a school's success to a single number.

Within this context, school reform, as this story reveals, is often a tortuous, nonlinear, and messy affair for three reasons. First, reformers must contend with a mix of student backgrounds, school expectations, district practices, and state mandates. This mix is even more chaotic, however, when the conflict between the philosophy of KERA and the reality of KIRIS is considered.

Second, reformers must also attempt to manage the interplay between internally generated strategies and externally imposed ones. This interplay is especially problematic when KERA and KIRIS strategies pull the school in different directions.

Third, reformers typically use both quantitative and qualitative data in assessing their success. Qualitative data lend themselves to formative evaluation and to a nontraditional research paradigm compatible with the concepts of KERA. The often more highly regarded "hard numbers" of quantitative analysis, however, lend themselves to summative evaluation and to the traditional research paradigm characteristic of KIRIS. Thus, the choice of evidence to document and defend success becomes problematic.

To understand West Middle School's tortuous, nonlinear, and messy journey toward school reform within the context of conflicting KERA and KIRIS paradigms, the story is divided into three sections: (1) the condition of the school when the journey begins, (2) the change strategies implemented during the journey and the problems that arise when the philosophy of KERA and the reality of KIRIS come into conflict, and (3) the current condition of the school. At the end of the story, we revisit the three reasons we believe have made this journey tortuous.

The Old School: West Middle School

When I accepted the principal's position at West Middle School, I knew the challenge of making a difference here would be difficult. The school had a long way to go before significant change could take place. I was the fifth principal in eight years. The school had one of the highest suspension rates and the lowest KIRIS scores of any middle school in the district. In fact, a colleague faxed me the regrettable story from a neighboring city newspaper that profiled the best and worst ten middle schools in the state. West was among the worst because of its lack of improvement in KIRIS scores. Indeed, West's lack of improvement in test scores had placed it in the position of being "in decline"—or even "in crisis" if it didn't show dramatic improvement at the end of the next two-year testing cycle. In Kentucky's high-stakes accountability arena, being declared "in decline" or "in crisis" would earn West, among other things, the dubious distinction of being assigned a "Distinguished Educator" (DE) to assist the school in improving its test scores in the next testing cycle.

Ironically, as I weighed whether to accept the principal's helm at West, the school's exceedingly low KIRIS scores were not a serious factor in my consideration. I had held a "KERA-compatible" philosophy prior to the passage of that landmark act, and at the time I was preoccupied with how to launch various change strategies that might facilitate the implementation of KERA, which I viewed as a means for long-term, systemic reform. I considered KIRIS to be a complimentary part of KERA that could help guide my efforts toward that aim. Indeed, I looked forward to the expertise a DE would offer me should my students' test scores fail to rise appropriately.

High on my list of concerns as I pondered how to implement KERA was the student population at West. West's attendance zones included some of the most poverty-stricken and crime-ridden populations in the metropolitan area. Moreover, parents of many of the most educationally oriented students in West's attendance zones applied to send their children to one of the district's magnet or traditional schools or to one of the area's many Catholic schools rather than to West. Consequently, West served a population of students who were almost 76% low socioeconomic, 15% learning and behavior disordered, and another 10% who were judged severe enough by the district to be self-contained in learning and behavior disordered programs.

A large number of the students came from homes that were characterized by unemployment and crises. Many of the students came to school hungry and very angry. They also arrived at school lacking the basic skills necessary to learn middleschool-level content, as well as lacking in foundational social and "readiness to learn" skills. The student body as a whole displayed apathy and cynicism toward learning and lacked a sense of belonging to the school. The students' parents were a voiceless group, few of whom involved themselves in school activities or affairs.

The teaching staff was a real mixture. A small group was skilled and dedicated to this population of children; others—though caring for the students— lacked the professional expertise to manage them; and still others just were not up to the challenge posed by this population. Thus, despite the presence of a small band of dedicated, caring teachers, the overall expectations of quality in teaching and learning were low. Many teachers were primarily concerned with simply controlling their classrooms rather than inviting and challenging students to learn relevant curriculum by engaging them with hands-on types of instructional strategies. With rare exception, enthusiastic, "growth-oriented" teachers assigned to West fulfilled an obligatory year or two of "battle duty" and then moved on to more highly respected and admired schools in other parts of the district. Indeed, in my early days at West, I had to constantly remind myself of this small group of dedicated teachers who were excited about teaching and learning and ready to take on KERA-friendly reform strategies such as alternative scheduling, interdisciplinary teaming, and hands-on instructional practices. I looked to this singular, talented group of staff to join me in implementing KERA at West.

The physical facility at West was symbolic of the neglect, chaos, and despair characterizing West and its culture. The building had been built as an elementary school and had never been modified for its adolescent occupants. In fact, because the building was small, approximately 230 West students were housed in the high school next door in a part of their building referred to as "the annex." There students had to cross two parking lots and walk up two flights of stairs to reach their classrooms. The high school administration would not allow these students to use a main building entrance, so they had to walk behind the gym along a partially uncovered path in rain and the snow. Moreover, the annex teachers had to escort these students across the two parking lots twice a day—for lunch time and related arts classes held at West. In addition to the extrasupervisory duties, teachers in the annex suffered other inadequacies such as lack of access to copy machines, collegial support, and school communication. Their students were largely isolated from the remainder of the student body. Needless to say, teacher and student alienation was especially high in the annex.

In the main building, area after area depicted a similar aura of neglect: stained and broken ceiling tiles; improperly laid floor tile that continually seeped glue leaving a dirty, mottled appearance; and dismal paint, devoid of color anywhere except for dirty beige. In classroom after classroom, broken and dirty water fountains, once used for elementary school students, hung on classroom walls as abandoned eyesores that communicated that no one cared enough either to replace or to remove them. Broken elementary classroom bathrooms were used primarily as closets for teachers' storage, with boxes shoved in and around old toilets.

Because in former days there were working toilets in most classrooms, the building had only one set of bathrooms in the hallway. These had to serve its entire population of more than 600 students. Expressing their disdain for the inadequate facility, boys obviously engaged in ritualized target practice by spraying the bathroom's radiators that reeked with the smell of vaporized urine.

Corridors were empty of any graphics or humor; the gym was dismal—no school mascot or colors were depicted. The library was a cluttered room of wall-to-wall stacks of books, old curriculum plans dating from 1975, and junk. In the cafeteria, torn, bent, and ugly brown Venetian blinds half hung across the windows. The cafeteria walls were painted an ugly beige that bespoke institutional efficiency with no regard for aesthetics or the spirit of children. There was nothing to spark learning or curiosity in this building—nothing at all.

Consequently, lack of commitment, leadership, and resources had rendered the school in crisis long before that label was used by KIRIS. Daily, several fights broke out in the halls. It was more the exception than the rule that teachers could teach classes without serious disciplinary interruptions. Chaos and disorder were the norm; respect for self and others and for the school itself was not evident.

The Journey of Change

In many ways, the journey of change at West was akin to an exodus from despair to hope, from neglect to caring, from constant struggle for survival to celebration and success.

The key to our future was what I took to be the creation of one of KERA's cornerstone components, a true learning community. We needed to strengthen our ties to each other and to our students. We needed to change our philosophy toward our students and toward each other. If we didn't believe in the promise of their future, how could they?

Key administrators and teacher leaders at West and I initiated several change strategies over the next four years that we believed could build the foundation for a learning community that eventually could lead to long-term, systemic reform of the school. Considering the dire environmental conditions at West, we decided the way to begin the process was with the facility itself.

Fortunately, the superintendent had the same perspective. In my first week as principal at West, I met with him. He and I were both new in our positions. I described the conditions at West as inadequate for a middle school population and suggested that the seriousness of the problem might necessitate closing the school if there were no funds for a new facility. The superintendent indicated he would see what he could do. In April of my first year at West, the school board authorized construction, within two years, of a new building for West at a site nearby. We later received permission to rename the new school "Springfield Middle School," a change we believed would assist in our process of school renewal. The promise of a new building with a new name fed a growing sense of hope about the school's future.

In the meantime, school leaders began a series of changes to reshape attitudes and expectations of both teachers and students. One key was to get teachers to seek ways to increase opportunities for student success rather than to blame students for their failures or to lower standards. We began with an examination of the high failure and retention rates of students. For example, on one of the instructional teams at West comprised of 90 students, nearly one half of the students had failed at least one grade level before coming to middle school. Many of our eighth graders were already 14 or 15; a few were even 16 years old.

One strategy we used was to select 10 seventh graders, behind two grade levels but capable as evidenced by grades and effort, to participate in a special summer program with the high school. We required these students to attend a four-week summer school. At the end of the four-week session, all 10 were successful in completing the requirements for promotion to the ninth grade. Follow-up conducted at the end of the first semester of the next school year revealed that all but 1 had earned grades of C or above, and 1 had achieved honor-roll status. Because of these positive results, teacher leaders began to focus on strategies to be used throughout the year that would help students succeed rather than fail.

Even though we slowly decreased student failure at West, the greater challenge was to increase student success by creating real challenge and high standards. And we needed to celebrate our students' actual talents by providing opportunities to showcase them.

The former principal had obtained a one-year grant to conduct career education focused on postsecondary training in order to raise expectations of students and teachers at West. The following year, we expanded this grant into the "Future Connections" project with funds obtained from the U.S. Department of Education. As part of the grant, the sixth-grade teachers and students undertook a "Kids to College" curriculum that engaged students in exploring careers of their choice, including visiting the local university. After this visit, the sixth-grade teachers reported awe at how well behaved and interested their students had been. The teachers were moved by the enthusiasm students exhibited about college. Collegial sharing of information about the results of this experiential learning adventure supported our view that this type of learning could be very powerful for our students.

Also as part of the grant, the seventh-grade students attended luncheons with community members who talked about their careers. As preparation, the students were taught traditional table etiquette that they were expected to exhibit while interviewing their guests during lunch. The students then wrote profiles about their guests as a follow-up activity.

One of the notable aspects of the luncheons was the quality of conversation that took place between the guest speakers and the students. For example, during one luncheon session the topic was "Careers in Law." A senior level public defender entertained questions from students about the many different kinds of law practices, the money to be made—and not made—in the practice of law, and about particular kinds of cases. The lawyer's statements were sprinkled with "inside information" about the actual experience of going to law school, taking the bar exam, and the importance of writing and research skills in practicing law. Many of these students were experiencing a type of "dinner conversation" that students in today's fast-paced society seldom experience.

The grant also provided support for eighth graders, including learning and behavior disordered students, to spend a week on a college campus, visiting classes, learning about financial aid and the requirements of college, and writing-related portfolio entries. Because of the inclusive nature of the project, all students were allowed to participate. Teachers were initially apprehensive about student behavior on field trips. However, an overwhelming majority of eighth grade students displayed appropriate behavior and high interest in the campus experience. Teachers later commented that they would not have been able to tell the students eligible for special education services from students in the "regular" program.

As part of the expansion of this project, West collaborated with United Parcel Service (UPS) to develop a curriculum for eighth-grade students that provided actual workplace learning opportunities at UPS. One of the most powerful vehicles for student and teacher growth was that the UPS staff had higher academic expectations for students than the teachers had held. At first, teachers did not feel the students could perform the math, technology, and other skills that the curriculum required. The UPS staff insisted that these real life skills were attainable by eighth graders. In the end, even some of the eighth graders at West who had been most notorious for exhibiting out-of-control behavior and lack of respect and low aspirations were giving presentations to an audience of UPS staff whom they had shadowed on their visits. Using technology and survey data that they had collected, students tackled a "challenge" scenario designed by the UPS staff that required application of knowledge about logistics management, contingency planning, and a number of other high-level skills. The teachers and UPS staff were highly impressed with the students' interest and success. We were beginning to challenge these students and the students were beginning to respond.

Two additional strategies that focused on school expectations became added stepping stones to significant change at West. First, the Sports Club, a program sponsored by the school district and a private foundation for students identified as "at-risk," featured former collegiate basketball players and teachers at West who conducted a Saturday morning sports and tutorial program. Club expectations required continuous improvement in grades, attendance, and discipline plus attendance on Saturday morning. The students who achieved these goals were rewarded with a series of incentives—T-shirts, sweatshirts, a bus trip to a professional basketball game out of town, amusement park season tickets, and pizza parties. The students in the Sports Club also received positive recognition and challenge every day from the teachers and collegiate participants who visited them in their classrooms.

This special recognition and opportunity for community quickly became the most popular program in the school. In its first year, the Sports Club participants at West earned the highest percentage of season tickets, the top prize for attendance, grades, and discipline of any of the Sports Clubs in the district. Again, in its second year, the Sports Club had the highest grade-point average, best school attendance, and lowest number of suspensions.

Second, while increasing school expectations was jump-started by Future Connections and the Sports Club, we needed to address the issue of behavior management directly. I asked the assistant principal to submit an application to the Model Schools Project, a behavior management project using national specialists. We became one of seven schools in the state invited to participate. The Model Schools project emphasized schoolwide expectations that all teachers were trained in and expected to model. To be sure, when we began the Model Schools project, we had already made some progress in behavior management. Running, loud talking, and disrespectful behavior had been minimized a great deal through a staff-developed, schoolwide behavior management plan. An indicator of improvement was the number of false fire alarms pulled each year: 1994–95, 22 false alarms, 8 bomb threats; 1995–96, 3 false alarms, 0 bomb threats; 1996–97, 0 false alarms, 0 bomb threats. In time, cafeteria and assembly behavior also improved. Students threw food and trash less often. Assemblies and pep rallies were increasingly conducted routinely with order and purpose. More and more, teachers at West were assuming responsibility for their students' behavior.

While we recognized the importance of creating high standards and expectations in building a learning community, we also knew that our students came to us from elementary school with very low basic skills. They would be unable to fully meet our expectations unless we gave them the basic foundation to do so. Students' inability to read the textbook was a major factor in the high rate of failure of students. Standardized tests for incoming sixth graders indicated the school's average literacy score was at the 13th percentile on the CAT/5 achievement test. Also, student performance on the KIRIS reading test had been very low. All these indicators suggested that teachers needed professional development in the teaching of reading and, more fundamentally, the total staff needed to accept responsibility for teaching students to read. Therefore, I organized a Reading Task Force.

We also recognized that if we were going to expect more from both teachers and students, the school needed to offer something more in return. A chief component of a learning community is its members' sense of belonging and pride in being a part of it. We needed to reshape West's identity from that of a bad school lacking in everything to that of a good school offering much. A renewed emphasis on the importance of sports and our athletic competitions—accomplished through assistance by the Sports Club and our volunteer coaches—helped us in this aim.

Initially, we experienced a number of false starts but eventually made impressive headway toward this goal. For example, I remember feeling awe at a basketball game I attended as I watched the band, cheerleaders, and dance team strut around the gymnasium with pride and hope for our school. The eighth-grade team once again prevailed in winning the school spirit stick, a practice that has become a tradition at the school. Coaches and teachers sponsored a schoolwide spirit chain contest. For twenty-five cents a link, a student could purchase a link in his/her team's chain. The team with the most links at the pep rally won the spirit stick. Already during this current school year, $400 has been raised for our athletic program, and the competition for the spirit stick has launched fun-loving rivalry between teams.

As part of raising the bar on student achievement at West, we encouraged performance-based learning and assessments. As an example of the type of instructional practice encouraged through this program—and the ensuing success to be gained from it—I remember watching our seventh grade team as they completed a team exhibition that could serve as a model for the type of learning that is possible in a true learning community. The students sat in groups of twos and threes around tables in the cafeteria. Each group of students had prepared for several weeks to conduct an exhibition of their work on Newton's laws of motion as demonstrated by the path of a marble on a roller coaster they had designed. Their task was to explain to a team of judges why the marble did or did not uphold Newton's laws and be ready to discuss what they had learned by trial and error about their design. Along with their verbal presentation, they had to provide a creative name for their "ride" and a brochure describing the properties of motion and the scientific processes and principles they had learned as well as the qualities of teamwork that had contributed to their work. The roller coasters that they had crafted were unique and creative.

I spent 20 minutes with one group of students who could answer most of my questions about inertia, friction, gravity, and Newton's laws. As I moved from group to group, nearly all students looked at me instead of hanging their heads, discussed their projects with interest, and attempted to answer my questions correctly. What struck me was how well they understood and valued their learning and how eager and proud they were to share it. Those students who had not tried or lived up to their potential were in the minority and were clearly embarrassed.

These change efforts are a sampling of the internal efforts of the staff at West to improve our school. In October 1996, my third year at West, an external change initiative was imposed on West with the publication of the state KIRIS test scores. Because of the scores, West Middle School was declared "in decline." This declaration was very demoralizing for the students and staff at West.

Staff were demoralized because many had just begun to believe their school was turning around and improving. Qualitative data collected by one of the Future Connections evaluators had begun to support this view. For example, data from a focus group with representation across roles and grade levels revealed that many staff had noticed that the hallways were now calm and safe places to be during the changing of classes and that students used less profanity in the hallways. Teachers reported that they were able to use the phrase "a Sports Club member wouldn't do that!" to bring students back in line and were getting results with it. Also, data from formal observations of eighth graders involved in the UPS units revealed the students had shown sincere enthusiasm and educational engagement when performing the work connected with the projects and during their presentations. Some students had actually used peer pressure to cajole their group members to show up for the group presentations and chided them for "letting the group down" when they were absent.

The labeling of their school as being "in decline" triggered a set back in the struggle to build staff morale. It caused staff to wonder whether all the hours of time and energy devoted to implementing the internally generated change efforts had been worth it or whether the school had improved at all.

Students were demoralized as well. Interview data connected with Future Connections suggested that students had also begun to believe that their school was "getting better." During the first year of the data collection for Future Connections, students never evaluated West as "a good school" and rarely said it was a place where "teachers cared about you" or "you learned stuff you needed to learn." In fact, students frequently commented on West's negative reputation in the county as a "bad school," compared it unfavorably to other schools in the district, and talked about transferring to "a better school" where the teachers could "control the kids" and "teach you something." However, during the second year of data collection, positive comments and favorable comparisons with other schools were beginning to crop up during both formal and informal interviews with students. The comments included such remarks as: "West is a better school than North," "there are teachers here that really care about you because they'll do extra stuff to help you when you need it," and "West is harder than St. Peter's because we have pre-algebra and they don't." The state's published declaration that West was "in decline" reinforced the beliefs of students who thought the West was a "bad school" and confused and embarrassed those who were beginning to believe the school was changing.

However, despite feelings of humiliation and disappointment, my staff and I looked forward to the personalized help the Kentucky Department of Education promised. Our understanding was that we would receive funds for enhanced instruction and would be assigned a DE to help us improve student performance on the KIRIS test. In particular, one program of assistance, School Transformation and Assistance Remediation (STAR) Program, required schools to produce a strategic plan for school improvement, to align their curriculum with the state tests, and to teach test-taking strategies for open response questions.

Initially, these tasks sounded like logical places to start. But we assumed we would eventually focus on strategies that would bring about the long-term, systemic reform that we had been seeking. We expected our DE to explore our ongoing efforts to restructure the school with us and offer guidance about how to either improve those efforts or implement new ones that would bring about systemic reform. We quickly discovered that this was not to be.

We were told that our own strategic plan had to be discarded and a new one had to be written. We soon realized this was but one of many innuendoes that, because we were in decline, we simply were not doing our job right. We—along with other staffs from schools in decline—found ourselves developing our transformation plan in a large auditorium led by several DEs who explained the format of the plan we were expected to write from a podium using overheads and a microphone. This format was hardly conducive to providing the kind of intimate, customized assistance that our school badly needed. As it turned out, West's DE, like most others, had to work with several schools and thus was not able to offer the customized assistance that this planning process required. Moreover, the plan we were to develop was very prescriptive and did not take into account the change strategies we had already begun at our school. Nor did it take into account our assessments of these strategies. We quickly discovered that funding would not be granted if a school did not plan "correctly."

Because so many schools had been declared in decline, the amount of money we could apply for was limited to $6,000. This amount was in sharp contrast to the $60,000 available in the previous test cycle. Thus, we were spending a lot of time refining a plan that would yield a maximum of $6,000—if we planned "correctly."

Nevertheless, we submitted our written plan, and it was approved. We then proceeded to the next step—the EIAC committee review. This committee, comprised of four or five community and KDE representatives, would make the decision as to whether our plan would be funded based upon a review of our written plan, a videotape we submitted, and an interview. Making the videotape took a considerable amount of time and effort, given that West did not have adequate video facilities. The tape had to be a response to five questions related to the Transformation Plan. A committee and myself scripted and rehearsed our responses and made our tape.

We sent our plan and tape to the committee prior to our interview, which we were told would be a question and answer session based on the materials we had submitted. The committee began by asking me to present our plan, a presentation we had already made in a written and videotaped format and for which we had not prepared. I launched into an explication of our plan anyway. We were awarded the $6,000 we requested, but I felt disheartened that I was spending so much time on the STAR process and so little time following through on the implementation of West's efforts to bring about systemic reform.

As I found myself diverted from our internal change efforts, my ability to lead the school was slowly eroded. My time and energy were spent trying to understand what the STAR process expected of me and how best to make it happen in the context of my school. STAR also consumed my staff's focus, time, and energy. For example, faculty meetings were devoted to STAR-related tasks rather than to holding committee meetings for such efforts as Future Connections, the Model Schools program, and developing a reading program.

The bureaucratic demands of my job tripled now that I had to deal with State Department regulations on top of my own district's regulations. Moreover, the regulations were in conflict, particularly in the area of finance. For example, whenever an activity required funding, we had to use the State forms and procedures and get the DE (who was in the building only once a week if we were lucky) to sign off before we could send it through our own district bureaucracy, which was already cumbersome.

For example, when we first tried to implement our plan by purchasing materials our staff was ready to use through STAR, we were repeatedly told by the DE that we had to wait until the money was received in the district. After weeks of delay, the DE called and told us that the money was available. However, when we tried to put through a purchase order, it was rejected by the district because they said that the money had not arrived.

The time lines of the state were seldom in sync with district time lines, so state documents would give us one set of directives while the district's documents would give another. Therefore, our school spent a lot of our time trying to deal with the "system" that was set up to help us. Consequently, I was in classrooms less than ever before and the DE did not have the time to work directly with teachers and students because of having to work at so many schools. The teachers were being asked by the state to implement change while only receiving minimal training and support.

Nevertheless, when I came back from Christmas break in 1996, I felt renewed and ready to move forward again. However, once again I was told by the DE that we had to write yet another plan for next year. So, in February, we began another series of meetings, this time for a more complicated plan. Except for my required classroom observations for evaluative purposes, I was seldom in classrooms in January, February, and March. Instead, I was involved either in writing a new plan or in managing and documenting the implementation of the plan we had just rewritten, which was our third plan in less than a year and a half.

Once again, we had to drive to a city one and a half hours away to appear before the EIAC to ask for more money. This time we were limited to $6,900. (Originally, we had been told we could ask for $7,500 and had written our plan accordingly; we had to revise the plan again because the DE was later notified that the funding had been lowered to $6,900.) We waited and waited and waited. An hour and a half after we were scheduled to appear before the committee, we were told that one member from the State Department had not arrived and that we would have to reschedule. I stated that we had driven more than 80 miles to present and that I didn't want to be out of my building again. A kind member of the committee, a superintendent, apologized for our inconvenience and arranged for the committee to sign off on our request immediately.

Despite the maddening bureaucracy of STAR, we did benefit from three STAR strategies. First, the DE suggested we have a Portfolio Night, an evening on which students and parents could come together and discuss portfolios. We had one of the highest parent turnouts ever. In addition, we began to practice with students on how to answer test questions. We initiated strategies to collect and analyze student work and, through teacher component managers, to monitor our improvement plan on a continual basis. We also initiated strategies to get students to buy into the test and to do their best. These efforts paid off. Students made clear efforts in test sessions. Hardly any student refused to try. The writing portfolios were much better than they had ever been. There were no off-task drawings, profanity, and one-liners that had previously characterized many of the portfolios.

I winced each time I read a portfolio at the end of the year, however. I sensed the hard work of the students and teachers that produced the portfolios, but I also recognized that, despite their laudable effort, the skill levels of our students were so low that the portfolios would still be scored "novice," the lowest score, even though we knew through follow-up interviews with students that they had worked hard and taken the test seriously. Still, with only four categories on the state scoring system, our students may not have shown enough improvement to move from one category to another.

A second way STAR helped the school was through a training session to align our curriculum with the state tests. The alignment process required teachers to establish entrance and exit criteria for class performance and to establish a sequence of learning. This process elicited good conversation among teachers about curriculum. While this strategy was helpful, the fact that it was prescriptive and not customized to our school rendered it less meaningful than the portfolio strategy.

A third key STAR strategy, training and practice for answering open response questions, was also useful. Because open response questions play such an important part in KIRIS testing, such training and practice were clearly needed. Unfortunately, some of the training was simply of too high a level for many of our students, thereby limiting its impact.

After our first year's involvement with the STAR process, we took stock of the overall situation at our school. The full impact of how completely STAR had diverted our attention from our own efforts to restructure has only recently crystallized. The implementation of many change efforts that we had launched prior to STAR had slowed considerably or stalled completely.

In sum, our involvement with STAR facilitated our understanding of the KIRIS testing process in a number of ways. We are far more clear now about just how low our students' level of performance on the KIRIS is and what it will mean to move their scores up enough to avoid the label of "in crisis." However, I do not know if we can move our scores up enough to avoid being declared "in crisis" while also resuming our focus on systemic reform. But, I also do not know if we can move the scores up without focusing on systemic reform either. My staff and I believe that long-term, systemic change is in the best interests of the school and our students. Therefore, we are now struggling to regain our momentum in implementing the change strategies that we believe will lead toward the kind of quality student and teacher performance that our students are entitled to.

The New School: Springfield Middle School

We've come a long way! Three sets of bathrooms instead of just one! Now the bathroom stalls, like everything else in our newly built school, speak of dignity and respect for our students. Banners hang in the lobby and corridors. They greet children daily with inspirational messages such as "U Do Matter" and "Dream BIG!"

We're a step closer to leaving the old image behind. New building. New name. New logo. We are launching two new programs next year—an advance program and a math, science, and technology magnet program. Our staff must undergo extensive training in these strategies in order to have a program that is on a par with other such programs in the school district. The community will be watching us to see how well we perform.

We have also begun implementing our new reading program in earnest again. Last spring, we conducted one professional development session in a specific reading strategy, and the staff agreed to try to use it. We also initiated a Pizza Hut reading initiative for the sixth grade and an Accelerated Reader program for the seventh and eighth grades. This year, in laying the ground work for staff buy-in for our reading initiative, the task force undertook a schoolwide inventory of the reading level of each student in the school. We used these data to guide the development of another school plan, and we purchased computer software to target specific remedial and accelerated needs of students in reading, software that will be in place next year.

The Reading Task Force, which changed its name to the Literacy Task Force to incorporate writing and math skills, provided a second staff development session in November 1997, in six other reading strategies. Teachers engaged in "table talk" conversations with colleagues about the success of specific strategies in their classrooms. Teacher leaders demonstrated the use of reading strategies in math, science, social studies, and language arts to show teachers models of strategies that worked in their subject areas. At a January 1998 staff meeting, the sixth-grade team discussed the schoolwide reading inventory of our sixth- and eighth-grade scores. The reading scores demonstrated no significant change in reading scores between our sixth- and eighth-grade students, thus underscoring the need for our focus on reading.

Now that we have moved past the planning phase and toward the implementation of our literacy initiative, we will be tracking and comparing reading scores for every class and organizing instruction accordingly. While I recognized two years ago the importance of this literacy initiative, I was delayed in getting the staff to buy into this focus because STAR focused primarily on test taking skills and curriculum alignment for the state tests. Now that we have generated our own reading data at the school level, staff are beginning to explore the teaching of reading as a key strategy for improving state test scores and student achievement. I have identified resource help in our district to help train our staff in these key areas. Meanwhile, I know many of our students still can't read. STAR never helped with long-term skills like reading and math. No matter how well students are trained to answer test questions, if they can't read and add they won't be able to perform on the test or in life. We've come a long way. And we've resumed our quest for systemic reform.

However, we still worry about test scores even though we know how far we've come. We know the test scores cannot describe the real change that has taken place here. Our scores may not be significantly higher despite all our efforts.

We can't get Sarah to school because after four weeks she still has head lice. We've had to get a court order to remove her from her home because it is infested with drugs and lice. Then there are the three sisters whose mother stabbed their grandmother in front of them last weekend—for drugs. Tim is still so angry due to his father's suicide last spring that we have to "time him out" daily. Gang behavior continues to compete with academic behavior.

Fortunately, we have the Sports Club and Future Connections experiences to help engage our students in learning and keep them connected to the school. The teachers are learning more every day how schoolwide behavior management in our Model Schools Project provides needed structure for our kids. And the STAR program has helped us focus our curriculum in ways that intentionally supports schoolwide academic performance.

When test scores come out soon, however, we may be labeled "in crisis" if we have not made enough gains to meet our original goal four years ago. In reality, we've been in crisis for a long, long time and are only now beginning to emerge. Unfortunately, such an official label will surely threaten the efforts we have made and may even threaten our new magnet and advanced programs. No one who knew West Middle school five years ago would recognize us as the same place. We've come a long way. What do these KIRIS scores really measure after all? Surely we are looking for more than a single number to understand what school reform is all about?

Discussion

Clearly, West Middle School's journey toward school reform has been tortuous, nonlinear, and messy. We now return to the three reasons earlier suggested for this messiness.

First, school reform is complicated by often divergent forces that make it difficult to achieve a unified focus. These forces arise out of varied student backgrounds, school expectations, district practices, and state mandates. Although these forces are sometimes in direct conflict, the more important point is that they give rise to divergent priorities.

The school, in its effort to effect reform, often cannot successfully address these priorities simultaneously. For example, West Middle School cannot maintain high attendance levels, a desirable goal, when students have to remain home because of persistent head lice or have to be removed from school because of possession of weapons. Nor can the school maintain consistent levels of on-task learning behavior when students come to school hungry and sleepy. And the school's principal cannot maintain her role as instructional leader of the school when she repeatedly has to turn her attention to compliance with the state's STAR assistance program.

In effect, each of these forces has presented its own agenda. The issue is *not* whether these agendas are legitimate or whether one necessarily takes precedence over another. Instead, the issue is that school reform cannot guarantee that all these agendas will be addressed in a way that will simultaneously satisfy those promoting them. Moreover, the attempt even partially to satisfy these varying priorities is further complicated by the other two reasons earlier alluded to.

School reform at West Middle School ultimately became a tension-filled interplay between internally generated strategies and externally imposed ones. The school's internal efforts in areas such as parent involvement, the Sports Club, and particularly Future Connections have all attempted to capture the attention of students, teachers, and parents. After all, these are the constituents of authentic reform. Without their involvement and cooperation, reform is not possible.

As these changes have unfolded, however, KIRIS results have increasingly dominated the change atmosphere, first as the school was judged "in decline" and now possibly "in crisis." To be sure, the principal's philosophy of change is compatible with KERA, but KERA's "evil stepsister," KIRIS, has imposed stringent demands from outside. The outside mandates that have accompanied KIRIS results have necessarily diverted attention away from carrying out internal change to meeting KIRIS requirements in the form of STAR planning and DE assistance. It is important to point out that these external mandates are not judged to be wrongheaded. Planning and assistance to meet state requirements that may ultimately produce better scores—and monetary rewards—are certainly welcomed. Rather, the point is that these externally imposed attempts at change, especially when they do not converge with internally generated change, dilute efforts in much the same way as does trying to respond to varied agendas.

Third, the use of both quantitative and qualitative data to assess school reform has become increasingly problematic. Especially in the case of Future Connections, the funding requirement made clear that an adequate evaluation of the project entailed a careful blend of both types of data. Thus, the evaluation has depended on routine evidence (such as attendance, retention, suspension, and test data), survey data (especially an annually administered questionnaire of students' beliefs about the importance of education and future educational and career plans); but also on interviews (especially of students and teachers), and observations (classrooms, lunchrooms, hallways, parent conferences, and PTA activities). Throughout the assessment of Future Connections, the assumption has been that no single measure fully captures what is happening.

This assumption is in stark contrast to the KIRIS approach, however. Not only is there no room in KIRIS for qualitative indicators of success, but even the quantitative data used to assess schools ultimately are reduced to a single number to represent the school's total educational performance. This "one size fits all" approach to assessment is disturbing in a school such as West Middle School, which is attempting school reform on many fronts at the same time and is learning to use multiple sources and types of data to improve the school. (Of course, this approach may not be so disturbing to advocates of high-stakes assessment.)

To be sure, the state uses a complicated (a term not to be confused with sophisticated) formula to arrive at a single number assessment of schools. This formula is—and for some time has been—open to criticism. More important, the criticism has been directed not merely at methodological issues but also at conceptual issues. We have repeatedly had to confront this issue in our journey: What do these KIRIS scores really measure after all? Surely we are looking for more than a single number to understand what school reform is all about!

Note

1. The data for this story come from three sets of experiences. The reflections of the principal encompass her years at the school and include data used in her doctoral dissertation. The reflections of the qualitative evaluator are based on her observations and on formal and informal interviews. And the reflections of the quantitative evaluator are based on his analysis of surveys and documents. For the sake of presenting a coherent story, we have expressed these reflections in the voice of the principal and her staff. The schools named in the story are of course pseudonyms.

7

Teacher Responses to Rewards and Sanctions

Effects of and Reactions to Kentucky's High-Stakes Accountability Program

PATRICIA J. KANNAPEL, PAMELIA COE, LOLA AAGAARD,
BEVERLY D. MOORE, AND CYNTHIA A. REEVES

Introduction

> All of this rewards business is reinforcing one of the greatest
> things that's wrong with our society: greed. . . . I try to teach
> well because it's the right thing to do. I've got a young kid's
> mind in my hands. . . . I don't give a hoot if somebody is going
> to pay me $3,600. . . . That money isn't going to make the
> school better. . . . You can't deal with [schools] as a business
> and have rewards and sanctions and stuff like that. . . . They
> forget the personal side that's attached—that you want these
> students to learn and that you care about them.
>
> —A Kentucky teacher

With these words, a Kentucky middle school teacher summed up the anger and insult that many Kentucky teachers felt in the early stages of Kentucky's new accountability program. Established in 1990 as the centerpiece of the Kentucky Education Reform Act (KERA), the accountability program requires schools to show a predetermined level of improvement on a new, challenging, performance-based assessment or face sanctions that could ultimately result in the dismissal of individual teachers and the voluntary transfer of students to more successful schools. Teachers in schools that improve beyond the goal set by the state are eligible to receive substantial financial rewards. Interviews with legislators as the reform law was being constructed (Kannapel, 1991) and since that time made it clear that legislators believed that high stakes attached to the accountability measures were necessary to compel teachers to make substantive changes in their practice.

Study Description

The information in this report of educators' responses to Kentucky's high-stakes accountability program is drawn from a longitudinal, qualitative study of KERA implementation in 20 schools in four rural school districts. The study began with baseline data collection in 1990–91 and extends through the year 2000. Data for this report were collected primarily between fall 1993 and spring 1996, although we have updated some information based on more recent data.

The intent of the longitudinal study is to inform policymakers, practitioners, and researchers about how state-mandated, large-scale restructuring plays out in local school districts. The study focuses on small, rural districts because KERA provided us with a unique opportunity to study systemic school reform in rural settings. While rural schools have frequently adopted reforms initiated in urban or suburban settings (Bohrson, 1982; Branscome, 1982a, 1982b; Gjelten & Cromer, 1982; Nachtigal, 1982; Rosenfeld & Sher, 1977), they have not typically initiated such reform (Keizer, 1988; Nachtigal, 1982; Schmuck & Schmuck, 1992). Moreover, the literature of systemic reform does not take into consideration the differences between urban and rural education (e.g., Schwartz, 1991; Smith & O'Day, 1991; The Business Roundtable, 1990; U. S. Department of Education, 1994), and the few attempts at systemic reform, such as the reforms in Chicago or Philadelphia, have been urban. In the statewide effort of KERA, however, whether or not the reform will succeed depends largely on the responses of rural districts to the reform, because Kentucky is predominantly a rural state.

The Districts

The study districts were selected to reflect a range of geographic, economic, and demographic conditions. One district is located in western Kentucky, one is in central Kentucky, and two are in eastern Kentucky. Three are county districts, and one is a small, independent district located within the boundaries of a larger, county district. The districts have been assigned pseudonyms to protect their anonymity. The districts range in size from about two schools serving 900 students to nine schools serving 3,800 students. Nearly 100% of the students are Caucasian in three of the districts, while the central Kentucky district has about 10% minority students, mostly African-American. Thirty to forty percent of the student body in each district is classified as economically deprived, except for the eastern

Kentucky county district, where the proportion rises to 60%. The central and western school districts are located in farming communities. The eastern county district is located in an area that formerly relied heavily on coal mining, but currently has no strong economic base. The independent district is located in a small town that serves as a marketing and medical center for the surrounding rural areas.

These districts generally were recommended to us for study as "average" school districts where there had been neither a great deal of innovation nor chronic management problems. As is true of many Kentucky school districts, the western and central study districts had followed a relatively traditional approach to education, which had been satisfactory to most educators and parents, and had produced results on standardized tests that were slightly above average. The independent school district, too, had followed a traditional approach, and had been rewarded by high student performance on standardized achievement tests. These three districts were not actively seeking to make substantial changes in their instructional approaches prior to KERA. Only the eastern county district, which had suffered from inadequate funding and had recently received management assistance from the state, had begun attempting major innovations on its own at the time KERA was passed.

Methods

The four person research team was an ongoing and regular presence in 20 schools in four rural school districts from 1990 through 1995. The first phase of research (1990–95) focused on five key components of KERA, one of which was instruction and assessment changes in Grades 4 through 12. This aspect of KERA became prominent during the 1993–94 school year with the release of the first comparative data from the state assessment. Data for this paper were drawn primarily from fieldwork activities in the school years 1993–94 and 1994–95, plus a round of interviewing with state and local respondents in the spring of 1996. Over this period of time, data were gathered from open-ended interviews with over 300 people, including state-level policymakers, district superintendents and key central office staff, school board members, school principals, teachers, parents, and students. Researchers conducted classroom observations of more than 100 teachers across grade levels 4, 5, 8, 9, and 11. In addition, school-based decision-making (SBDM) council meetings, school board meetings, faculty meetings, and staff development meetings were attended periodically by members of the study team. Research staff also reviewed key documents such as reports of KIRIS scores, local and state newspapers, minutes of all SBDM council and school board meetings, and rewards certification forms from schools receiving rewards. At the state level, researchers attended nearly all meetings of the State Board of Elementary and Secondary Education since 1992 and reviewed state documents related to the KERA accountability measures.

Research Focus

This chapter considers two key questions relative to the KIRIS program:

1.) How have the accountability measures affected school practices?

The first question is concerned with the extent to which the accountability measures have produced behavioral change among educators in schools and classrooms. It was the intent of the legislation that the KIRIS testing and associated accountability system would drive instruction by holding schools accountable for student achievement on a performance-based assessment instrument. Because KIRIS is designed to measure higher-order skills, the rationale was that teaching to this sort of test would result in teachers changing their practices to develop students' abilities to think, solve problems, and apply and integrate knowledge. Thus, schools were expected to align curriculum and instruction with what was contained in the KIRIS assessments. Because the use of performance-based tests in high-stakes accountability programs is relatively new and limited, there are only a few studies (such as Koretz, Stecher, & Deibert, 1992—in Vermont—and Almasi, Afflerbach, Guthrie, & Schafer, 1994—in Maryland) that document whether or not the positive outcomes envisioned by supporters are beginning to occur. Our first research question was aimed at adding to this database by examining how instructional practices had been influenced by KIRIS in our study schools.

A second focus of this research question concerned whether or not school practices had been affected by the KERA tenet that schools should expect high levels of achievement of *all* students. The KIRIS assessment is designed so that all students must take the test, and so that educators will feel compelled to push all students to achieve at high levels. Schools receive a "novice" score for students who do not take the test. All special education students participate in KIRIS through adaptations (such as having the test read aloud to them) or through an "alternate portfolio." We wanted to know if these requirements had led educators to focus their efforts on all of the students in their schools.

In addressing the first research question, we gathered evidence that schools were changing in some of the ways that were intended by the assessment and accountability system, but discovered there also were some unintended (but not entirely unexpected) effects of high-stakes accountability.

2.) How do local educators and parents view and respond to the KERA accountability measures?

The second question deals with attitudes toward and opinions about the accountability measures held by local respondents. The analysis of these results indicated that many of the attitudes and beliefs about the new system were quite negative, to the extent that they could become impediments to reform. We looked specifically at: (1) educators' beliefs about children's ability to achieve at high levels; (2) attitudes toward accountability's effect on educator professionalism; and (3) educator difficulties with KIRIS itself and policy decisions regarding it.

Research Findings

Effects of Accountability on School Practices

We first consider the aspects of school reform that KIRIS was intended to drive and the extent to which they were occurring in the study schools. We then describe some unintended consequences of the accountability program that we witnessed or heard about in the study schools.

Intended curricular and instructional changes. We observed a moderate degree of change in school curriculum and instructional practices, most of which appeared to be assessment-driven. The most conspicuous change was a much greater emphasis on writing and the writing process to help students develop writing portfolios. In addition, teachers placed increased emphasis on open-ended problem-solving exercises to help students develop mathematics portfolios, students were engaged in practice of answering open-response questions, and schools were incorporating content that is tested on KIRIS but not previously emphasized in many rural school districts, such as the arts and humanities.

The increase in the amount of writing taught was in direct response to the strong writing component of KIRIS. KIRIS includes (or has included during the course of this study) a writing portfolio, a math portfolio with a strong written component, and open-response questions that require students to write. Currently, the accountability index is designed so that writing portfolios count for 75% of the school's writing score, while on-demand writing prompts count for the remaining 25% of the score; open-response questions count for 100% in other content areas. Thus, there was a strong incentive for teachers to focus on writing, and many did so. Even when teachers made few other instructional changes, most assigned more writing than previously.

It is unlikely that many teachers would have emphasized writing to the degree that they did had they not been forced into it, yet many teachers saw the benefits and reported that they would continue to emphasize writing even if KERA were not in effect. This seemed to be especially true of the teachers in our study who had served as writing portfolio "cluster leaders"—teachers who received regional and state-level training and information about portfolios, which they were to pass along to their colleagues. An eighth-grade writing portfolio cluster leader explained why she has become a portfolio enthusiast:

> For years we have been so concerned with [teaching] English in parts. You did a unit and then you went to another one and you never brought it all together. Somehow the kids never understood, "Why am I doing this?" So to me, actually seeing that they can communicate and use these skills is great.

However, many teachers in our study reported that writing consumed so much classroom time that they did not have time to teach skills or cover the amount of content they felt they should. Teachers of content areas other than writing and math seemed to be especially resentful of having to spend so much time on writing. Two comments, the first from a junior high science teacher in 1993–94 and the second from an elementary physical education teacher in 1994–95, illustrate this:

> They [portfolios] are taking away from valuable classroom time with nonsense that doesn't help anybody. . . . Give us some money to build us a middle school science lab, and you watch these state test scores! We don't have to have portfolios and all this wasted time.
>
> My number one concern, since I teach P.E., is that we have 80% of the American public overweight, and now they're trying to get us to write and do all this other stuff in our P.E. time. We only have 30 minutes three times a week [with each class]. If we go to junior high, they're only [in P.E.] for six weeks and don't have any the rest of the year. And now they're taking what little time we have and trying to get us to do other things. I'm sure that's well and good, but if they're going to get overweight and fat and die at 30, it's not going to do them very much good to be educated.

Another assessment-driven change was the use of open-response questions on tests and in classroom assignments. Because of the heavy weighting given to open-response questions in the accountability formula, teachers in all schools in the study were teaching students to answer these questions. Many of our study schools required teachers to post in their classrooms a list of steps to answering an open-response question. Some of the schools in our study held minicourses for students in answering open-response questions. The latter practice appeared to be the type of activity that had potential for inflating test scores rather than actually improving student abilities because the skill of answering open-response questions seemed to be taught out of context of specific subject matter students were learning. However, most teachers we interviewed supported the use of open-response questions in general and many reported that they had always included them on tests. Thus, the use of open-response questions in and of themselves was something teachers easily accepted, but the pressure of the accountability measures sometimes compelled educators to teach open-response questions in an unnatural way.

A curriculum change that appeared to be driven almost entirely by the assessment program was expansion of the curriculum to include arts and humanities courses. This content is not traditionally covered in any depth in rural schools, but two high schools in our study made plans to add arts and humanities courses to the curriculum when art and humanities questions on KIRIS began to count in the accountability formula.

It should be noted that the developers of KIRIS envisioned a system in which assessments were embedded into classroom instruction. For the first five years of reform implementation, it did not appear that many teachers in the study schools were integrating instruction and assessment. In general, teachers tacked writing activities onto their existing curriculum or supplanted other content in order to squeeze in writing. This suggests that coverage of traditional content may suffer, a possibility also proposed by Fenster (1996).

The perceived loss of "basic skills" became an increasingly prominent concern in the four study districts throughout the course of our study. The concern stemmed from a de-emphasis on the traditional, content-based "scope and sequence" in favor of broad learning goals that emphasize integration and application of knowledge. As teachers struggled to teach children to write and to think rather than to simply memorize and recite, they became more and more fearful that they were not spending enough time teaching basic content. During the 1996 round of interviewing, for instance, 30% of local respondents identified the loss of basic skills as a major weakness of KERA. There is little evidence to date to substantiate or refute the claim that basic skills are being lost under KERA.

These curricular and instructional changes that we noted in our small study sample seemed to have taken place in other schools around the state. Similar findings were produced from both the statewide RAND survey (Koretz, Barron, Mitchell, & Stecher, 1996) and a smaller study involving interviews at six central Kentucky schools (Kelley & Protsik, 1996). Bridge, Compton-Hall, and Cantrell's (1996) conclusions about writing practices also were analogous to ours.

With regard to teaching every child, interview data revealed that at least a few teachers were pushing all students to do well on KIRIS in direct response to the accountability measures. One teacher commented:

> I've always felt like I had enough experience with children to know which ones to push, which ones to encourage, which ones to say, "I can't accept this." Now I have to push every one of them, because it's not that they're accountable—I'm accountable. I have to.

An elementary school principal described how the combination of rewards/sanctions and student results led teachers at his school to look more closely at all students:

> I think we are becoming more aware of all the students than what we have in the past. I think it has been fairly easy in the past to say, "Well, Johnny is just not interested so just let Johnny sit there and the rest of us go on." I think the teachers are more aware now: "Yeah, Johnny isn't interested, but let's see if we can do some things to pull Johnny into it to get him interested." [This shift in attitude occurred] partially because they know that schoolwide we're under the gun to do this. . . . rewards and sanctions hanging out there over the top of us. Another big part of

it is that most teachers are really buying into the fact that, "Yeah, we do need to try to reach these kids, even if it's only a little bit. If we don't, who will?"

In 1995, these sorts of reactions were not expressed by more than a few teachers, however. It is too soon to tell if these responses will become a general trend as educators develop a better understanding of what they must do to earn rewards and avoid sanctions.

Unintended consequences. Measurement-driven instruction has been viewed as problematic when norm-referenced tests are used because teaching to these tests tends to lead to a narrowing of the curriculum to the kinds of isolated skills covered on such tests (Bracey, 1987; Haertel, 1994; McLaughlin, 1991; Shepard, 1991). When high stakes are attached to norm-referenced tests, teachers often teach in ways that violate their own beliefs and values about how and what students should be taught (Hatch & Freeman, 1988; Urdan & Paris, 1994). In contrast, performance-based examinations, such as KIRIS, are meant to reflect higher-order skills. It is believed that if tests are changed to require higher-order skills, the negative effects of previous MDI efforts will be offset (Haertel, 1994; Linn, 1993; Noble & Smith, 1994; Shepard, 1991). When performance-based examinations are closely linked to a "thinking curriculum," teaching to the test is considered desirable (Linn, 1993; Noble & Smith, 1994; Shepard, 1991).

Even with the introduction of performance-based assessments, however, many people (Bracey, 1987; Darling-Hammond, 1991; Freedman, 1994; McLaughlin, 1991; Shepard, 1991; Torance, 1993) continue to have grave reservations about using an assessment program to drive instructional reform because of possible onerous, unintended consequences of high-stakes testing, most of which would affect students who are not likely to do well on the assessment. For instance, fears have been expressed that schools may retain low-achieving students in nonaccountable grades (Haertel, 1994), encourage them to drop out of school (Darling-Hammond, 1991), place them in special education so they won't be tested (Darling-Hammond, 1991), or reject them entirely (Darling-Hammond, 1991; McLaughlin, 1991; Shepard, 1991). In addition, school administrators may shift the best teachers to the accountable grade levels (Haertel, 1994), or teachers may try to transfer to schools that have a better chance of doing well on the test (Darling-Hammond, 1991).

Some of the unintended consequences listed above have been avoided through the KIRIS requirements that all students be tested, and that schools move a certain percentage of low-scoring students to higher categories. Koretz et al. (1996), however, reported that "appreciable minorities" of teachers in their statewide survey reported inappropriate test administration practices, such as rephrasing test questions or answering questions about the content of the assessment during administration. In only one case did we find convincing evidence of a questionable practice: one school administrator reported that teachers typed students' portfolio entries and corrected them; it was his impression that "everyone" did this. While we have heard very few of these kinds of reports in our study schools, we have seen and heard evidence of unintended side effects that resulted from the pressure imposed by the accountability measures.

Haertel (1994) predicted an unintended outcome of KIRIS that apparently occurred at two schools in our study: disproportionate numbers of students were retained in the primary program an extra year to give them more time to prepare for the fourth-grade assessment. A more common occurrence is that in some of the study schools the strongest teachers have been moved to the accountable grade levels.

Our data supported another unintended adverse consequence of high-stakes assessment programs identified by Haertel (1994): that the test scores themselves become the goal of education rather than the "intellectual attainments those grades are meant to represent" (p. 70). While KIRIS was designed such that scoring well on the assessment should represent actual educational achievement, we found evidence suggesting that the pressure of the accountability program caused some educators to focus more on assessment scores—and the resulting salvation or loss of their jobs—than on the welfare of their students. For instance, a principal expressed concern about the amount of time eighth-grade students devoted to the band program and athletics:

> Like it or not, band's not going to do anything for us as far as us reaching our threshold. But we've got half of our eighth grade out today to a band camp when we need to be in our classrooms getting ready for our KERA testing. . . . I told our basketball coach the other day, "I'm sorry, but your 18 wins a year in junior high school is not going to help me one darn bit to keep my job."

At one school, parents reacted negatively to the school council's plan to increase the number of credits required in core subject areas in order to improve KIRIS scores. Parents feared students would not be able to take needed elective courses. Discussion of the proposed plan at a council meeting revealed that teachers were focused almost entirely on test scores while parents focused on student needs. A parent council member stated:

> I have a concern because so much of what I'm hearing about curriculum is an echo of a test score rather than our children's current needs or future dreams.

Teachers agreed they were focused on the test. A teacher commented:

> The only thing that counts under KERA is test scores. That's one of the flaws of KERA. . . . We end up doing exactly what they tell us to do because we don't want to be [sanctioned], and that's the only way you

can go. And that chokes off stuff that is extremely valuable, like what [the parents] are saying.

At another school where special activities were planned prior to KIRIS testing to encourage students to do their best on the test, a parent expressed concern that the emphasis on doing well on the test was for the benefit of teachers more so than students:

> Are we as council members going to encourage parents to get their kids ready to be tested so the teachers can get more money, or is that money going to be put back into the system as a whole to help the whole school?

A fourth-grade teacher spoke of how her concern about improving assessment results almost caused her to lose sight of student welfare:

> At the beginning of the year when I first got the test scores, I was really worried and I was trying to push. And then one day I talked to a mother [whose] husband had kicked her and five children out of their home. She was taking these children to different places every night to live. She and her daughter were living in a car. And I said, "I don't care what that child does on the test; I want him to know that I care about him. And I want him to know that school is a safe place for him to be." That put me back on track for knowing what the kids need. . . . I believe they all will do the best they can, but as for me putting the pressure on them to succeed, I'm not going to, and I'm going to try to stop putting it on myself.

Attitudes toward KIRIS

Beliefs about All Children Achieving at High Levels

The basic premise underlying KERA is that all children can achieve at high levels. This issue is addressed at least three times in KERA: (1) The introductory section states that the legislature's intent was to create a system of public education that will allow *all* students to acquire the specified capacities; (2) the section listing KERA goals states that schools must expect a high level of achievement of *all* students; and (3) the section describing the accountability measures states that the legislature intends for schools to succeed with *all* students (Kentucky Department of Education, 1994).

This underlying premise of the law runs counter to the experience and ingrained beliefs of most professional educators (Barzun, 1959; Bowles & Gintis, 1976; Brown, 1991; Lortie, 1975; Spring, 1976; Wilcox, 1982). Teachers have been socialized into an educational system designed to sort students rather than to insure high achievement for all (Barzun, 1959; Bowles & Gintis, 1976; Brown, 1991; Lortie, 1975; Spring, 1976; Wilcox, 1982), and they generally have been inculcated into a deeply ingrained belief that some children have the innate capacity to achieve at high levels and others do not.

In the schools we studied, the notion of holding higher expectations for all students became equated with the perceived KIRIS demand that all students score proficient on the state test at some point. Teachers roundly rejected this demand, while often agreeing that expectations for students should be raised. That is, while teachers did not necessarily believe that all students could perform at a proficient level on an external test on a given day (or perhaps ever), they generally did believe that all students could improve their performance with respect to given standards.

These nuances of meaning rarely emerged without targeted questioning, however. Teachers tended to focus more on the KERA catch-phrase, "All children can achieve at high levels," which they almost universally rejected. Over the course of the study, educators and parents alike occasionally volunteered comments about this philosophy, often indicating their skepticism. During the 1994–95 school year, we made it a point to ask those we interviewed what they thought of this philosophy. Eighty-five percent of the 70 or so educators and parents who were asked directly about this philosophy said they did not subscribe to it.

A high school teacher we interviewed dealt with the issue of expecting all students to reach a specified level of performance:

> I think that students should be expected to achieve at the highest level that they are capable of, but I do not believe that all students can achieve at the same level. Every student should be given the opportunity to do their best, to learn as much as they can, to excel, but they're not all going to be proficient writers or proficient mathematicians, much less distinguished.

Others commented that home background or lack of student motivation would keep some students from attaining high levels of achievement. A junior high teacher commented:

> No, I don't think all students can achieve at high levels. I think they can achieve at *their* high level. But if you're going to say "This is high level and everybody can reach it," I'm sorry, it just won't work. Not unless you're going to give them to us when they come out of the hospital and we're going to be here 24 hours a day, maybe. But you're fighting a whole other world out there, sometimes; a world that doesn't value education.

Even when not asked directly about their philosophy, some educators' responses to other interview questions revealed that they did not believe all children would improve into the proficient or even the apprentice category on KIRIS.

A principal expressed the view that the extended school program, which was designed to assist students who need extra time to meet KERA goals, should be offered to only those students who had the potential to move from the "novice" to the "apprentice" performance category. He felt that the extended program was wasted on students who, in his view, would never score higher than "novice."

An eighth-grade teacher in another district spoke of the temptation to focus her efforts only on students who were capable of advancing to the next performance category:

> I have kids who are novice students, and that's all they are ever going to be. But I worked probably harder with those novice students, and they worked as hard as any of the other levels to come up with their finished [portfolio] product. . . . but yet, at the novice level, they only score zeroes. All they'll ever score is a zero. We don't get any credit at all for the improvement that they made—and they made a lot of improvement, but they're just never going to be at that next level. I just feel like, as a teacher, this kid is a novice, whatever I do with him isn't going to help that score. Just forget him, let me work with these [who can reach the next level]. And I think that's going to happen to a lot of kids.

Even though it did not appear that most educators believed that all children could achieve at high levels, there were instances when it appeared that student performance on KIRIS was convincing some educators that students were capable of performing at higher levels than they had imagined. An eighth-grade teacher in another district described how one of her students had progressed through working on portfolios:

> I had a kid last year who couldn't write a sentence. In his letter to the reviewer he said, "I never thought I would be able to do this." I look at him and I think, "What if all I had stressed had been grammar skills and punctuation skills but he had never transferred that?" . . . Last year he was the slowest kid I had, and I thought, "I'll never get a portfolio out of him." We had no problem. He's the first one to hand his portfolio in.

In summary, it appeared that the majority of educators either did not believe that all children can achieve at high levels, or believed that it was not within their power to ensure that all students scored proficient on the KIRIS test. However, student achievement on KIRIS made believers out of a very few people, or at least opened their minds to the possibility that they could expect more of students. Koretz et al. (1996) reported some similar, albeit rosier, findings in their statewide survey of teachers and principals. They reported that only about half of their survey respondents disagreed with the tenet that all children can achieve at high levels. However, they also found that fewer than 10% of teachers agreed that all students can reach the *same* level of performance, so phrasing of the question may account for differences in results. Another Koretz et al. finding was that 68% of the teachers surveyed reported expectations had increased for students since KERA passed, although teachers reported that expectations had increased more for high-achieving students than for low-achieving students. Few of the teachers interviewed in our study spoke about expectations for high-achieving students, which may explain why our results regarding increased expectations look more pessimistic in comparison.

Attitudes Regarding Accountability's Effect on Educator Professionalism

In a preceding section, we described the extent to which the accountability system forced change to happen in the four districts we studied. Many of these changes may have a positive effect over time if teachers come to see the value of them and implement the changes for their own sake. At present, however, educators' attitudes toward the accountability measures may act as a barrier to their acceptance of the assessment-driven changes. As a rule, the accountability program was strongly resented by educators in the four districts. For instance, in the 1996 round of interviewing, 30% of local respondents identified the accountability program as a weak point of the law, and an even higher percentage (51%) said the assessment program in general is a weak point in the reform effort.

Almost across the board, the educators we spoke with resented the accountability measures as an insult to their professionalism. They often told us that educators are motivated by intrinsic factors and that extrinsic rewards will not transform an incompetent, uncaring teacher into a competent, conscientious one. Many teachers said they try to do their best because that's their job. When asked if she was driven by the promise of rewards or threat of sanctions, a high school teacher remarked:

> I haven't really thought that much about it either way. I think that I work . . . as hard as I work because of who I am; that's just me, [and] this is what my job is . . . that's more my motivation than thinking about sanctions or rewards. Obviously, I don't want to be a school in crisis, but I don't think . . . about that so much as simply doing what I'm supposed to do.

Many teachers initially said they were not driven by the promise of rewards because they did not believe the rewards would actually be conferred. Even after the first round of rewards were dispensed, virtually no teachers with whom we spoke indicated that the promise of rewards had inspired them to work harder or change their approaches.

While the majority of teachers we talked to about this issue said they were not driven by the promise of rewards, over one third of the educators we spoke to on this issue in 1994–95 admitted that the threat of sanctions had compelled them to make changes in instruction and to push students to the limits of their capabilities. Thus, many educators found the threat of sanctions motivating in the negative sense. A high school teacher in one of our study schools explained:

> The thought of losing your job is far more threatening, far more intimi-dating than receiving rewards. You want to make sure you keep your job and keep the school open. Distinguished Educators [can] come in and they're going to have dictatorial powers to close down the school. . . . When the powers-that-be make a change and they say you've got to do something, then you've got to do it because they have the power to make life miserable for you if you don't.

Researchers in other states have also reported a diminished sense of profes-sionalism on the part of teachers experiencing externally-mandated tests associ-ated with high-stakes accountability (Noble & Smith, 1994; Shepard, 1991; Torrance, 1993). Our findings regarding the relative importance of rewards versus sanctions to teachers in Kentucky were similar to those reported by Kelley and Protsik (1996) and the Evaluation Center at Western Michigan University (1995).

Difficulties with KIRIS Particulars and Policies

The timelines built into the legislation have also created impediments to effec-tive implementation of the accountability system. Kentucky educators commonly joked rather hostilely about the state's "building the airplane while they are flying it"—a reference to (among other things) the fact that high-stakes testing was implemented before the test was fully developed. Kentucky policymakers have been responsive to complaints from the field and have revised the KIRIS program each biennium. These revisions have been designed to make the assessment more reliable while also trying to keep it performance-based. The revisions include: taking out, then reinstating multiple-choice questions; removing group adminis-tered, hands-on performance events; delaying the imposition of the most severe sanctions for two years; removing math portfolios from the assessment to allow for more research and development; and expanding the accountable grade levels in response to educators' anguish over teachers' and children's stress and work over-load at Grades 4, 8, and 12—the grades originally specified in the reform law. The revisions have generally made the assessment program more manageable for teachers, but have also made it difficult to maintain consistency. Teachers have sometimes expressed the feeling that they were shooting at a moving target as the assessment pieces changed from one biennium to the next. The difficulties of maintaining consistency in the face of these changes have been exacerbated by the fact that performance testing is a new field nationally and there are not yet a set of generally agreed-upon standards—everyone is learning from Kentucky's efforts.

Educators in the study districts also were skeptical about many aspects of the assessment, including the comparison of two different groups of students to determine school progress, the reliability of scoring, and the validity of the test for individual students. Some teachers questioned the validity of KIRIS because individual student scores were sometimes inconsistent with student performance in the classroom. In addition, they wanted a test that provided useful student diagnostic information; they did not understand how KIRIS could be reliable for schools but not for individual students, as educators were initially told by the Kentucky Department of Education.

Many teachers questioned the validity of KIRIS because they often could not identify what, if anything, they had done to cause the school's scores to go up or down. When asked to explain their scores, the educators we talked to usually attributed the scores to something outside the school's control—most commonly, having an unusually bright or slow class in the accountable grades that year, or the general makeup of the student body (e.g., having deprived vs. stimulating home backgrounds). Educators from schools that failed to meet their thresholds sometimes attributed their lack of success to having a high baseline score. A junior high teacher at a school where the high school scores fell below the baseline described the reaction of high school teachers to the assessment results:

> They don't know why they dropped. . . . They're all thinking it's the composition of the kids that made this difference here. . . . We've scrambled around. . . . Nobody knows quite what to do, so everybody is coming up with ideas, some of which get tried, some of which have a longer life span than others, but there's not a cohesive sort of plan. . . . We don't know what the hell is going on, all right? And so [teachers] say, "One thing I know is that [the state is] weak legally." Really, this is what goes through people's heads. . . . They're long since over, "What can we do in here as a group to make these better?" and they're into, "How can I protect my [job]?"

The reluctance to attribute scores to something positive that teachers had done in the classroom carried over when educators were asked about the scores of other schools. In a district where it happened that the most innovative school was the only one that was not successful, several teachers in successful schools stated with some measure of satisfaction that they had done better because they had eschewed much of KERA. Sources in three of the four districts privately accused other districts or schools that had been rewarded of previewing the test, setting artificially low baseline scores, or otherwise "cheating" on the test. Some educators in nonreward schools in two districts were so incensed about the whole business that they reported grossly inaccurate comparisons between their own schools' scores and those of reward schools.

Discussion

In this chapter we considered two large research questions: (1) How have the accountability measures affected school practices, and (2) How do local educators and parents view and respond to the KERA accountability measures? Our data from 20 schools in four school districts provided evidence that the accountability measures had begun to drive the reform effort in that teachers had changed their instruction to focus on writing and some schools added new courses to the curriculum. In addition, at least a few teachers were making stronger efforts to reach all students. In some instances, educators seemed to be internalizing the philosophy behind the changes they had made because they saw the positive effects on students. More commonly, however, educators taught to the test because they must, and many resented this.

The designers of KIRIS hoped that the test would mirror "good" instruction to such an extent that teaching to the test would be a worthwhile endeavor. Many educators and parents have reported that students' writing abilities have improved tremendously as a result of the increased emphasis on writing, and that students are better thinkers through practice in analyzing and explaining their work. Thus, early indications are that some of the goals of the program are being realized.

It is disheartening, however, to find educators more preoccupied with the test than with helping students achieve high standards. It is likely that the framers of KERA envisioned an educational system in which everyone worked together toward the ultimate goal of helping all students achieve at high levels, with the assessment program serving as an instrument for measuring whether that occurred. What has happened so far is that there is a movement toward everyone working to help students do well on KIRIS as an end in itself. While it is hoped that KIRIS mirrors the right kinds of instruction and high levels of achievement, a single assessment instrument can never measure everything that should be taught in school. The temptation and reality for Kentucky teachers is to concentrate on the changes likeliest to raise KIRIS scores in the short term.

Others who have studied measurement-driven reform have also been troubled by the wrong-headed focus that results when assessment drives instruction. Noble and Smith (1994) charged that tying performance-based assessment with high-stakes accountability for teachers is philosophically inconsistent because, while the assessment promotes a constructivist view of student learning, the accountability that is tied to the assessment is based on a behaviorist view of teacher learning because teachers do not feel in control of their professional lives. Torrance (1993), who studied measurement-driven reform in Britain, does not believe that assessment should drive instruction because it is difficult, if not impossible, to capture all of the elements of good teaching in a single teaching and assessment package.

A question that has been inadequately explored pertains to whether KIRIS is a valid measure of KERA implementation. Two evaluations of the KIRIS assessment and accountability program recommended that its reliability and validity be more strongly established (Hambleton, Jaeger, Koretz, Linn, Millman, & Phillips, 1995; Western Michigan University, 1995). While our study sample is too small to provide a basis for studying the validity of KIRIS as a measure of school success, we have been in the study schools for several years and have become familiar with their leadership, administrative, and instructional structures. Thus, we expected that we might see some hint of a connection between the level of KERA implementation and student performance on KIRIS, should one exist.

After the first biennium, we were surprised that we could perceive no pattern whatsoever to how the schools performed on the assessment. After the second biennium results were in, however, we closely examined our data from the three schools in our study that had earned rewards for both accountability cycles. This time, we found some common characteristics. Educators in all three schools held high expectations for students. In addition, they had a relatively consistent instructional approach over time, with most educators in the schools adhering to a common approach (whether traditional or innovative). There were few factions among the teachers in the three schools, and they tended to willingly follow the lead of the building principal. Interestingly, the general level of KERA implementation did not seem to be a deciding factor. In fact, two of the three schools had remained relatively traditional in their approaches, not necessarily focusing their curriculum around KERA goals and expectations. These data clearly are not generalizable, but they suggest to us that it is too soon to know if KIRIS is an accurate measure of KERA goals.

To summarize, KERA has resulted in many changes, some of them substantive. Systemic reform, however, has not yet occurred in the sense that all the pieces of the reform effort are working in concert toward the goal of improved student achievement. Instead, many educators are strongly focused on bringing up test scores in the short run. While some would argue that the accountability program will eventually force systemic reform (Steffy, 1993), it is possible that the accountability measures may actually impede the philosophical changes that are required to effectively implement KERA. If all students are to achieve at high levels, then the focus must be on students—not on an instrument that is supposed to measure their achievement. KERA is a step in the right direction in that it provides substantial money and resources to helping teachers focus on meeting the needs of individual students. The change effort might be even more successful if the focus were placed more singularly on building teacher capacities to help students achieve high standards than on rewards and punishments as they are now conceived. A more wholehearted acceptance of the reform measures might have been achieved if there had been an initial period of several years during which the KIRIS test was developed to the point of general credibility and teachers and educators were provided professional development that built their capacity to develop curriculum and instructional approaches that would enable students to achieve the high standards mandated by KERA.

References

Almasi, J. F., Afflerbach, P. P., Guthrie, J. T., & Schafer, W. D. (1994, April). *The impact of a statewide performance assessment program on classroom instructional practice in literacy.* Paper presented at the annual meeting of the American Educational Research Association, New Orleans, LA.

Barzun, J. (1959). *The house of intellect.* New York: Harper & Row.

Bohrson, G., Jr. (1982). Taking education to the crossroads: Texas' Regional Education Service Centers. In P. M. Nachtigal (Ed.), *Rural education: In search of a better way* (pp. 101–116). Boulder, CO: Westview Press.

Bowles, S. & Gintis, H. (1976). *Schooling in capitalist America: Educational reform and the contradictions of economic life.* New York: Basic Books.

Bracey, G. W. (1987). Measurement-driven instruction: Catchy phrase, dangerous practice. *Phi Delta Kappan, 68*(9), 683–686.

Branscome, J. (1982a). The Teacher Corps in Mississippi: Washington strategy against Delta dilemmas. In P. M. Nachtigal (Ed.), *Rural education: In search of a better way* (pp. 47–60). Boulder, CO: Westview Press.

Branscome, J. (1982b). The Urban/Rural Program: Can the government buy change in rural schools? In P. M. Nachtigal (Ed.), *Rural education: In search of a better way* (pp. 139–156). Boulder, CO: Westview Press.

Bridge, C. A., Compton-Hall, M., & Cantrell, S. C. (1996, January). *Classroom writing practices revisited: The effects of statewide reform on classroom writing practices.* Lexington, KY: Institute on Education Reform, University of Kentucky.

Brown, R. (1991). *Schools of thought: How the politics of literacy shape thinking in the classroom.* San Francisco: JosseyBass.

The Business Roundtable (ND). *Essential components of a successful education system: The Business Roundtable Education Public Policy Agenda.* New York: The Business Roundtable.

Darling-Hammond, L. (1991). The implications of testing policy for quality and equality. *Phi Delta Kappan, 73*(3), 220-225.

Fenster, M. J. (1996, April). *An assessment of "middle" stakes educational accountability: The case of Kentucky.* Paper presented at the Annual Meeting of the American Educational Research Association, New York, NY.

Freedman, S. W. (1994, June). *School reform through examinations: Lessons from the British experience.* Occasional Paper No. 38, National Center for the Study of Writing. Berkeley, CA: University of California.

Gjelten, T., & Cromer, D. (1982). Getting on the bandwagon: Maine schools discover the National Diffusion Network. In P. M. Nachtigal (Ed.), *Rural education: In search of a better way* (pp. 117–138). Boulder, CO: Westview Press.

Haertel, E. H. (1994). Theoretical and practical implications. In T. R. Guskey (Ed.), *High stakes performance assessment: Perspectives on Kentucky's educational reform* (pp. 65–75). Thousand Oaks, CA: Corwin Press.

Hambleton, R. K., Jaeger, R. M., Koretz, D., Linn, R. L., Millman, J., & Phillips, S. E. (1995, June). *Review of the measurement quality of the Kentucky Instructional Results Information System, 1991–1994*. Frankfort, KY: Kentucky General Assembly, Office of Education Accountability.

Hatch, J. A., & Freeman, E. B. (1988). Who's pushing whom? Stress and kindergarten. *Phi Delta Kappan, 70*(2), 145–147.

Kannapel, P. J. (1991). *Education reform in Kentucky: Expert theory, folk theory, and the Kentucky Education Reform Act of 1990*. Unpublished master's thesis, University of Kentucky, Lexington.

Keizer, G. (1988). *No place but here: A teacher's vocation in a rural community*. New York: Viking.

Kelley, C., & Protsik, J. (1996). *Risk and reward: Perspectives on the implementation of Kentucky's school-based performance award program*. Madison, WI: University of Wisconsin-Madison.

Kentucky Department of Education (1994). *1994 Kentucky school laws*. Frankfort, KY: Kentucky Department of Education.

Kifer, E. (1994). Development of the Kentucky Instructional Results Information System (KIRIS). In T. R. Guskey (Ed.), *High stakes performance assessment: Perspectives on Kentucky's educational reform* (pp. 7–18). Thousand Oaks, CA: Corwin Press.

Koretz, D. M., Barron, S., Mitchell, K. J., & Stecher, B. M. (1996). *Perceived effects of the Kentucky Instructional Results Information System (KIRIS)*. Santa Monica, CA: RAND.

Koretz, D., Stecher, B., & Deibert, E. (1992, August). *The Vermont portfolio assessment program: Interim report on implementation and impact, 1991–92 school year*. Los Angeles: National Center for Research on Evaluation, Standards, and Student Testing (CRESST), Graduate School of Education, UCLA.

Linn, R. 1993). Educational assessment: Expanded expectations and challenges. *Educational Evaluation and Policy Analysis, 15*(1), 1–16.

Lortie, D. (1975). *Schoolteacher: A sociological study*. Chicago: University of Chicago Press.

McLaughlin, M. W. (1991). Test-based accountability as a reform strategy. *Phi Delta Kappan, 73*(3), 248–251.

Nachtigal, P. M. (1982). Rural school improvement efforts: An interpretive history. In P. M. Nachtigal (Ed.), *Rural education: In search of a better way*. Boulder, CO: Westview Press.

Noble, A. J., & Smith, M. L. (1994). Old and new beliefs about measurement-driven reform: "Build it and they will come." *Educational Policy, 8*(2), 111–136.

Popham, W. J. (1987). The merits of measurement-driven instruction. *Phi Delta Kappan, 68*(9), 679–682.

Rosenfeld, S. A., & Sher, J. P. (1977). The urbanization of rural schools, 1840–1970. In J. P. Sher (Ed.), *Education in rural America: A reassessment of conventional wisdom* (pp. 11–80). Boulder, CO: Westview Press.

Schmuck, R. A., & Schmuck, P. A. (1992). *Small districts big problems: Making school everybody's house.* Newbury Park, CA: Corwin Press.

Schwartz, H. (1991). Putting the pieces together: A systemic approach to educational reform. *Planning and Changing, 22*(3/4), 231–239.

Shepard, L. A. (1991). Will national tests improve student learning? *Phi Delta Kappan, 73*(3), 232–238.

Smith, M. S., & O'Day, J. (1991). Systemic school reform. In S. H. Fuhrman & B. Malen (Eds.), *The politics of curriculum and testing: The 1990 Yearbook of the Politics of Education Association.* London: Falmer Press, 233–267.

Spring, J. (1976). *The sorting machine: National educational policy since 1945.* New York: Longman.

Steffy, B. E. (1993). Top-down—bottom-up: Systemic change in Kentucky. *Educational Leadership, 51*(1), 42–44.

Torrance, H. (1993). Combining measurement-driven instruction with authentic assessment: Some initial observations of national assessment in England and Wales. *Educational Evaluation and Policy Analysis, 15*(1), 81–90.

Urdan, T. C., & Paris, S. G. (1994). Teachers' perceptions of standardized achievement tests. *Educational policy, 8*(2), 137–156.

U. S. Department of Education (1994). Systemic education reform. *The ERIC Review, 3*(2).

Western Michigan University, The Evaluation Center. (1995, January). *An independent evaluation of the Kentucky Instructional Results Information System (KIRIS).* Frankfort, KY: Kentucky Institute for Education Research.

Wilcox, K. (1982). Differential socialization in the classroom: Implications for equal opportunity. In G. Spindler (Ed.), *Doing the ethnography of schooling* (pp. 268–309). New York: CBS College Books.

Part III

Alternative Approaches to Accountability

8

A Teacher Appraisal Invention Process

Developing Commitment to Accountability

LINDA SHELOR

How can a school system develop commitment among teachers for accountability measures? It can happen when the school system establishes a culture that focuses teachers on modifying their work to "fit" the students rather than on trying to modify the students to fit the teacher's work. So how can a school system promote the necessary urgency among teachers to be committed to supporting and leading such a culture? Impossible in one lifetime you say? A growing number of school districts disagree—as does the Center for Leadership in School Reform (CLSR).

CLSR is a private, nonprofit, national organization that provides technical assistance and support to school reformers. CLSR's work grows from the belief that schools need to be more clearly focused on providing quality work to children and that districts need to enhance their capacity to support and sustain such reform at the building and classroom levels. CLSR developed the Teacher-Appraisal Invention Process (TAIP) in its role as a change agent to support districts in establishing teacher standards and evaluation processes while building local ownership and commitment within each district to these standards and processes.

The TAIP model shifts from the traditional administrative-driven annual rite of evaluation organized around generic checklists and capturing "Kodak moments" to teacher-driven, continuous assessments aimed at improving the quality of the work that teachers provide to students.

CLSR's Teacher-Appraisal Invention Process (TAIP) is a design process for creating a locally developed teacher evaluation system. In our experience with four school districts in the Southeastern United States,[1] it takes about 15 months

149

to develop a local version adapted from a suggested CLSR model. The initial model was created during a 24-month collaboration with one particular school district.

The CLSR model provides candidate standards and procedures based on a beliefs-based framework as a seed bed from which local districts shape local standards for the work of teachers. An accompanying "invitation to invention" design process encourages local adaptations. Organized peer groups focus their attention on designing districtwide accountability procedures aimed at improving the quality of the work provided to students. Invitation to invention strategies—in contrast to "mandate to implementation" strategies—focus district attention on providing a supportive structure for practitioners to use a "let's try something and see if it works" method for developing a system of accountability.

Each use of TAIP has led to improvements based on lessons learned and has provided fresh examples of formats and procedures. While the model is based upon a specific beliefs-based framework (see Schlechty, *Inventing Better Schools: An Action Plan for Educational Reform*, 1997), it is designed to promote local ownership and encourage local adaptations, thus gaining commitment. Teachers in one district using this model refer to these adaptations as "[district-name]-izing the model."

The Foundation

The logic of the TAIP design reasons that teachers understandably reject accountability systems that hold them responsible for factors in the learning process outside of the teachers' control. The TAIP design argues that teachers should be held accountable only for those factors over which teachers have control and that affect student learning. There are many factors not in the teachers' control that affect student learning. But the one factor that teachers can control is the work or assignments they provide to students.

The guiding assumption is based on the belief that raising the quality of the work that teachers provide to students will raise the quality of the work that students return to the teachers. In raising the quality of the students' work returned to teachers, the students will increase their own learning and will achieve academically. Students will do junk work when they are given junk work to do. While such work may keep students busy, it does not lead to academic achievement.

If his or her students are not learning and achieving, the teacher should reexamine and modify the work or assignments provided to the students. The effect is a cycle of continuous improvement. The teacher continuously monitors the effects of the assignments and modifies those assignments to increase the effects of those assignments—student learning and achievement.

This logic changes the focus of teacher inquiry and accountability. Teachers do not focus on "what's wrong with Josh?" or "what are we going to do about

Josh?" Such discussions often provide solutions outside the control of the teachers. On the other hand, focusing on "What's wrong with the work that we are
providing Josh?" or "What are we going to do about the work that we have for
Josh?" changes the inquiry. And these discussions result in solutions that are
within the control of the teachers—improving the quality of the work assigned to
the students. From this paradigm, when students are provided high-quality assignments, the work itself ends up "fixing the student."

An Overview of the Model

TAIP is an invitation-to-invention process that structures time and processes for
a coalition of district educators to bring a sense of professionalism and control to
their often seemingly bureaucratic and uncontrollable lives. It is not a model that
views teachers as herds of cattle with trail bosses discussing whether it is best to
drive them or lead them when—no matter which technique is used—the final
result is hamburger meat. TAIP is a model that views teachers as leaders and
designers of intellectually challenging work for students—that is, work that will
cause students to engage, persist, and gain satisfaction from doing the work as
they learn what their parents and community value.

The TAIP processes focus on finding middle ground on the "painting" continuum that has emerged in education where one end finds university-bound the-
orists who sit around all day long and discuss what color to paint rooms but never
get to paint them, and the other end finds classroom-bound practitioners who
paint rooms all day long but never get to pick the colors.

The process builds a culture that nurtures teacher commitment through district support for local, teacher-led creation of teacher standards in areas that
teachers can control—the assignments or work that they provide to students.
Also, discussions begin to center on the quality of the assignments given to students. What does a high-quality assignment look like? How do you know? Are
ditto sheets high-quality assignments? Can you provide quality assignments in 55-
minute blocks of time? Do quality assignments need to be interdisciplinary or
cross-disciplinary? How do you measure student engagement?

The TAIP processes support the notion that the development of collegial
relationships increases a sense of mutual support and responsibility. Therefore,
the processes promote teacher commitment to (*a*) a reflective dialogue between
teachers and administrators, (*b*) the assistance of collegial support teams, and (*c*)
the development of professional portfolios in the search for answers to their questions. Repeatedly, both teachers and administrators in every district used the
words *substantive* and a sense of *growing trust* to describe their conversations. As
one teacher pointed out, "I now see conversations with my principal as helpful
rather than being under investigation." Other teachers have pointed out the
important changes in their reliance on fellow teachers for assistance. They

express good feelings about "being on a structured support team and not wondering if you were bothering someone if you needed help."

This change in focus also promotes group inquiry as it is much more acceptable to teachers to discuss and assess jointly their assignments for students rather than to discuss and assess their personal performances in the classroom. The former seems to promote cooperation among teachers while the latter seems to promote competition.

This logic has been applauded intellectually by teachers in all four districts. However, it is an internal shift of logic that most teachers have found difficult to make. While discussing indicators of quality student assignments, teachers have trouble letting go of their own performances, and they cling to indicators of quality such as "The teacher greets the students as they enter the room." These teachers find it difficult to focus on the performance of the students in relation to the assignments provided to them. This focus produces indicators such as "The students knew what they were supposed to do and why they were doing it." While both activities are important, the first continues a focus on the behavior and performance of the teacher while the second advances discussions on the quality of the work provided to students.

The exploratory nature of the TAIP design supports teacher discussions concerning this logic and helps teachers to make this shift in focus. As one principal pointed out, "For the process to take hold, you have to take the time to watch the grass grow. Patience is very important." Put differently by a teacher who commented, "This last year I was concerned with *whose* [support] team I would be on; next year I will be more concerned with *what* my [support] team is working on. To me, that's growth."

Another added that "The outcome has been unbelievable commitment and an atmosphere of professionalism." And still another teacher stated, "Honest evaluations are helpful to teachers, especially when the goal is to help the teacher improve, not just to evaluate the teacher."

A Closer Look

To create the local version of the CLSR model, districts organize three levels of interactive teams: a districtwide Advisory Committee, a districtwide Design Team, and school-based Invention Teams. The teams provide direction and focus for the involvement of significant internal constituency groups—teachers, administrators, union representatives—over a likely 15-month time frame.

The role of the districtwide Advisory Committee is to articulate the purpose of the to-be-created teacher appraisal system and to create "candidate" teacher standards. These two elements lay the foundation for the school-based invention process. From experiences in the four districts, it seems the makeup of the Advisory Committee can fit into the local context in various ways. For example, one district found the teachers' union leading the charge; another was led by one of 12 districtwide strategic planning task forces; another by the superintendent as a strategy for promoting a districtwide school reform initiative; and the fourth by the director of Curriculum and Instruction taking proactive action on upcoming state mandates.

However, two factors are critical: (*a*) the support of the superintendent and local teachers' union, and (*b*) sufficient time spent in serious dialogue and developing trust.

The statement of purpose communicates the intent of the new accountability system. It must solidify the intention of creating an appraisal system that views evaluation activities as a *means* to improving continuously rather than the ends for inspection. For example, one district declared its intent to build "a system committed to supporting teachers as professionals as they continuously improved their craft" and concluded that "the building of commitment of teachers to inventing their own evaluation system was vital if that system was to become anything more than a checklist as the old evaluation system had become."

This changes the focus of evaluation from an annual "gotcha" by the principal to one more concerned with continuously assisting teachers to improve the work that they design. Teachers and administrators in the four districts wholeheartedly welcomed this approach. At the same time, they often doubted that it was possible as it was so different from past practices. Initially, most approached the task very apprehensively, looking for signs from the top leadership that either supported or disavowed the stated intent.

CLSR suggests candidate teacher standards that provide a "Jell-O-like" starting point. These will solidify only after they have been examined carefully by the affected groups. The candidate teacher standards that CLSR uses initially include:

- The teacher supports the beliefs, commitments, and vision adopted by the _____ Public Schools.
- The teacher designs knowledge work for students containing customer-focused design qualities. [The student is the customer.]
- The teacher manages the resources of time, people, space, information, and technology in order to enhance the quality of the work provided to students.
- The teacher continuously *monitors* the extent to which students are engaging in the work, persisting with the work, experiencing satisfaction in the products of the work, and learning what is expected as a result of doing the work, and *modifies* the work accordingly.
- The teacher demonstrates leadership patterns that are consistent with the expectations of outstanding teachers in the _____ Public Schools.

CLSR suggests that clear beliefs concerning the focus of teachers' work and the focus of accountability systems guide the creation of teacher standards. District beliefs must be compatible with the notion that teachers are leaders and designers of quality work and accountability systems should focus only on those areas over which teacher have under their control.

In two out of the four districts, the TAIP processes were slowed down until the board of education could come to agreement on these beliefs and commitments. In one of these districts, the Advisory Committee announced their intention to go forward without sanctioned districtwide beliefs by stating that "the beliefs were under construction." This same committee supported teacher development of belief statements by stating, "The beliefs under construction would be consistent with . . . " and inserted beliefs developed by the involved constituency groups. It is interesting to note that while all four districts generally embraced CLSR's teacher standards, the emphasis across the districts varied. For example, one district focused on teachers as designers of *knowledge work* while another focused on teachers as designers of *customer-focused* work.

At this point, the Advisory Committee issues a districtwide invitation for schools to participate in the invention of the districtwide accountability system. Once schools have been identified, the Advisory Committee forms a Design Team made up of representatives from each of the schools and from the Advisory Committee.

The Advisory Committee then becomes a mentor to the Design Team. Their role shifts to ensuring that the developed policies and procedures are consistent with state and local regulations and agreements or to leading the changes needed to achieve such consistency. Later in the process, they also provide support for the final recommendations to the superintendent and for board of education approval.

The Design Team and School-Based Leadership Teams

The Design Team organizes leadership at the schools through the development of school-based leadership teams. The Design Team then develops candidate indicators of meeting the teacher standards for the school-based invention teams to consider.

More substantial and divisive dialogue occurs when the Design Team begins to develop specific indicators of what knowledge work or quality work looks like. Agreement within the Design Team that any listed indicators are illustrations of things you *might* see rather than a checklist of what you *must* see allows divergent opinions to arrive at consensus.

For example, as a starting point for one of the teacher standards, CLSR suggests:

- The teacher structures product-oriented, quality-work containing the qualities of clearly articulated and compelling standards, protection from the adverse consequences for initial failures, affirmation of performance, opportunities to affiliate with others, novelty, choice, authenticity, organization of knowledge and substance and content.

Suggested indicators include:

- The work has a product-focus. That is, the work:
  - is clearly linked to a product, performance, or exhibition;
  - provides a connection between student learning and a product, performance, or exhibition;
  - others;
- The work provides protection from the adverse consequences for initial failures. That is, the work provides:
  - a nonthreatening means for determining progress;
  - feedback about progress toward the completion of each part;
  - support to enable the student to complete each task successfully;
  - opportunities to practice and revise in order to improve the demonstration of learning;
  - an atmosphere that encourages creativity and risk taking;
  - others.

One district reformatted this teacher standard to read: "The teacher designs knowledge work containing customer-focused design qualities. They then listed indicators such as, "The work contains clear and compelling standards, protection from failure," and so forth. Another district altered the standard to read, "The teacher designs quality work." Thus far, districts have participated in rich dialogue but not altered the underlying concepts. They have, however, leaned toward more concise language than proposed by CLSR.

Concurrently, the Design Team suggests a candidate annual cycle of supportive peer and administrative interactions designed to support teacher achievement of the standards. The school-based invention teams then develop "little tries" and make adaptations based on the results of the little tries.

Generally, a reflective practice cycle focuses on organizing district-supported dialogues among teachers and administrators around improving the quality of the work for students. The following graphic outlines CLSR's candidate starting point as a "Reflective Practice Cycle."

In this example, the first annual procedure for a teacher is a self-assessment of meeting the teacher standards; the second a conference between the teacher and an administrator to discuss the self-assessment; the third the assignment of the teacher to a collegial support team, and so on.

From this tentative set of procedural activities, questions begin to arise such as:

- What should a teacher's professional file look like?
- What is the role of the administrator?
- How are teachers assigned—if they are assigned at all—to support teams?
- What instrumentation is needed?

Figure 8.1. A Reflective Practice Cycle

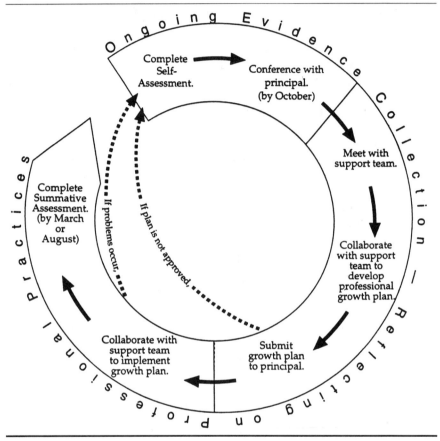

- What instrumentation goes into the district personnel file?
- How is the evidence of meeting the standards evaluated?
- Who approves what? When?

The Design Team then organizes activities designed to explore answers to these questions. These activities are the basis for the "little tries" at the school-based invention sites. As one teacher commented, "This is democracy in action and if we don't pull it off, we have no one to blame but ourselves . . . we [teachers] must promote accountability to ourselves."

At this stage, the Design Team's main task becomes one of coordinating and supporting school-based activities. The team focuses on capturing successful "little tries" and developing recommendations and adjustments based on consensus-based agreements of best practices.

School-Based Leadership Teams organize activities within their respective schools. There are numerous little tries to be explored as the local teacher appraisal system is invented. Schools can limit their activities so that no one school must participate in the invention of every aspect. Communications among all of the schools, however, is critical. During the invention process, the little tries are focused on three progressively more detailed phases of activities.

Schools concentrate first on activities designed to assist their staff in understanding the teacher standards and in developing varying avenues for collegial support. For example, one district's school teams outlined four different types of support teams. These included a Coach/Advisee Team where one individual with particular expertise leads the team; a Collegial Friends Team where peers agree to explore an issue; an Administrator/Teacher team where new teachers, prospective principals, and teachers who need extra support work more closely with an administrator; and a District Cohort Team where teachers from different schools work on districtwide issues. Other districts focused on fewer distinct types.

After the school staff have a conceptual understanding of the teacher standards, the school teams concentrate on developing ways that teachers can display evidence of meeting the teacher standards. These activities shape and develop local examples and illustrations of varying styles of professional files or portfolios.

Once schools have gathered evidence of meeting the teacher standards, the school teams focus on a method for evaluating that evidence. These activities have resulted in a rubric-type instrument for both self- and district assessments.

For example, CLSR suggests five candidate components for teacher leader indicators: vision, integrity, self-knowledge/self-awareness, communication, and expanding leadership opportunities for students and colleagues. A sample rubric designed around the vision indicators may be seen in Table 8.1.

Reflective Thoughts

It is not uncommon during the invention process for individuals on the respective teams to report initially that they feel they are managing chaos. They are. It is a messy nonlinear invention process. For example, one teacher commented,

> I would not have believed that you could do something like this with the size of the group that we have [9 schools; 35 individuals on the Design Team]. I had expected a select group of seven to eight teachers to work on it. There are just so many ideas floating around. I really didn't think that you could manage a group this size and come to agreement. Yet we are.

And another commented,

> It's totally different. I've been with several different school districts in several different states, and I've never done anything like this before. I

Table 8.1. Sample Rubric

Vision			
1	*2*	*3*	*4*
Has little sense of purpose.	Has some sense of purpose but little direction.	Has a sense of purpose and direction but does not always inspire and motivate others.	Models a sense of purpose and direction that inspires and motivates others.
Sees no avenue to influence affecting the system.	Knowledgeable of policy decisions affecting the school system.	Sometimes influences policy decisions affecting the system.	Often influences policy decisions affecting the system.
Has little knowledge and expertise about teaching/learning.	Is gaining knowledge and expertise about teaching/ learning.	Often engages in dialogue about teacher/learning.	Contributes to the knowledge base about teaching/learning issues.

think it's exciting and will be good for the district, the teachers, and, of course, for the kids. This is pretty revolutionary.

Revolutionary, yes, as it requires the building of communications and trust among the respective teams as the evaluation system is redesigned from a "gotcha" system to a system that supports and nurtures continuous professional development.

At this point it would be fair to question the time and energy that it takes to coordinate such a large-scale effort. Couldn't a small committee head for the hills and create a similarly supportive and redesigned evaluation system? The answer is, of course, yes—and no. An appraisal system could be developed, but then time and energy would be needed to market the system to teachers. If history is any indicator, teachers would then focus on "looking good" rather than using the processes to "do the right thing."

Taking the time and energy to develop the processes in the manner described not only results in creating teacher commitment to the accountability measures, but pressure is also put on the district to embrace other necessary and complementary systemic changes. For example, the TAIP process requires the district to have a well-defined set of beliefs concerning the purpose of school, the role of teachers and students, and so on. It also requires the district to be clear about expected student learnings. Both of these actions are large tasks in their own right but are critical components.

A Model with Sensitivity

The TAIP processes seem complex when confined to linear explanations. They are dynamic in action, however, and follow a natural and logical progression. Once the intent of the accountability measures is clear and the teacher standards are developed, the process used to design the remaining components can be adjusted to fit the constraints in the local context.

For example, one district limited the number of schools who could participate in the invention process so they could limit the amount of released time needed for teachers on the districtwide teams and to ensure good communications. Two districts felt that it was important to allow as many schools to participate as possible. One of these districts had enormous difficulty in maintaining good communications among schools. Even with this problem, the district felt it had made the right decision. The other district made use of its computer capabilities and developed a private electronic network to ensure good communications.

Another district—carrying baggage from an unpleasant history with seeming top-down decision-making—shifted the Advisory Team tasks of articulating the purpose and developing candidate teacher standards into the school sites. This facilitated a more bottom-up approach. The CLSR model outlines the necessary components but it becomes a strategic decision as to where the components are developed.

Unintended Consequences

No model is without consequences—both beneficial and worrisome. The beneficial ones are welcomed and often touted as part of the initial plans. It is the worrisome ones that demand attention, and this model is no different. Several worrisome consequences for school districts have been observed.

First, the participating teachers become marketable. Perhaps through documenting evidence of their activities and growth, they develop confidence and a sizable portfolio of accomplishments. One teacher related that she put her portfolio on her personal Web page and sent out letters inviting district personnel officers to visit her Web page. She received numerous offers. When teachers in one district began to assume the principalship and credit was given to their organized portfolios, the word about the importance of the portfolio spread quickly.

Additionally, all four districts recognized that new skills are needed by administrators to participate in conferences with teachers as professional colleagues. In one district, this change in expectations originated at the district level while in another district, it originated from the principals themselves.

Facilitating collegial discussions takes different skills from those needed as an evaluator. In the past, most evaluation approaches have been concerned with documenting what teachers are doing in the classroom—teacher behaviors and performances—rather than focusing what the teachers have created—work for students that engages the students, causes them to persist with their work, and learn those things that are of value to the community. With this profound change of focus, the evaluators' previously learned "documenting" behaviors become liabilities.

To meet these challenges, one district's staff development department organized "quarterly dialogues" for principals and their school leadership teams. These forums focused on the latest literature on leadership and leading change and provided a stimulus for collegial discussions. The initial session was required, but additional attendance was voluntary. In this district, attendance continued. The staff development staff were surprised and delighted. This must be credited in no small part to the capacity and skill of the district's staff development department to lead and support this type of inquiry.

These quarterly dialogues were referenced often by principals as a place where "a myriad of ideas are being promoted" and found them to be "a major stimulation." As one leadership team member stated, "Working with individuals from other schools has created a district 'idea pool' and helped me see things from other points of view."

Additionally, carving out the time necessary to not only invent but to sustain these activities requires a re-delegation of time. Time is required not only for teachers to meet in small groups, but the passage of time is needed for teachers to internalize and reflect on the standards and question the implications. As one teacher commented when asked about the evaluation process, "I like the train that we're on, but I'm not sure if I like the direction that it's headed in."

A Parallel but Separate Track

The TAIP model recommends that official documentation procedures of teacher deficiencies aimed at sanctions or dismissal be developed along a parallel but separate track. This logic stems from a belief that all teachers—as well as all students—can learn and should be focused on continuous improvement in an atmosphere that builds trust. It would be difficult to maintain such a trustful atmosphere when an individual is fearful of losing his or her job.

However, there is a reality that not every teacher will meet the minimum levels of attainment specified by a local school district. The TAIP model encourages districts to face this issue from the beginning. Districts should consider developing specialized plans of action that ensure targeted support and due process and that meet union contractual agreements. Any teacher who is officially on this "nonrenewal track" could then participate the "normal" reflective practice cycle, remain on a support team—perhaps the Administrator-Teacher Team—and yet gain the extra attention that a district plan of action might provide.

A Few Final Words

The TAIP seems to be a powerful strategy for involving a significant number of people in designing a local teacher evaluation system. The experience suggests that the TAIP has the potential to initiate serious dialogue and change. While the redesign of evaluation systems can a powerful component in a school reform effort, it is still just one component. A next question concerns the capacity of each district to sustain the potential long-term changes suggested by this design.

Just as important, TAIP was designed as an invention process. Yet each succeeding district is eager to see preceding versions, and thus focus on modifications. Do the models provide enough structure to provide a safety net of assurance while the process encourages flexibility and innovation? Do the time factors involved in a serious invention enhance the practicality of adaptations?

While experiencing success, the TAIP model and design process are in their infancy. Two of the districts are currently in the middle of their invention activities. Just as in the stock market, current returns do not guarantee future earnings. Difficult questions are being raised in several districts for which there are no pat answers. Will state-mandated performance pay for teachers promote competition among teachers and destroy collegial support systems in their infancy? Will the public accept continuous improvement rather than checklist evaluations for teachers? Will the acceptance of accountability for continuous improvements extend beyond teachers and include students? Can school accountability measures be understood to include more than student test scores? Will school accountability systems measure what matters? While there are no guarantees, this model places its commitment and faith in the hands of a critical mass of local district teachers who view their roles as professionals and have the support of top leadership in inventing new solutions.

Notes

Many thanks and much credit go to the districts who supported personal and focus-group interview sessions that provided many of the quotes used in this paper. Without their help, much less evidence would be available to support the conclusions drawn.

1. By the fall of 1998, four school districts had applied the principles discussed in this article. Each successive use has resulted in increasingly more sophisticated instrumentation. The Cincinnati (OH) Public Schools (50,000 students in 79 schools)—in collaboration with the teacher's union—helped crystallize the standards of teaching performance. The Newport News (VA) Public Schools (32,000 students in 41 schools) embraced the invention process supporting six

school faculties (4 elementary; 2 middle) and one high school team in developing many of the lessons learned for his article and has been the first district to take the process districtwide. The Citrus County (FL) Public Schools (15,000 students in 19 schools) focused activities in 9 schools (8 elementary; 1 middle) while the Forsyth (GA) Public Schools (14,200 students in 19 schools) focused activities in 14 schools (8 elementary, 3 middle, and 3 high schools). Both Citrus County and Forsyth County plan to implement the process districtwide in 1999 and have begun a similar invention process focusing on accountability for administrators.

9

The View from Maine

Developing Learner-Centered
Accountability in a Local Control State

DAVID RUFF, DEBRA SMITH, AND LYNNE MILLER

We approach this chapter as educators who have long been involved in school reform in Maine. As in other parts of the country, our state is wrestling with issues of student achievement, assessment and accountability. Unlike many other states, Maine holds local control as a central value. As a result, efforts to raise student achievement and monitor progress are a blend of state and local responsibilities, with the large proportion of discretion and control placed at the local level. In this chapter we describe how a school-university partnership helps district and schools, within the broader policy initiatives of the state, develop the capacity to design and implement local systems of learner-centered accountability and assessment. In doing so, we offer a view of school reform that places considerable faith in local educators and their communities. Such faith is a double-edged sword. It gives educators the power over practice that they desire and, at the same time, requires the utilization of skills and knowledge that few have had to opportunity to learn and practice.

The Maine Context

Maine, like Kentucky, is a poor, rural state where many workers have relied on employment in industries that are disappearing in the emergence of a global, information-based economy. Maine has the second most dramatic increase in the number of children living in poverty (from 15.3% to 19.3%) since the last census as well as increases in the rate of teen pregnancy (up 23%) and juvenile arrests (up 34%) (Annie B. Casey Foundation, 1995). There are dramatic gaps in per pupil expenditures between high and low spending districts (Maine Educational Policy Institute, 1997).

Since 1984, the State of Maine has been embarked on an ambitious agenda to reform schools and raise student achievement. The Reform Act of 1984 increased graduation requirements, upgraded teacher certification procedures, and lessened inequities among districts. This legislation also called for the creation of the Maine Educational Assessment program in which all students in Grades 4, 8 and 11 are tested in writing, reading, and mathematics, and matrix sample tested in science, social studies, health, humanities, and fine arts. The writing portion of the test is scored by Maine teachers, and test results are reported back to schools and communities.

In 1987, the state supported school restructuring with a competitive grant program. Ten schools were awarded from $10,000–50,000 per year for three years to pilot restructuring efforts. Over the life of the grants, the pilot schools challenged some of the regularities of schooling. They experimented with block scheduling in the high school, multi-age primary classrooms, new curricula and assessment programs, innovative professional development approaches including increased time for teacher learning, inquiry-based models of instruction, interdisciplinary studies, alternative student grouping patterns, and full inclusion programs. Many of these experiments have become routine practices in schools throughout the state.

The publication of Maine's Common Core of Learning in 1990 was a first attempt to articulate a framework of knowledge and skills for all Maine students across traditional subject-matter boundaries, to be used by local districts to guide their curriculum planning. Such a document was a major event in Maine, where any hint of a state curriculum raises the hackles of local control advocates. The state was adamant in its statements that the common core was not a curriculum guide. As a result, its effect on curriculum and instruction was inconsistent and scant. In 1996 session, the Maine legislature passed the Learning Results Law (SP701-LD1791), which calls for the Department of Education, in consultation with the State Board of Education, to establish and implement a comprehensive, statewide system of Learning Results and comprehensive assessment no later than the 2002–03 school year. These Learning Results are stated in terms of six broad guiding principles: Each Maine student must leave schools as:

- a clear and effective communicator
- a self-directed and lifelong learner
- a creative and practical problem solver
- a responsible and involved citizen
- a collaborative and quality worker
- an integrative and informed thinker (State of Maine, 1997)

In addition, more specific content standards are stated in eight content areas: career preparation, English language arts, foreign languages, health and physical education, mathematics, science and technology, social studies, and visual and performing arts The content standards are designed to reflect high expectations for all students and to be benchmarked to "world-class standards."

As a hedge against being viewed as establishing state curriculum, state officials are very careful to point to the Learning Results as the agreed-upon ends of an education for Maine students, not as the means. The actual curricular and instructional programs of districts remain in firm local control. This bow to local control is particularly evident in the statewide comprehensive assessment system that is supposed to measure individual achievement of the standards and lead to standards-based high school diplomas. While the Maine Educational Assessment (MEA) will be expanded to include all eight content areas, its portion of the comprehensive assessment system is limited to 10%. It is not, by any means, a high-stakes assessment, having no rewards or sanctions for schools nor specific consequences for students attached to it. An Assessment Design Team made up of K–12 and university educators has made recommendations to the commissioner, and specifications for a redesigned state test that is aligned with the Maine Learning Results is in the process of development. The new MEA will be implemented in the 1998–99 school year. The Maine Educational Assessment will provide a snapshot of school performance at three key points (Grades 4, 8 and 11) and will serve as a validation tool for the local comprehensive assessment system, which comprises the other 90% of the comprehensive assessment system. Local assessment systems must be keyed to the Learning Results' content standards and should include multiple measures over time. They may include performances, portfolios, demonstrations, standardized tests, and other records of achievement. Assessments will vary district to district, as will requirements for the high school diploma. Finally, the law calls for a statewide plan for professional development for implementation of the Learning Results, with funds allocated to districts on a per-pupil basis.

The Southern Maine Partnership

The Southern Maine Partnership is a school/university collaborative that links thirty school districts, two private schools, and three institutions of higher learning in what John Goodlad calls, "the simultaneous renewal of schools and the preparation of educators" (Goodlad, 1988). Established in 1985 and housed at the University of Southern Maine, its original higher education partner, the partnership was an original member of Goodlad's National Network for Educational Renewal. It has grown from a group of eight schools and one university to its present size and configuration. It has achieved a regional, statewide, and national reputation as a center for reform in member schools and in teacher education. With formal affiliations with the Coalition of Essential Schools, the Foxfire National Outreach Network, the National Center for Restructuring Education, Schools, and Teaching, and the National Education Association's Center for Innovation, the partnership is a regional collaboration with national connections. It is supported by annual dues, an in-kind contribution from the University of Southern Maine, and outside grants and gifts. Its executive director is a tenured faculty member from the university, who is granted released time for partnership work.

The partnership has built a reputation as an organization that respects the professional knowledge of educators and tacitly acknowledges both their skills and the trying conditions under which they work. At the same time, the partnership nurtures teachers' potential as inventors and change agents. It is a place where ideas are exchanged, where teachers show their work and prod and encourage each other, where administrators engage with new learning rather than constant problems, where university and public school faculty inform and enrich one another's practice, and where educational research gets examined through the lens of daily school experience.

The central concern of the partnership is similar to that of reformers in Kentucky: to raise achievement for all students and to guarantee a rich educational experience to everyone, not just an elite few. While Maine's students fare well in national and international comparisons (our fourth graders are first in writing, second in reading on the NAEP), there are still an unacceptably high number of them who do not have basic skills, and a slim proportion who are fluently literate in any content area.

We want all of our students to leave high school with the knowledge, skills, and habits of mind that will enable them to participate fully in their communities and our society at large. At present, we are long way from achieving this goal, but we are steadily moving in that direction.

The Southern Maine Partnership has identified eight challenges that must be faced in order to support children reaching higher achievement:

- development of local comprehensive assessment systems;
- guaranteeing the integrity of the high school diploma;
- development of rich, integrated, connected curricula;
- development of an expanded teacher repertoire in instruction and assessment;
- development of community connections;
- development of quality leadership;
- development of organizational capacity to support and sustain change; and
- communication and dissemination of information about best practices.

As schools approach these challenges, the work of the partnership is guided by a coherent theory of change. All of the partnership's work is based on a vision of education that assumes that all students can learn and achieve high levels of performance when they, their teachers, and their parents have the knowledge, resources, and tools to support this. Our approach is based on research that supports teachers as the linchpins of successful school reform. These theories are resonant with the strong history of local control in Maine and other northern New England states, which reflects a deep belief that decisions need to be made by those people most immediately affected by them.

The partnership uses a variety of strategies to address the challenges schools face in attaining the outcome of higher achievement for all students. Some of the strategies are general and are aimed at "going broader" and involving a wide and diverse range of participants; other strategies focus more on a group of schools or districts that are engaged in "going deeper" (Miller & O'Shea, 1996) with focused work in a particular area. General, broad-based activities that are available to all interested members include our monthly calendar, newsletter, Dine and Discuss sessions, and workshops. Superintendents, principals, and curriculum directors groups meet on a regular basis to address issues of common concern. All of these activities are linked to the challenges we have identified.

Other "going deep" strategies are embodied in funded projects in which schools and districts work intensively to develop tools and processes in support of schools' work toward the common outcome of increased student achievement. While these projects may appear to be distinct and separate, they are in actuality a family of strategies, and schools may be involved in several concurrently. Because partnership initiatives emerge from the identified needs of members and are built on a set of common theories of change, there is a level of coherence across projects. We have chosen to highlight one of these strategies, the School Quality Review process (SQR), in some detail. In addition, we present less detailed descriptions of two other strategies, the Learner-Centered Accountability High School Network (LCA), and the Electronic Learning Marketplace (ELM), that continue and expand the work of SQR. All three of these strategies share common goals: helping schools and districts raise student achievement, developing and expanding teaching practice, and designing local systems of accountability and assessment that drive instructional decisions, rather than certify, label, and sort students.

School Quality Review Network (SQR)

In the early nineties, the partnership began to explore the notion of "learner-centered accountability." This conception of accountability is based on the idea that schools are ultimately responsible to their communities—not state agencies and other proxies—both for student achievement and for ensuring quality teaching and assessment. A group of our members decided on the School Quality Review (SQR) process as the vehicle for testing this notion in practice. Originally based

Southern Maine PARTNERSHIP
linking school renewal and teacher development

Outcome:
To increase achievement for all students

Theories of Change:
- When teachers perceive that changes in teaching practice result in increased student growth and achievement, they commit to these changes in their own practice.
- Professional communities in which teachers discuss practice, examine and assess student work together, observe each other, and engage in joint planning teaching and evaluation produce higher student achievement.
- Strong administrative leadership that leads to an emphasis on instruction by teachers, leads to higher achievement on the part of students.
- When there is teacher "buy-in" to change (either up front or later) the change is maintained and sustained over time.
- Depth and sustainability of change require initial training, opportunities for practice, and ongoing classroom support and assistance from both internal and external resources.

Challenges:
a) development of local comprehensive assessment systems (1, 3, 5, 7, 8, 17)
b) guaranteeing the integrity of the high school diploma (7, 11)
c) development of rich, integrated, connected curricula (2, 5, 11, 15)
d) development of an expanded teacher repertoire in instruction and assessment (1, 2, 3, 4, 5, 7, 11, 14, 15, 16)
e) development of community connections (1, 2)
f) development of quality leadership (4, 8, 9, 11, 12, 14, 15)
g) development of organizational capacity to support and sustain change (3, 4, 7, 8, 9, 11, 12, 17)
h) communication and dissemination of information about best practice (1, 4, 5, 8, 13)

* lettering of challenges does not imply priorities; it is intended for identification

Strategies:

ELM (1)   SQR Network (3)   Dine & Discuss (5)   Policy Work (6)   LCA (7)

Superintendents' Group (9)   National Networking (10)   CES Center (11)   CFG Program (4)

Curriculum Coordinators Think Tank (8)   Principals' Group (12)   PRIM (2)

SMP Publications (13)

Collaborations with USM—Graduate Courses (14) PDC (15); ETEP (16); CEPARE (17)

* numbering of strategies does not imply priorities; it is intended for identification

Figure 9.1. Southern Maine Partnership's Theories of Change

on the work of Her Majesty's Inspectorate in Great Britain and adapted by David Green in New York State, SQR provided the opportunity for partnership educators to design and create a way to examine their practice, understand how to look at and talk about student achievement, and how to move their schools towards higher levels of work. We formally initiated the School Quality Review process in 1993–94.

Three key elements undergird the partnership's SQR design: a set of common principles; a process and inquiry tools that are adaptable to each school's unique context; and a network of critical friends. The School Quality Review Network places special emphasis in the development of local comprehensive assessment systems, development of organizational capacity to support and sustain change, and development of an expanded teacher repertoire in instruction and assessment. Over 100 partnership educators worked collaboratively in a series of all day sessions to develop three broad "learner-centered principles" to lay a firm foundation for the SQR process:

1. *Academic focus*: The school has a clear academic focus where teachers choose appropriately from a range of strategies to promote student learning. A core set of skills and knowledge for all students is clear and can be explicitly stated by teachers, students, parents, and community members. All teachers and students can answer the question: What are you doing and why?

2. *Assessment and accountability*: The school holds itself accountable for ensuring that all students can demonstrate quality standards of literacy in all knowledge areas. It organizes and reorganizes itself accordingly. Appropriate forms of assessment that reflect high, public standards for learning are used to document student progress and achievement. The school uses multiple mechanisms for reporting frequently and publicly to parents, students, and the community on how well the school is meeting its stated outcomes.

3. *Community*: A sense of community permeates the school. Parents, teachers, students, and other members of the school community are partners in learning. All members of the school community are treated with dignity and are valued, honored, encouraged, and supported in their development.

Participating schools commit to using these principles to guide their own inquiry and planning; visiting teams use them to focus and organize their review of teaching and learning in a school. The common principles enable teachers to share a language and stance toward teaching and learning that provide opportunities for deeper thinking and learning concerning the educational lives of children.

After initial whole school agreement to participate, each school develops a focus question with an accompanying Inquiry Plan, and commits to actions based on inquiry, evaluation of their work, and dissemination of their knowledge to their communities. Each school identifies a coordinating team (which may be an existing body, such as a school improvement team) that includes teachers, administrators, support staff, at least one parent or community member, and students if appropriate, to facilitate and document their school's work. Below we briefly describe the elements of the inquiry process.

The school's focus question, along with the learner-centered principles, guides their self-assessment for a particular year. This question comes from the school's ongoing work and is developed from extensive faculty dialogue about what is most central to their work at this point in time. For example, one school asked, "How does assessment drive our instruction?" Another asked, "How does student reflection inform our practice?" A third asked, "How are our six common beliefs reflected in our school?"

Based on their focus question, each school then develops an Inquiry Plan, defining how it will collect and analyze data about the focus question and how the learner-centered principles are reflected in the school. As appropriate to their focus, schools use a variety of tools for this, such as:

- exploring student work through use of processes such as the Tuning Protocol, Collaborative Assessment Conference, or Descriptive Review;
- classroom observations;
- student shadowing (accompanying a student guide through his or her daily schedule);
- interviews with faculty, parents, students, and community members;
- review of student performance data, documents and policies; and
- a visiting team review.

As can be expected, Inquiry Plans change as the work progresses, but the initial plan serves as a yearlong map for the inquiry process.

As schools gather and analyze data relevant to the learner-centered principles and their focus question, they can make decisions about teaching based on a solid understanding of the educational experiences of children. These actions are ongoing and intertwined with the inquiry process. They may take the form of small adjustments in teaching practice, as well as larger decisions about programs and practices across the school that may be decided by the whole staff.

Throughout the process of inquiry and action, the school engages in evaluating its own work. This evaluation both informs the ongoing process within the school and serves as a vehicle to communicate with the broader school community. This may take a variety of forms (some of them already in place) such as newsletters, reports, parent forums, presentations, and cable television shows.

In support of these school efforts, the Southern Maine Partnership has designed and implemented the Collaborative Inquiry Summer Institute to provide school and visiting team members with an overview of SQR, opportunities

Figure 9.2. Ongoing Self-Assessment for Continuous Improvement of Teaching and Learning

Southern Maine Partnership School Quality Review Initiative

1. The School conducts its own ongoing inquiry and hosts a Visiting Review Team every few years.

2. Includes:
   - exploring student work
   - observations
   - student shadowing
   - interviews
   - review of documents and policies

3. The Annual School Profile is a five- or six-page document that summarizes background information about the school, its mission and learner outcomes, progress toward its mission/outcomes, and the SMP Learner Centered Principles, and next steps.

4. Each school develops ways of reporting its progress to its community.

5. Tools and processes such as the Collaborative School Protocol, Tuning Protocol, Collaborative Assessment Conference, and Descriptive Review of Work may be used as appropriate for dialogues focused on teaching and learning.

to explore the learner-centered principles, practice using various inquiry methods and tools, and time for team planning. Institute facilitators are teachers and administrators who have been actively involved in developing the SQR process and who have played leadership roles in schools and visiting team reviews.

At the same time they are learning and practicing inquiry processes, participants are forming a community of critical friends with strong commitment and trust. This community develops as school teams share their work, problem-solve together, and continue to practice using new inquiry tools through networking meetings throughout the school year. Visiting team members are included in meetings as appropriate. In addition, teachers from the lead schools serve on visiting teams to other schools. The strength and safety of these connections enable teachers to share both successes and failures from their classrooms. This honest dialogue provides great learning opportunities for teachers, and in turn, begins to impact the learning experiences of children.

While not required, all schools involved in the network have undertaken a visiting team review. A visiting team review provides the school with the opportunity to receive outside critical feedback on the learning experience of their students.

Partnership staff coordinate the construction of visiting teams composed of educators (teachers, administrators, specialists), support staff, and at least one parent/community member whenever possible. Each team has a chair and assistant chair, or co-chairs, depending on how the leaders choose to define the responsibilities for facilitating and managing the visiting team review process. The size of the team depends on the size of the school and the team's profile is matched with the school's focus question as closely as possible.

The visiting team spends a week exploring teaching and learning in the school through student shadowing (following a student for a day); classroom observations; interviews with teachers, students, parents and other members of the school community; and examining student work. The precise schedule of activities is developed by the school coordinating team and varies from school to school.

Data collection, analysis and reporting are organized around the learner-centered principles and the school's focus question. The team describes evidence and examples of the principles and focus question in operation and generates findings/statements from these. They deliberately do not make recommendations, but pose questions that emerge from the review process for the school's consideration. Report highlights are presented orally to the entire staff and others the school invites on the fifth day. A final written report is prepared by the team and a discussion with the school staff follows within a few weeks following the visit.

In writing the final report, the visiting team strives for honesty and sensitivity. Positive and negative findings are reported in tandem. For example, at one school, the team reported:

In the Advanced Placement courses, teachers and students are able to articulate clearly the knowledge and skills expected of students, In Phase II to IV courses, the teachers, and students' abilities to articulate clearly the required knowledge and skills vary widely.

The overwhelming majority of students reported there was at least one adult they could turn to for help. Some noted, however, they felt that some teachers "want to get out of their class as quickly as possible."

Since the first year of development, six schools from all levels have undertaken both internal reviews of their work and five-day visiting team reviews from outside critical friends. Over 90 southern Maine educators and community members have attended extensive summer training institutes and become involved either within their own school or on visiting teams. When the original funding ended in June of 1996, the network of schools decided to continue its work and, in fact, to expand to other members. Schools have used their own financial resources to support the work.

School Quality Review has become the basis of and laid the foundation for much of our future work in the area of assessment and accountability and teacher practice. Schools involved with SQR helped move thinking within the partnership beyond a single concentration on assessing student achievement to include the impact of teacher practice and school structures on students' learning. By examining both student achievement and teacher practice, schools were able to use data to make decisions about ongoing development and changes. In undertaking such an intensive investigation of schools and their practices, participants came to understand the demand for more accurate classroom assessments, and they developed a willingness to openly analyze and investigate instructional practices. Finally, the knowledge gained through the SQR process inquiry was shared and used by a broad teacher audience; this is in sharp contrast to conventional practice when a select few administrative leaders have access to information and hoard it. Such broad-based access promotes the development of learner-centered accountability at the level of the whole school, where each member of the school community feels responsible for the success of every child.

The Learner-Centered Accountability High School Network (LCA)

Growing out of the pioneering work done by schools in the SQR process, the Learner-Centered Accountability High School Network focuses specifically at the high school level. Six LCA schools are working to meet the state mandate for locally developed graduate standards as part of a districtwide comprehensive assessment system. As in SQR, this initiative looks to both enhanced student achievement and quality teacher practice as the goals of the work. To reach these ends, the six schools spend significant time and effort developing both classroom and whole school assessment practices, making special efforts to guarantee the integrity of the high school diploma. Throughout, special attention is paid to involving the entire school faculty, not just a few chosen leaders, in order to sustain the intended change at a whole-school level.

After a school year of dialogue, network principals and teachers focused their efforts on collaborative inquiry as a means to develop learner-centered accountability systems. Building on SQR, the schools defined learner-centered accountability as a system of assessment tools and processes that enables a school to publicly understand student achievement as well as the learning structures that support it. We expected, and have seen, tremendous variation in the initial design of these systems. Such variety is heartily encouraged because it acknowledges the diverse needs of the schools.

Each of the six participating schools has identified an on-site leadership team to coordinate its efforts, beginning with the drafting of a yearly inquiry plan. Based on concerns raised by the school, the inquiry plan details outcomes for the work, actions to be taken, use of staff development time, and overall financial considerations. The partnership provides a small implementation grant of $2,500, but each school is expected to greatly supplement this money with local professional development funds and time.

A partnership staff member is assigned to work with each school as a "school coach." In this role, the staff members work neither as a consultant nor as an unbiased facilitator; rather, they promote co-discovery with each school. The two partnership staff members working in this role have past experience working with assessment tools and protocols. They have found that the establishment of accountability systems designed to meet standards for student achievement that are externally developed and internally assessed is new territory for both the state and its schools. The school coach's charge is to share ideas and concerns with the school faculty without taking over control of the change process. It is in this new territory that we find the greatest potential for developing schools' capacity for increasing student achievement in substantive ways.

Schools receive ongoing training through participation in the Collaborative Inquiry Summer Institute and networking meetings throughout the school year. As described in the SQR section, the Collaborative Inquiry Summer Institute provides participants with inquiry tools and skills to implement and use these tools. Schools send teams of 4–6 members (including the building principal) to networking meetings that provide both additional training and the sharing of ideas between schools. Using such strategies as school protocols, schools present their work, including successes and areas of concern, and receive support and feedback from other schools. While not every school has the opportunity to present their work at each gathering, those serving as critical friends in the audience are able to pick up new ideas and reflect on their own work through the efforts of others. The networking meetings also provide a forum to share statewide updates concerning the Maine Learning Results and structured time for school teams to work on their own issues.

While we do not expect schools to have developed or implemented a complete system of assessment for high school graduation in one year's time, we do expect to see initial implementation of various assessment tools and processes. These tools should begin to reveal the richness of student achievement and the teaching and learning structures in place at each school. To this end, each school is expected to complete a brief written report at the end of the first year that identifies areas of student achievement and the processes in place for analysis and action. The report will be used in numerous ways including sharing between schools and their communities. Additionally, the reports should form the foundation for locally developed templates to explain the work of students and teachers in the school to the broader community. The work has far to go, but a network of schools owning and taking responsibility for student achievement holds great promise for providing a model for how local schools can make sense of state initiatives and incorporate the Learning Results into local practice.

The Electronic Learning Marketplace

The Electronic Learning Marketplace (ELM) represents an idea that was germinated in our earlier work around learner-centered accountability and grew in response to the Learning Results. Over time, we had come to see assessment as a powerful lens for helping teachers and schools to focus on student learning. With support from the partnership mini-grants program and the School Quality Review process, teachers and schools had developed tools and knowledge that had been shared across the region through dialogues, institutes, conferences. But involvement in any of these activities was constrained by time and space: if you were not present for a dialogue that took place from 4 to 6 p.m. on the first Wednesday in February, you did not have access to the information and ideas discussed at that time. Publications made some of the rich work going on in classrooms accessible to a larger audience, but their cost in terms of time and money limited the range of work that can be shared. While several districts had begun development of systemic approaches to standards-based reform, this practice was not widespread and little of what had been developed was easily transportable and accessible. We were seeking a way to support our members' efforts to interpret the state standards in meaningful ways, to support good teaching practice and student learning, and to use the tools of collaborative inquiry we had developed and refined in SQR. We wanted to build on the work that had already been developed and tested, and we wanted to find a way to accomplish the interaction and collaboration we had achieved on a small scale (through the summer institutes and site visits associated with SQR) on a larger scale.

The Electronic Learning Marketplace (ELM) uses technology to achieve the ends we seek. It exemplifies "the authentic use of technology" (Means, 1993) and is conceived as a lively World Wide Web–based center for the exchange of ideas, information, and high-quality products related to Maine's Learning Results. Funded by a five-year U.S. Department of Education Technology Innovation Challenge Grant, the ELM grant connects the university's Engineering Department, a demonstration school district, five multimedia production studios dispersed across the partnership, and ultimately every teacher in every school in the region to high-quality assessments and information and resources about learner-centered accountability. The project has defined the following objectives:

1. Demonstrated improvement in student learning;
2. Demonstrated change in teacher assessment practices;
3. Permanent, self-sustaining website that focuses on assessments geared to Maine's Learning Results;
4. An established network of website users and contributors;
5. Coherent K–12 systems of assessment and accountability that meet the requirements of the Learning Results;
6. Fully operational demonstration district that models website use to improve student learning and change assessment practices;
7. Software processes and products that promote knowledge and use of performance assessments and learning resources related to the Learning Results.

In order to meet these ends, the ELM project is in the process of developing a user-friendly and accessible website. It is also establishing procedures and protocols for the development of assessments and is providing diverse and multiple opportunities for teachers to engage with each other and with quality products that assess student learning and guide teacher practice. Central to the work of ELM are the collaborative inquiry tools originally developed by SQR. Teachers depend on design templates and scoring guides, which are collaboratively developed, to guide their assessment work. They use tuning protocols to refine their products and to ready them for publication on the website. And they engage in site visits and collegial conversation by way of electronic communications.

The ultimate goal of ELM is the same as the goals of SQR and LCA; that is, the development of learner-centered accountability systems that derive from the practical work of teachers in classrooms and that are held to high standards of quality through peer review and feedback.

Conclusion

We began this chapter by acknowledging the challenge that Maine educators face in establishing accountability systems in a local control state. Unlike Kentucky, where most of the work is done at the state level with the assumption that local schools and districts will comply, in Maine educators are given the major responsibility for designing student assessments, setting standards and benchmarks, and establishing criteria for graduation within the parameters set by the Learning Results legislation. We then described the efforts of a school-university partnership in helping local schools and districts build the capacity to do the work. We introduced, and through example elaborated upon, the notion of learner-centered accountability. We conclude here by framing what we consider the general principles that undergird this kind of accountability.

- Schools are ultimately accountable to local students, parents, and community rather than to distant political entities.
- Schools are accountable for providing high-quality teacher practice as well as for high quality student achievement.
- Schools and districts are capable of building assessment systems that both guide instruction and measure progress toward achievement targets.
- The most powerful, useful, and transportable assessments are teacher-developed, teacher-critiqued, and teacher-refined.
- Collaborative tools and protocols enhance teacher capacity for conducting systematic inquiry, deepening teacher practice, and designing assessment and accountability systems capable of improving student learning.
- Reciprocity, sharing, and nonhierarchical patterns of authority create an environment where teachers can talk to and learn from each other, exchange ideas and products, set standards and assess student work against those standards, and develop the capacity for doing the assessment and accountability work.

We believe that there is nothing "soft" about these principles. In many ways, they lead to the most stringent standards and high-stakes consequences that the harshest critics of education advocate. Learner-centered accountability clearly places the responsibility for effective learning and teaching with teachers. When teachers publicly establish standards and hold themselves and their students accountable for meeting them, they are opening themselves and their practice to public scrutiny and evaluation. This is the meaning, and the power, of learner-centered accountability.

References

Annie E. Casey Foundation (1995). *Kids count data book: State profiles of child well-being, 1995.* Baltimore: Annie E. Casey Foundation.

Goodlad, J. (1988). School-university partnerships for educational renewal: Rationale and concepts. In K. Sirotnik & J. Goodlad (Eds.), *School-university-partnerships in action: Concepts, cases, and concerns* (pp. 3–31). New York: Teachers College Press.

Maine Education Policy Research Institute (1997). *The condition of K–12 public education in Maine, 1997.* Gorham, ME: Center for Educational Policy, Applied Research and Evaluation, University of Southern Maine.

Means, B., Blando, J., Olson, K., Middleton, T., Morrocco, C. C., Remz, A. R., & Zorfass, J. (1993). *Using technology to support education reform.* Washington, DC: U.S. Government Printing Office.

Miller, L. & O'Shea, C. (1996). School-university partnership: Getting broader, getting deeper. In M. W. McLaughlin & I. Oberman (Eds.), *Teacher learning: New policies, new practices.* New York: Teachers College Press.

10

A New Look at School Accountability

ANNE WHEELOCK

Introduction

School accountability in various forms has been of interest to education policy-makers and professionals for decades (Kirst, 1990). In the early part of the century, pressures for school accountability sought greater uniformity of practice in classroom design, curriculum, and instruction. With an increase in federal and state legislation to expand schooling to those formerly excluded from schools, accountability has also come to involve the monitoring of states, districts, and schools for compliance with particular laws, frequently in exchange for federal or state funding. In recent years, managerial, or bureaucratic, approaches to school accountability have been proposed as part of a larger agenda for performance-focused reform, with rewards and sanctions attached to school progress or lack thereof. In this era, "accountability" is seen as the "stick" that will drive schools onward to meet the "standards" for student achievement and school improvement, measured primarily by test scores and set at the state level.

However, as this book demonstrates, the managerial model of school account-ability that seeks to coerce schools into improvement through the gathering and reporting of "outcome data," and the allocating of rewards and sanctions based on those data is inadequate to realizing long-lasting reforms in teaching and learn-ing. This managerial model assumes that teachers can and will apply themselves to boosting student achievement only when the state offers them incentives for doing so. It further assumes that if incentives are not strong enough in them-selves, public scrutiny and threats of state intervention will scare schools into bet-ter practice. This book has documented some of the consequences of those assumptions in terms of the model's impact on real teachers and students in real schools. Although a high-stakes system, whether for schools or teachers, may appear to motivate some educators in some schools to improve student achievement, it falls short of helping teachers develop the knowledge and skills they need to help an increasingly diverse student population learn at deeper levels of understanding. At the same time, the ways in which schools adapt to such policies often prove to be counterproductive to developing a strong professional community within each school that can promote effective practices within reorganized school structures. Yet such a professional community is essential if schools are to develop and sustain the effective classroom practices and school routines that result in improved student achievement and school holding power.

Reframing the Notion of Accountability

Skepticism about the current bureaucratic accountability model does not imply a rejection of the notion of accountability per se. However, the shortcomings of current managerial models beg for further discussion of what educators and the public can expect from an effective accountability model. If, in considering the consequences of existing approaches, the costs of the bureaucratic model appear to outweigh the benefits, policymakers must reconsider the assumptions that drive current policy. They must also consider how alternative approaches might better serve both the objective of reporting to the public on the progress of reform as well as the larger purpose of improving student learning.

The failure of the managerial approach to school accountability is rooted in several of the approach's assumptions about the factors that foster school improvement. Grounded in the notion that "only outcomes matter," the model ignores the importance of the daily life and culture of the school and district context within which teachers teach and students learn. Yet school structures, norms, relationships, and regularities that shape students' access to knowledge, motivation to learn, and the school culture itself merit equal attention given their well-documented impact on student achievement and teachers' professional practice (Corbett & Wilson, 1997; Mac Iver & Plank, 1996; Oakes, 1989; Sarason, 1996). The model's second assumption that performance assessments implemented in a high-stakes context will leverage better teaching is equally ill-founded. Indeed, as Noble and Smith (1994) found in their examination of teachers' responses to new state testing in Arizona, the assessment-measured, outcomes-driven reform strategy was not only inadequate to move teachers toward instruction for reasoning, analyzing, and problem-solving; its behaviorist tenets undermined reformers' broader goals of enhancing teaching for understanding. In practice, when performance-based tests are used to measure outcomes, only schools that already have a healthy supply of the "will" and "skill" necessary for reform are able to organize time for and implement the extensive professional development needed to adapt curriculum and instruction to assessments that focus on higher-order understandings (Shepard, 1995).

If policymakers hope to use "accountability" to improve teaching and learn-ing, they must move away from an approach that relies on measures of schools' progress toward meeting test score goals. Instead, a more promising approach to accountability focuses not only on the results of teaching, but on classroom prac-tices that conform to standards set by the teaching profession itself. Such an approach requires professionals to describe the standards of practice they honor and account for decisions they make and actions they take in relation to those standards and the needs of their students. The setting of learning goals and assignments, selection of materials, balance of didactic instruction, Socratic dis-cussion, and "hands-on" learning, grouping of students, scheduling of classes, and use of classroom assessments are the "stuff" of such decisions.

"Accounting for" decisions related to professional practice means that edu-cators must not only report the aims and results of their work to their constituents but also explain how they execute their work in accordance with the ethical responsibilities of the profession to their students (Haney & Raczak, 1994; Darling-Hammond, 1992). These responsibilities include selecting practices that reflect up-to-date research related to school organization, classroom practice, and learning theory. But they also go beyond selecting the means of reaching goals to include the setting of learning goals themselves. For example, Mitchell (1989) argues that the professional practitioner must take responsibility for school reform and renewal, determine the kinds of outcomes that are desirable, and select appropriate interventions for achieving those outcomes in line with what is known to be effective. He notes (pers. comm.):

> In authentic professional settings (law, medicine, architecture, account-ing, etc.) we do not measure performance by outcomes. Thus, for exam-ple, we expect criminals to be found guilty, despite outstanding defense. Accountability means accepting responsibility for pursuing the results on the basis of work strategies that have known effects.

This is not to say that new forms of accountability should deny the impor-tance of outcomes. Serious educators are intensely interested in what their stu-dents learn and how well they can demonstrate what they have learned, practice thoughtful habits of mind, and contribute to school life. However, a purely man-agerial approach to accountability may generate school profiles that indicate progress in relation to what is "expected," but the emphasis on results alone offers no incentive or guidance for teachers themselves to review and reform their own classroom practices. Teachers can not realize the promises of school reform with-out regular opportunities to make sense of their students' learning, and to weigh student assessment results against the context of the teaching, curriculum, orga-nizational structures, and learning opportunities in their school. Moreover, teachers can not boost student achievement without knowledge of the practices that are likely to produce better learning. Only a combination of information about student outcomes and knowledge of effective practice can guide decisions regarding which practices are worth keeping and which should be discarded to improve student achievement.

An alternative approach to accountability would more effectively serve the larger goal of making schools places where every student produces work that meets standards of excellence. If accountability is to serve this end, policies must be fashioned within a broader school reform strategy that strives to ensure that all students, regardless of where they live, which school they attend, or the social circumstances in which they find themselves, receive a high-quality education. However, in a society that is increasingly unwilling to tax itself to provide public services, especially when those services might benefit a community's most vulnerable members, accountability is more often offered as a means to assure a cynical public that schools are providing adequate return on the tax dollar. In this climate, an accountability model that focuses only on outcomes prevents the public from developing deeper appreciation for the conditions within which teachers and students work together to develop and expand learning and understanding.

A new accountability model would not equate school success with test scores but with the work students produce and the practices teachers employ to engage every student in creating that work. A focus on test scores tells students, parents, or the public little about the quality of projects, writing, artistic expression, problem-solving, or scientific experimentation that students do. Test scores say little about the progress students make in producing work that shows thoughtful revisions or effort toward excellence. Nor do test scores reflect the quality of teaching in a given school. A new accountability model must allow for a focus on the knowledge and skills students demonstrate in work that can be displayed publicly and used by multiple constituencies.

A new model of accountability would also go beyond viewing teachers as responding only to rewards and sanctions for success or failure as measured by test scores. Instead, it would embrace the notion of teachers as professionals and call on them to "account for" their practice—to their colleagues and to the public— in light of the knowledge and norms of the larger teaching profession and the needs of their students. Such accountability policies would put teachers in situations where they would, on a regular basis, discuss professional issues of teaching, weighing and assessing their own practice in light of student outcomes. In this way, accountability would begin to serve the goal of strengthening the capacity of schools to reform themselves and enhance schools as communities of learners.

A new accountability model would emphasize teachers' accountability to the values, norms, and ethics of the profession within which they work. Those ethics require teachers to consider everything they do in light of its effect on their students. Moreover, they require teachers to go beyond their school-based peers to share successful practices with the wider profession and develop new skills and knowledge that reflects new research in the field. Such a model would reject professional or school competition as being at odds with the interest of every student to receive high-quality instruction. It would foster professional collegiality so as to expand the knowledge of the profession as a whole and the access of every student to competent teaching.

A new accountability model would reflect the reality that teachers in schools are also accountable to constituencies beyond their own profession. They are accountable to their employers, parents, and the public that entrusts them with the community's children. They are accountable to federal and state laws and the terms of their contract. Given this reality, a new accountability model would be a hybrid, promoting teacher responsibility for outcomes on the one hand while also enhancing teacher capacity to explain those outcomes in terms of the best practices that research identifies for the profession and an ethic of professional responsibility for pursuing those practices within larger mandates. Such a model would not exempt schools from examining data that highlight the skills and knowledge students have learned and what they can do as a result. To the contrary, it would expand the sources of data available to teachers for such examination and, at the same time, insist that teachers reflect on those data as a basis for improving practice.

In short, a new approach to accountability emphasizes capacity-building over coercion and professional reflection about data over simplistic reporting of data. Such a shift widens the lens used to examine schooling to include both "background" and "foreground," engaging teachers in explaining both outcomes and also the conditions of the teaching to the public. This approach requires understanding of key concepts of "standards of practice" based on "duty of care," and school "enabling conditions."

Standards of Practice

While many school reform policies of the 1990s have emphasized a managerial model of accountability as a primary strategy for influencing school reform, a number of educators have argued that more effective leverage for reforming teaching and learning lies in strengthening professional responsibility and practice (Astuto & Clark, 1992; Darling-Hammond, 1988, 1994; Darling-Hammond & Ascher, 1991; Firestone, 1991; Hall, 1991; Levin, 1991a, 1991b; McDonnell, 1991; Mitchell, 1989; Noble & Smith, 1994; Shepard, 1995; Sirotnik, 1987; Sirotnik & Goodlad, 1985). This emphasis reframes accountability in terms of "standards of practice" and an ethic of what Darling-Hammond (1992) calls "duty of care." "Duty of care" as the grounding responsibility central to all forms of accountability refers to the obligation of professionals to apply knowledge and practice in wise and responsible ways to advance the learning of every child; it also includes the responsibility to avoid practices that would damage students. This duty puts student welfare at the center of all practice and policy decisions. In this way, standards of practice direct attention not to outcomes alone but also to those professional processes of teaching that enhance student learning and welfare.

A notion of accountability that encompasses standards of practice based on a duty of care thus expands to include what Darling-Hammond (1992) describes as:

> [A] set of commitments, policies, and practices that are designed to: 1) heighten the probability that schools will use good practices on behalf of students; 2) reduce the likelihood that schools will engage in harmful practices; and 3) encourage self-assessment on the part of schools and educators to identify, diagnose, and change courses of action that are harmful or ineffective. (p. 40)

This broader definition of accountability protects educators from the trap of confusing a high stakes, test-based accountability policy with a comprehensive accountability system. Incorporating the notion of "standards of practice" into broader demands for accountability pushes policymakers and educators in each district and school to account for the enabling conditions that research tells us help or hinder learning.

Enabling Conditions

Standards of practice as part of accountability policies force policymakers and educators to examine the context of schooling in order to assess and understand the conditions that contribute to specific outcomes. Research locates those conditions that "enable" student achievement in three areas of schooling: access to knowledge, press for achievement, and professional conditions for teaching (Oakes, 1989). These conditions are manifest and play out in a variety of observable school practices, routines, and norms in different local contexts and as they vary from school to school. For example, "access to knowledge" may be gauged by the percentage of students who use a school's library for computer-assisted research on questions of their choosing, the percentage of eighth graders enrolled in Algebra 1 or the equivalent, or the percentage of fifth graders who engage in scientific experiments in partnership with a working scientist. Likewise, "press for achievement" is reflected in different schools in different ways, including, for example, in the percentage of students participating in debate or math competitions, the number of students who do work that "really matters" to constituencies outside of the school, the number of times students use "extra help" opportunities to boost their grades, or the opportunities the school provides for students to revise their work for public exhibit. Reduced numbers of students assigned to each teacher, opportunities for collegial planning and collaboration in which teachers support one another as learners, or numbers of teachers engaged in study groups may indicate the extent to which school norms value professional conditions for teaching.

Assessing the enabling conditions in a school can provide meaning to otherwise sterile outcomes that stand on their own in a public report. Indeed, without an examination of the "context indicators" of schooling, information on outcomes alone can not help answer questions about how to apply existing resources to benefit students, peel away ineffective practices, or pursue new resources. "Accounting for" those school practices, norms, and routines that reflect students' access to knowledge, press for achievement, and professional conditions for teaching helps the public and teachers themselves understand the reasons for improvement or decline in achievement; attention to these school context factors can feed a process of continuous school improvement. When teachers analyze the enabling conditions at work in their schools, then consider the data on student outcomes in light of those conditions, they begin a process of informed reflection about "what we're doing right" and "what we're doing wrong." As teachers begin to tell the stories of their practice in terms of enabling conditions, they can begin to see that they have choices about how they organize their school to facilitate stronger professional practice and improved student learning. Such conversations are key to developing professional responsibility for student success.

A high-stakes, outcomes-based, managerial accountability policy is ultimately unlikely to provide most schools with incentives to examine and reflect on the enabling conditions that contribute to student outcomes. The process of "setting standards," "teaching to those standards," "assessing learning," and "reporting results" is a process that puts teachers largely on the sidelines of decision-making. It separates accountability from professional practice and the unpredictable conditions of the schoolhouse that teachers contend with daily. It is a process that defines teachers as little more than technicians. It is a model of accountability that stresses reporting and monitoring, squeezing teaching and learning out of the picture.

Professional accountability does demand the reporting of data that highlight academic achievement and schools' investment in students' learning; but the ways in which professionals in each school use these data to inform practice is what ultimately leads to greater school capacity to promote meaningful learning for all students. Unless professionals have the time and support to reflect on data and research in light of their own day-to-day practice, the long-term impact on teaching and learning, and thus on student performance, will be limited.

A Professional/Managerial Accountability Model for School Improvement

Accountability approaches must reflect educational purposes. They should stimulate school improvement, create and sustain educational equity, create support for schools, and inform policy, with the primary goal being improved student learning for all students in all schools (National Education Association, 1991;

National Association of State Boards of Education, 1988). Given the limitations of high-stakes managerial approaches to accountability, an alternative model grounded in an examination of multiple indicators of student achievement, including student work, considered in light of each school's enabling conditions and standards of practice offers greater promise of meeting broad educational goals than an approach that relies on data reporting and monitoring alone. Indeed, the managerial and professional approaches to accountability are not mutually exclusive. A hybrid system that accommodates features of both managerial and professional accountability models may hold the greatest potential for effecting school reform (McDonnell, 1991). Such a hybrid would merge the benefits of a managerial orientation to gathering and monitoring outcomes data with an orientation to promoting professional responsibility for selecting and using effective practices that meet the needs of every student.

This hybrid model presumes that districts and states will gather and monitor data on multiple indicators selected in consultation with practitioners in each school within parameters that educators and the public agree constitute meaningful aspects of schooling. It requires methods of reporting data that involve practitioners in explaining their practice to their constituencies. It also relies on districts and states providing technical assistance that can guide practitioners in using data to bring about meaningful reform. Linking the notion of professional responsibility for practice to larger discussions of school accountability ultimately emphasizes that accountability must be seen as a *process* for continuous quality improvement rather than an after-the-fact reporting event (Darling-Hammond & Ascher, 1991). A combined managerial/professional model of accountability that respects this process offers a much improved chance of building the capacity of all schools to improve student performance than either one model alone. It provides a framework that allows for differential treatment of schools, with technical assistance provided according to schools' own varying capacity for engineering reform. It also pushes schools to devise their own strategies to improve student performance outcomes and strengthen the enabling conditions that contribute to such outcomes. Such a system would engage all schools in reform not *after* data is gathered and reported but as part of an *ongoing* process that explicitly sets out to improve both student outcomes and teacher practice.

High Standards Focused on Student Work

Standards for professional practice and student achievement lie at the core of the hybrid model of accountability. The notion of "standards" means different things to different people (*Education Week*, 1995). In executing a hybrid model of accountability, standards would be understood as images of excellence that inform a commitment to continuous improvement. As Wiggins (1993) observes:

Standards are *always* out of reach; that is the point. The standards of performance and the standards of self-discipline in one's work are always "ideals" for all but the world's best performers in every field. Thus I do not "expect" most people to meet the standards set by the best. My "expectation" is that everyone will strive to improve his or her work by studying what is best and working continuously to narrow the gap between the current level of performance and the ideal level of performance. (p. 285)

Within this definition, then, it is the work students produce, not test scores, that indicates both the quality of student performance outcomes and professional practices. And it is student work that forms the basis for "accounting for" how professional practice will change to improve the quality of that work. As Wiggins (1993) asks us to imagine:

What if each teacher had to display monthly the best work from each student in a public place of the school? What if academic teachers (as many vocational teachers now do) had to meet yearly with a "consultant committee" of professionals from their field to review their work? What if performance appraisals were centered on teacher self-assessment in reference to a range of student work from a major assignment? These are the kinds of mechanisms that would improve accountability immediately and forcefully. (p. 264)

For accountability purposes, student work represented in projects, portfolios, exhibitions, and other demonstrations of competence should ultimately allow teachers, parents, students, and policymakers to make an assessment of school performance that represents a truer picture of student achievement than test scores can reveal. But relying only on an external assessment of work misses the point. It is the process teachers use to examine the work and critique it against images of excellence that offers promise for greater professional accountability and student achievement. Such a process engages teachers in discussing the quality of student work, when work is "good enough," and what student work reveals about teaching and assignments, curriculum and opportunities to learn. At the school level, the process of studying student work in light of standards that are "images of excellence" is the basis for reviewing and revising teaching aims and strategies and refining teacher expectations, with a focus on moving all students toward high standards (Darling-Hammond, 1994). At the district level, the process of establishing standards through districtwide critique of student work can result in a blueprint for excellence in achievement and professional practice for an entire system of schools (Barth, 1994). Regular opportunities for parents and the public to view and critique the work students have produced extends the notion of teachers as accountable to all school constituencies.

Use of Multiple Indicators

Any accountability designed to promote reform must rest on multiple indicators of both student performance outcomes and conditions for learning (Kirst, 1990; National Association of State Boards of Education, 1988; National Education Association, 1991; Oakes, 1986; Office of Educational Research and Improvement, 1988; Shavelson et al., 1989; Sirotnik & Goodlad, 1985). Thus, along with a process for examining and describing the quality of the work students produce, managerial/professional accountability models should include reporting on school performance indicators that describe schools' "holding power." These include attendance and dropout patterns, grade retention and suspension rates, and rates of student placement in substantially separate special education settings. Some policymakers and school staff will argue that these indicators are not important, that if student work is of high quality, other data bear little significance. That is not the case. Indeed, the ethics of professional practice call on educators to be concerned about the events of inclusion and participation that all students experience in the daily life of schools and that these indicators describe.

Reporting should also include background indicators related to the inputs of education such as budget information and community, teacher, or student demographic data. These provide a broader context for understanding overall conditions of schooling. Of particular relevance is information related to school resources, defined not simply in terms of per pupil expenditure, but in terms of how resources are actually used. As Oakes (1989) observes:

> It is important to monitor resources and how schools spend them, not because resources directly influence results but because they provide basic information about what schools have available to them. . . . When measures of resource *level* are juxtaposed with measures of resource *use*, (for example, on up-to-date textbooks and curriculum materials, science laboratories for hands-on activities, field trips, etc.) their power to demonstrate school quality is likely to increase dramatically (p. 187)

In addition, accountability reports should include the process (or "context") indicators reflecting school conditions that enable high achievement: access to knowledge, press for achievement, and professional conditions for teaching (Oakes, 1989). These indicators highlight practices that shape students' experiences in relation to, for example, instructional time (hours spent in credit-earning classes); curricular emphasis (the proportion of teaching time devoted to academic and vocational subjects); grouping practices (percentages of students in academic programs); and extra support (availability of one-to-one help, computer-assisted instruction, and enrichment opportunities). Such data begin to explain school performance, but these clues still provide only partial understanding of how to craft improvement efforts.

Qualitative data derived from ethnographic studies, case studies, and surveys of students, teachers, and parents are also important for expanding practitioners' thinking about school conditions that contribute to student outcomes. School self-assessment tools such as the Effective Schools Battery developed by Johns Hopkins University's Center for Social Organization of Schools, surveys developed by the School Effectiveness Project of the Connecticut Department of Education, and the Middle Grades Assessment Program (MGAP) developed at the Center for Early Adolescence at the University of North Carolina have been found to be effective tools for developing a school profile, suggesting research-based directions for change, and involving teachers and students in their own plans for reform (Gottfredson, 1986). Schools working with the Center for the Study of Testing, Evaluation, and Education Policy at Boston College have found that student drawings, executed in response to a request that students draw a picture of their teacher at work in the classroom, can promote serious reflection about teaching practices (Tovey, 1996).

The Program Quality Review Process of the California Department of Education (1994) takes schools beyond the "checklist stage" to gather information about teaching and learning through a systematic examination of student work. Establishing a network of "critical friends" committed to a supportive assessment of school functioning can provide schools with a "running sort of accountability" (Sizer, 1989). Cross-school visitations based on the British inspectorate system can enlighten both visiting teams of educators and those in the schools visited about professional practice (Darling-Hammond, 1994). These approaches are currently incorporated into New York's School Quality Review Initiative, a comprehensive professional accountability model in which schools' knowledge about teaching and learning and commitment to continuous improvement grows through self-assessment and give-and-take with other professionals (Ancess, 1996).

Data from such sources can provide schools with insights about school quality that would not be so easily recognized by a managerial accountability system alone. Moreover, the use of multiple indicators more accurately reflects the multidimensional challenges of school reform. With student work included, teachers maintain a focus on authentic student achievement. With enabling conditions highlighted, teachers have data that can guide them toward changing practice to improve student work.

A District-School Partnership

A professional/managerial accountability system that includes indicators of both outcomes for student learning and enabling conditions that foster achievement calls for different actors to undertake complementary roles and responsibilities. Together all constituents act to strengthen a school reform process in light of information generated by accountability reporting. For example, Sirotnik (1987) notes that educators at the school level must engage in their own process of improvement while those at the district level should articulate the overall goals of that process, provide schools with resources adequate to achieve those goals, promote professional practice in line with those goals, and conduct evaluations of "lessons learned" to inform further improvement.

A professional/managerial model of accountability would combine such leadership and guidance at the district level with empowerment at the school level. This two-tiered design acknowledges that different levels of a school system use information gathered about school processes in different ways. For example, school principals and teachers may use the process of gathering and reviewing data to assess school strengths and weakness and target efforts for reform in particular curricular areas or grade levels. At the same time, district leaders may use data on both outcomes and enabling conditions to assess policy initiatives, inform budget decisions, and work with schools to design new programs that affect teaching and learning, including professional development.

District Guidance and Technical Assistance

In addition to collecting meaningful cross-school indicators, district staff should be involved in outlining the broad parameters that reflect a commitment to those enabling conditions most likely to contribute to reform of teaching and learning. These should follow Oakes's (1989) typology of access to knowledge, press for achievement, and professional conditions for teaching. District staff must also be involved in assuming leadership for communicating goals and standards throughout the district, providing technical assistance to schools as they assess results and context descriptors for their school, linking schools for shared professional examination of student work, helping identify new resources needed, and empowering principals and teachers with the necessary skills, and resources (including time) necessary over a multiyear period to support, nurture, and sustain reform to improve student work.

A system committed to a managerial/professional accountability model would also review all functions of the larger system in light of the goal of promoting reform in all schools. For example, districts that are serious about accountability must review their management information systems, assessment programs, curriculum frameworks, instructional and professional support, budget, and specialized school renewal projects in light of standards set for student work. The district itself may call on its own "critical friends" for a periodic, independent review of schooling outcomes and conditions in the system as a whole or in part, assessed in terms of access to knowledge, press for achievement, and conditions for professional practice. District leadership would convene study groups within the district office itself for the purpose of assessing districtwide policies and practice.

The district has a special role in relation to promoting equity across a district. Because different schools have different capacity for reform and different resources to draw from, the district must act to address the inequalities in capacity. In this context, the district has a key role to play in contract negotiations and other arenas to ensure that staff conditions in schools are conducive to developing a professional community of learners. Such a community can only develop when leadership is stable, teacher turnover is minimized, and teacher attendance is high.

The managerial/professional model of accountability would require increased district willingness to be partners with schools rather than top-down managers of schools in the intensive effort necessary to examine student work to improve student achievement. Such an effort would involve developing a climate that allows for the review of student work to improve quality without high-stakes consequences. At the same time, the district would reserve for itself the responsibility for intervening more directly in schools that do not demonstrate the capacity to meet standards of practice that will help students produce better work.

School Selection of Indicators for Reporting

Collecting data is one thing. Putting it to use is another. Educators are more likely to use data if they are involved in the selection of indicators and assessments that answer questions they deem most important (Malen, 1988; Sirotnik, 1987). By making teachers responsible for selecting indicators for monitoring, educators within each school can begin to develop norms and habits of shared inquiry so that the process of examining student work and other data becomes part of the school culture. Just as teachers must examine student work in light of agreed-upon standards, teachers must select indicators (and directions for improvement) that reflect their own goals for improvement developed with research-based "images of excellence" in practice in mind.

This principle falls well within tenets of current school reform organizations. Leaders of the networks of schools like the Coalition of Essential Schools, Accelerated Schools, and Partnership for School Renewal have consistently emphasized a commitment to participatory, school-based approaches that require each school to take responsibility for deciding what it aims to achieve and how progress toward that vision will be measured. In this model, then, school-based educators assume responsibility for shaping the objectives of reform from the beginning, not simply for determining the technical means for realizing objectives defined outside their purview. The commitment to involve teachers in planning for accountability reporting is also compatible with principles of school-based management and continuous quality improvement.

Simply putting decision-making authority in the hands of school staff does not mean that the decisions they make will be good decisions. However, locating this authority within a managerial/professional accountability framework boosts the potential for decisions made in light of research findings and standards of practice. Given direction, technical assistance, and professional development, school staff become partners with district staff in a school reform strategy that focuses on meeting standards through a process of examining student work without standardization.

Technical Assistance for Professional Networks and Study Groups

Professional accountability requires that educators become their own best critics of practice and supporters for risk-taking to make change. To this end, districts are increasingly developing professional networks across schools and with other districts, supporting whole faculty study groups, promoting subject area collaboratives, and pooling resources for professional development (Lieberman, 1995; Little, 1995; McLaughlin & Talbert, 1993; Murphy, 1998; Useem et al., 1995). Such approaches increase the likelihood that teachers actually use new strategies. Networks may be organized around clusters of particular kinds of schools, like the small, teacher-directed schools participating in the Center for Collaborative Education in New York City, or around "pathways" of elementary, middle, and high schools that work together to develop a consistent and shared culture as promoted by the ATLAS Project. Networks for principals encourage leaders to share information about school-based approaches to meeting standards.

District staff have a key role to play in providing technical assistance for such professional development. Subject area administrators may highlight resources and research related to particular curriculum areas or link school staff with university-based academics. Instructional experts may assist in areas like writing across the curriculum that are identified as being of broad concern and develop within- and across-school teacher study groups. Professional development experts may provide training for principals in whole school change strategies; some may serve as coaches and facilitators for teachers within and across schools as they examine students' work. In this way, district staff become boundary spanners, supporting school goals through resource development and networking.

Developing Assessments and Reporting Progress

A managerial/professional accountability model would assign the job of developing assessments for student progress to a joint district-school partnership making decisions about the kinds of assessments that would be required as a shared exercise and providing overall policy guidance for classroom and school assessments. While standardized tests would have a place in gauging the "broad brush" progress of the district and highlighting patterns that signal the need for greater attention, most assessments would focus on student work. In addition, the district would convene groups of teachers to examine student work to develop broad, usable rubrics to guide classroom teaching and learning. The assessment system would develop apart from high stakes, so would have full potential to become part of instruction. As in assessing school performance, indicators for student performance should be multiple, so that students have numerous chances to demonstrate what they know and can do.

A hybrid model of accountability would also require district and school staff to become partners in reporting information to constituents. With teachers selecting indicators and reviewing student work against district expectations and standards, information-gathering becomes part of a continuous improvement process. Information about school and student performance is a regular topic for discussion at faculty, parent, and community meetings, with teachers empowered to explain performance patterns to parents and the public. Written reports prepared in partnership with the district would include information on outcomes, including samples of student work, and enabling practices of schooling. They would also include information reported over time so that both educators and the public could assess the direction of change in outcomes and learning conditions.

Schools committed to an accountability ethic may also hold themselves accountable to their constituents through regular public displays of student work. Practice precedes policy in this respect, as some schools already hold regular "open houses" or organize student-led conferences during which students explain the work they have completed to parents, community visitors, and sometimes incoming students. In some schools, student work is so oriented to "real life" that it becomes its own report on the school's success. For example, when students who have engaged in a study of their community's water quality or tested for radon in the neighborhood surrounding the school also compile their results and communicate them in ways that are understandable to everyone, the work itself either "succeeds" or "fails" on its own merits. Schools like New York City's Central Park East and some others that have joined the Coalition of Essential Schools sometimes involve professionals from the community in assessing student work according to standards for their profession. Teacher affiliated with Foxfire work with students to see that their writing is "at standard" for publication in journals that reach wide audiences.

Rewards and Recognition

Rewards and recognition play an important role in supporting the aims of school reform inherent in a professional/managerial model of school accountability. Within this framework, rewards are allocated in the service of capacity-building and professional development to strengthen student achievement. Under this rubric, multiple awards might include stipends for teachers who agree to facilitate professional networks, serve on quality review committees and report back to their own school on their findings, or engage in teacher-based action research; or they might include legal relief from restrictive regulation (Firestone, 1991; Fuhrman & Elmore, 1991). Other rewards could include assistance (in terms of financial help, professional support, and release time) for groups of teachers to apply for certification by the National Board of Professional Teaching Standards or support for attendance and presentations at professional conferences.

Given multiple indicators of a hybrid accountability model, districts could recognize schools for success on multiple indicators. In particular, they could recognize high standards of practice that strengthen the school as a learning community, using discretionary funds to highlight school successes in expanding access to knowledge, intensifying press for achievement, and nurturing conditions for professional development. Districts could also award mini-grants to groups of teachers to introduce innovations that promote these enabling conditions. They could also invite all schools to apply for additional funding to pilot such achievement-oriented approaches as new standards-based curriculum or restructured library resources.

In such a system, school rewards would not only benefit individual schools and teachers, but would advance school reform throughout a larger system of schools. As the district looks for excellence deserving of recognition, a system of awards creates the means to identify, disseminate, and replicate innovations so that all schools understand that they are expected to contribute.

The Role of the State

An accountability model that combines features both the reporting features of the managerial approach and the capacity-building features of the professional approach assigns most of the roles to the district and its schools. However, this does not dismiss the role of the state. In fact, the state's leadership in providing a broad policy context within which districts and schools can develop their own accountability mechanisms is critical to the overall success of the system. Within the larger goal of strengthening both student achievement and every school in a state, the state must work with educators to establish those indicators that will be reported across all schools. In addition, the state would assist districts in identifying a "menu" of indicators within the categories of enabling conditions—access to knowledge, press for achievement, and professional practices—from which districts and schools could choose to monitor depending on local conditions.

The state also has a critical role to play in promoting equity in professional practice across all schools. For example, based on data gathered on learning conditions and outcomes, the state is in a position to promote equity by directing funding to districts with large numbers of students who are in danger of being left out of reform to strengthen the capacity of an entire district to respond to those needs. Likewise, the state would have a continuing responsibility to promote research-based practices that use federal funding for specific programs or groups of students, going beyond the simple monitoring function that has failed miserably (see, especially, National Assessment of Chapter 1 Program, 1993; Millsap, Moss, & Gamse, 1993) to embrace a role of technical assistance in helping districts develop better knowledge about "best practices." As part of such technical assistance, states have an important role to play in convening "equity teams" from district offices, including staff responsible for special education, Title 1, and bilingual education to meet with curriculum and professional development staff.

With a diminished role in implementing statewide assessments for high-stakes rewards or sanctions, states would be free to direct more resources toward developing professional capacity for change through statewide networks, and networks of like-minded schools. In this role, the state would orchestrate professional development for and facilitate a school quality review process. It would also take the lead in banking exemplars of student work prepared in response to common assignments and facilitate development of common rubrics for use statewide. The state would also assist districts when their efforts do not result in school improvement. In this context, the state would give up direct control over schools but would gain influence in professional development.

Conclusion

In many states, the pressure is now on districts to "scale up" their efforts. In this context, a managerial model appears seductive as a way to force teachers into compliance with expectations of new assessments. But the experiences of schools that have engaged in deep reforms to improve teaching and learning for all students suggest that there are no quick fixes. Experience further suggests that, even in a hospitable policy climate, school reform occurs one school at a time. A hybrid managerial/professional accountability model offers an alternative to the coercive bureaucratic approach that has become the new conventional wisdom and that, in the absence of a learner-centered ethic or attention to those conditions that enable learning, demands much but may produce little, especially in those schools where children are most in need of authentic accountability.

References

Ancess, J. (1996). Outside/inside, inside/outside: Developing and implementing the School Quality Review. New York: National Center for Restructuring Education, Schools, and Teaching, Teachers College, Columbia University.

Astuto, T. A., & Clark, D. L. (1992). Challenging the limits of school restructuring and reform. In Ann Lieberman (Ed.), The changing contexts of teaching: Ninety-first Yearbook of the National Society for the Study of Education. Chicago: University of Chicago Press.

Barth, P. (1994). From crisis to consensus: Setting standards in Chicago. *Perspective*, 7(1), Fall.

California Department of Education. (1994, September). *Guide and Criteria for Program Quality Review*. Sacramento: California Department of Education.

Corbett, H. C., & Wilson, B. L. (1997a). *Cracks in the classroom floor: The seventh grade year in five Philadelphia middle schools*, Philadelphia: Philadelphia Education Fund.

Darling-Hammond, L., & Ascher, C. (1991). *Creating accountability in big city school systems*, New York: ERIC Clearinghouse on Urban Education/ Institute on Urban and Minority Education and National Center for Restructuring Education, Schools, and Teaching.

Darling-Hammond, L. (1994). Performance-based assessment and educational equity. *Harvard Educational Review*, 64(1), 5–30.

Darling-Hammond, L. (1992–93). Standards of practice and delivery for learner-centered schools. *Stanford Law and Policy Review* Winter: 37–52.

Education Week. (1995). Struggling for standards. Special report, April 12.

Firestone, W. A. (1991). Merit pay and job enlargement as reforms: Incentives, implementation, and teacher response. *Educational Evaluation and Policy Analysis*, Fall.

Fuhrman, S. H., & Elmore, R. F. (1991). *Takeover and deregulation: Working models of new state and local regulatory relationships*. Paper presented at the annual meeting of the American Educational Research Association, April 3, Chicago.

Fuhrman, S. H., with Fry, P. (1989, December). *Diversity amidst standardization: State differential treatment of districts*, New Brunswick, NJ: Consortium for Policy Research in Education, Rutgers, The State University of New Jersey.

Gottfredson, D., Hybl, L.G., Gottfredson, G. D., & Costaneda, R. P. (1986). *School climate assessment instruments: A review*, Baltimore, MD: Center for Social Organization of Schools, The Johns Hopkins University. July.

Hall, G. E. (1991, April). *The local educational change process and policy implementation*. Paper presented at the annual meeting of the American Educational Research Association, Chicago.

Haney, W. and A. Raczek. (1994, February). *Surmounting outcomes accountability in education*. Unpublished paper. Chestnut Hill, MA: Boston College Center for the Student of Testing, Evaluation, and Education Policy.

Kirst, M. W. (1990, July). *Accountability: Implications for state and local policy makers*. Washington, D.C.: U.S. Department of Education, Office of Educational Research and Improvement.

Levin, H. M. (1991a). Accelerated visions. *Accelerated Schools*, 1(4), Fall.

Levin, H. M. (1991b). *Building school capacity for effective teacher empowerment: Applications to elementary schools with at-risk students*, New Brunswick, NJ: Consortium for Policy Research in Education.

Lieberman, A. (1995). Practices that support professional development: Transforming conceptions of professional learning. *Phi Delta Kappan,* 76(8), 591–596.

Little, J. W. (1995). Teachers' professional development and education reform. *Policy brief.* New Brunswick, NJ: Consortium for Policy Research in Education.

Mac Iver, D. J., & Plank, S. B. (1996). *The talent development middle school. Creating a motivational climate conducive to talent development in the middle schools: Implementation and effects of student team reading.* Report No. 4. Baltimore/Washington, DC: Johns Hopkins University and Howard University, Center for Research on the Education of Students Placed at Risk.

Malen, B. (1988). Book review of Michael Quinn Patton, Utilization focused evaluation. *Journal of Educational Finance,* 13(4).

McDonnell, L. M. (1991). *Accountability and decentralization in public education: Resolving the dilemma.* Paper prepared for delivery at the 1991 Annual Meeting of the American Political Science Association, The Washington Hilton, August 29–September 1.

McLaughlin. M. W., & Talbert, J. E. (1993). *Contexts that matter for teaching and learning.* Stanford, CA: Center for Research on the Context of Secondary School Teaching.

Millsap, M. A., Moss, M., & Gamse, B. (1993). *Chapter 1 in public schools: The Chapter 1 implementation study. Final Report.* Prepared by Abt Associates, Inc. and Policy Studies Associates, Inc. Washington, DC: U.S. Department of Education, Office of Policy and Planning.

Mitchell, D. E. (1989). Measuring up: Standards for evaluating school reform. In T. J. Sergiovanni & J. H. Moore (Eds.), *Schooling for tomorrow: Directing reforms to issues that count.* Needham, MA: Allyn and Bacon.

Murphy, C. (1998). *Whole faculty study groups: A powerful way to change schools and enhance learning.* Thousand Oaks, CA: Corwin Press.

National Assessment of the Chapter 1 Program. (1993). *Reinventing Chapter 1: The current Chapter 1 program and new directions.* Washington, DC: U.S. Department of Education, Office of Policy and Planning, Planning and Evaluation Service.

National Association of State Boards of Education. (1988). Effective accountability: Improving schools, informing the public. Alexandria, VA.: National Association of State Boards of Education.

National Education Association. (1991). *Education accountability initiative: Basic assumptions.* Washington, DC: National Education Association.

National School Boards Association. (1991). Pitfalls to avoid in designing an accountability system: Excerpt from *Straight A's: Accountability, Assessment, Achievement.* Reston, VA: National School Boards Association. Author.

Noble, A., & Smith, M. L. (1994). Old and new beliefs about measurement-driven reform: "Build it and they will come." *Educational Policy, 8*(2), 111–136.

Oakes, J. (1989). What educational indicators? The case for assessing the school context. *Educational Evaluation and Policy Analysis, 11*(2).

Office of Educational Research and Improvement. (1988). *Measuring up: Questions and answers about state roles in educational accountability,* Washington, DC: U.S. Department of Education, Office of Educational Research and Improvement, November 1988.

Sarason, S. B. (1996). *Revisiting "The culture of school and the problem of change."* New York: Teachers College Press.

Shavelson, R. J., McDonnell, L.M., & Oakes, J. (Eds.) (1989). *Indicators for monitoring mathematics and science education: A sourcebook.* Santa Monica, CA: RAND Corporation.

Shepard, L. A. (1995). Using assessment to improve learning. *Educational Leadership, 52*(5), 38–43.

Sirotnik, K. A. (1987). Evaluation in the ecology of schooling: The process of school renewal. In J. I. Goodlad (Ed.), *The Ecology of School Renewal: 86th Yearbook of the National Society for the Study of Education.* Chicago: University of Chicago Press.

Sirotnik, K. A. and J. I. Goodlad. (1985). The quest for reason amidst the rhetoric of reform: Improving instead of testing Our schools. In William J. Johnston (Ed.), *Education on trial: Strategies for the future.* San Francisco: Institute for Contemporary Studies.

Sizer, T. R. (1989). Diverse practice, shared ideas: The essential school. In H. Walberg, & J. J. Lane (Eds.), *Organizing for Learning: Toward the 21st century,* (pp. 1–8). Reston, VA: National Association of Secondary School Principals.

Tovey, R. (1996). Getting kids into the picture: Student drawings help teachers see themselves more clearly. *Harvard Education Letter, 12*(6), 5–6.

Useem, E., Buchanan, J., Meyers, E., & Maule-Schmidt, J. (1995). *Urban teacher curriculum networks and systemic change.* Paper presented at the Annual Meetings of the American Educational Research Association, San Francisco, April.

Wiggins, G. (1993). *Assessing student performance: Exploring the purpose and limits of testing.* San Francisco: Jossey-Bass.

Part IV

Reactions

11

State and School Level
Accountability Dilemmas

JON SNYDER

The preceding chapters explore the issues and dilemmas inherent in the uneasy relationship between state-level and school-level responsibility for the formal education of children. While the state of Maine, as Ruff, Smith, and Miller point out, makes a conscious effort to distribute responsibility to the local district, most states, in reality if not rhetoric, assume significant state-level responsibility.

There are, at least, three compelling reasons for the state to assume a significant responsibility for schools. One rationale is legalistic in nature. The state, through its elected officials, owes an accounting to the citizens of the state for the money they forward to schools. We are not talking peanuts here—well over half of every state budget goes ultimately to fund public education. A second rationale is individually ethical in nature. Since the state, by law, compels parents to send their children to school, the state has an ethical responsibility for what happens to those children (the caliber of care and of educational opportunities) once there. If my son has a teacher—with a license granted by the state and with a paycheck from the state—who physically or emotionally abuses him, I believe the state is guilty of the crime of compelling my child to be harmed. A third rationale, both legal and ethical, is more social in nature than the first two. Public education is a socially agreed upon right that we, as a people in each state in the country, have agreed is necessary for the welfare of a democratic society—and for the individual child's future, liberty, and pursuit of happiness. Public education, we have agreed with our votes and our pocket books, is both a social necessity as well as a socially agreed-upon protection of a child's inalienable rights—rights upon which our country's existence is premised.

Despite a convincing case for state responsibility, we know (and if we do not, by now there is certainly no excuse) that those external to the schools cannot do the work of schooling. The work of formal education is done in classrooms and schools in the moment to moment efforts of children, their families, and the adults who interact with them daily. The last time I checked, I found no evidence that a child learned anything solely because a state legislature decreed it.

The lack of a direct relationship between legislative intent and effects on public education is, as alluded to in the Wheelock chapter, a consequence of a series of false assumptions. Legislative mandates hope to find the "one best system" (Tyack, 1974), codified by law and specified in regulations, by which all students may be educated. They assume that: (a) students and educators are standardized so that they will respond in identical and predictable ways to the "treatments" devised by policymakers; (b) sufficient knowledge of which treatments to prescribe is both available and generalizable to all educational circumstances; (c) this knowledge can be translated into standardized practices, which in turn can be maintained through regulatory systems; and (d) administrators and teachers can and will faithfully implement the prescriptions for practice (Darling-Hammond & Snyder, 1992). The validity of each of these assumptions is, as made abundantly evident in the classroom-based chapters of this volume, questionable at best.

Ultimately, states cannot ignore the basic educational fact that the work of schools happens in schools—but, neither can schools ignore the influence of state accountability efforts on their work. Accountability responses at the state level such as standards, curriculum frameworks, and assessment decisions, profoundly influence what does happen, the nature of the work that students and adults do in schools. State-level decisions regarding credentialing policies and approved textbooks profoundly influence who, and whose ideas, are even allowed in classrooms.

My response to reading the chapters in this book is to see what lessons can be learned from the Kentucky experience about how the two, equally essential, accountability locations can work together to support their mutual goals. In simplest terms, the Kentucky accountability plan includes three components: define outcomes, assess outcomes, attach stakes to those outcomes. One of the first lessons from Kentucky is that there are mutual goals. That is, when extremists on either side of any ideological debate are heard but eventually overruled in the interest of children over ideology (for instance, "back to basics" proponents who do not want children to learn to think, or "whole language" proponents who burn skill-based books), the populace can, and often does, come to agreement about a set of goals for public education that will enable students to be productive members of a democratic society and to construct a future of their own choosing. At least initially, state and school could both agree on the defined outcomes. That agreement, however, changed because of the way in which the state decided to assess those outcomes.

Meet the New Boss, Same as the Old Boss

There are major incongruencies between state-level decisions regarding assessment and school-level beliefs regarding assessment. As Calvert, Gaus, and Ruscoe point out, "The implementation of KIRIS, the state's use of mandated, performance-based assessments, continues to hold on to conventional notions of reliability and validity and to reduce the assessment of a school's success to a single number." School-level educators, in these chapters, tend to think of accountability as requiring more grounded information gathered over time. They seem to subscribe to the evaluation principle that any sound decision requires multiple sources of evidence collected over time (Snyder, Chittendon, & Ellington, 1993). As Calvert, Gaus, and Ruscoe put it, "Surely we are looking for more than a single number to understand what school reform is all about." The state sees teacher knowledge as bias to overcome because of a traditional psychometric notion that reliability requires standardization. Classroom-based educators see teacher knowledge as essential to sound decision-making.

This incongruence between state and local accountability beliefs regarding appropriate assessment instruments has several outcomes. First, as Jones and Whitford point out, it destroys the agreement regarding educational outcomes. For instance, a single assessment (whether "performance-based" or otherwise) simply cannot assess the learning of the "Throw-Up Incident" described by Brooks in his chapter. Yet, the kind of respect for the human rights of others authentically documented in that incident, is surely an educational outcome with nearly universal public support. Even within the realm of more "purely" academic outcomes, the state's assessment decisions diminish the ability to assess such valued educational outcomes as constructing an extended argument; framing a question; defining and collecting data to respond to a question; and storytelling narrative as a form of analysis, a way of knowing, and an essential component of language development and reading comprehension.

Secondly, as Fickel documents particularly well, the state's assessment decisions may actually hinder the kind of teaching and learning environments that support the initially agreed upon goals. When students ask, "Is this on the test?" they exhibit knowledge of another basic educational fact—what gets tested is what gets taught. In effect, teachers are asking the same question of the state's outcome assessments. This is the way that the content and format of an assessment system drives instruction to the point where teaching is testing and learning is practicing for the test. To use assessments as a lever for educational change requires constructing over-time and multiple-source assessments to mirror, support, and assess significant learning outcomes. The state's decisions invert the process in Kentucky—limited assessments mirror, support, and assess limited learning.

As usual in such a complex social endeavor as public education, the issue is not a simple one. For instance, is the "problem" the assessment choices or a more fundamental one? That is, whether the assessment system is limited or powerful may not matter because in both instances, state-level psychometric decisions drive instructional practice. Perhaps valued educational outcomes can best be achieved if the strengths, interests, and needs of students drive practice—not assessments. Traditional notions of psychometric reliability, as well as the scope and sequence inherent in most sets of standards (and perhaps even assessments driven by more "authentic" principles) are linear and logical. Learning is human and psychological. Therein lies a challenge to any state-driven assessment system.

Within the chapters presented, however, evidence exists that, limited though the state assessments might have become, they do enhance certain of the consensually agreed upon educational outcomes. The Kannapel et al. chapter points out that student writing improved in response to the assessments' reliance on short written answers to open-ended questions. The McGee chapter suggests that students write better and in more genres. In addition, the Fickel chapter documents a school using the assessments to enhance curriculum through developing a collaborative community. Kannapel et al. quote a junior high school principal informing a basketball coach that because of KIRIS, practicing open response questions was now more important than an eighteen-win season. Though a serious basketball fanatic, I happen to believe this is an educational advance.

Another incongruence issue is that the function of "accountability" differs at the state and local levels. The state needs large-scale data sets to make annual large-scale decisions. Classroom-based educators need minute-by-minute student-by-student finely honed information to make instructional decisions. State legislators and policymakers cannot, and should not, possess the quality and quantity of information regarding student achievement that the adults who work with students daily possess. Still, they need to have some kind of information in order to make the decisions for which they are responsible. The solution may be in the form of systems that summarize complex data such as the Primary Language Record (Darling-Hammond, Ancess, & Falk, 1995) and humanistic-based standards systems such as developed by New Haven, California (Snyder, 1998; Waters, 1998). In these systems, assessments are grounded in the day-to-day enacted curriculum and are dependent upon multiple checks and balances on teacher judgment yet still are capable of generating reliable large-scale data sets for decision-making far removed from children.

Trailing Clouds of Glory or Nasty, Brutish, and Short

The state of Kentucky attached stakes to educational outcomes—a maximum of an approximately $100 monthly increase in the paychecks of teachers who "won," a few dollars a month, and a "distinguished educator" into a school that "lost." To some, particularly when a $100 per month is aggregated statewide, these seem high. Yet these stakes for educators are certainly minimal compared to the stakes for the children and the hopes of their families.

Thus, the issue is not attaching stakes, it is in the kinds of stakes attached. Attaching stakes involves assumptions about human nature. What is going to motivate people? At opposite ends of the continuum stand the notions of humanity as nasty, brutish, and short and motivated by coercion (primarily punishment with a dollop of bribery) to do things right versus humanity as entering life trailing clouds of glory who will do the right thing if given only a smidgen of an opportunity to do so. The nasty, brutish, and short end of the continuum tends toward behaviorist modes of motivation. The trailing clouds of glory end tends toward humanistic modes of motivation.

Accompanying these assumptions about human nature are concomitant assumptions about the nature of teaching (not surprising given the core role of motivation in learning). The differences are captured in the difference between doing things right versus doing the right thing. Doing things right emphasizes "things"—a particular way of acting. Doing the right thing emphasizes "right"—a moral issue much more difficult to ascribe to an action and thus more difficult to assess.

Educators, like their students, are neither angels nor devils—just people who most likely have needs for both kinds of motivation. Herzberg (1966) posits that the more behaviorist modes of motivation serve as dissatisfiers, and that their lack can decrease effort, while the more humanistic modes of motivation serve as satisfiers in that their presence can increase effort. He argues that optimal human functioning requires a healthy balance of both. It is difficult to ascribe a view of humanity to a location (i.e., a state legislature versus a local school). Still, in general, those responsible for an outcome who cannot do the work (state legislators and the work of schooling, teachers and the work of learning) certainly have more opportunities for frustration with human nature.

The way KIRIS has operated, over time, definitely tends toward the coercion end of the continuum. Its basic assumption is that educators can be motivated by rewards and punishments to do things right. To exacerbate the imbalance, the real stakes in KIRIS are not the financial rewards. The high stakes in Kentucky are the punitive public flogging of "failing" schools accompanied by the loss of school-level discretion, the equivalent of professional imprisonment. As McGee; Jones and Whitford; Calvert, Gaus, and Ruscoe; and Kannapel et al., all point out, schools experienced many more "controls" than "supports." The threat of punishment serves more as a dissatisfier than as a spur to greater effort. As Kannapel et al. write, "Virtually no teachers with whom we spoke indicated that the promise of rewards had inspired them to work harder or change their approaches. . . . Many educators found the threat of sanctions motivating in the negative sense."

In those cases where the system "worked," the threats were still present, but educators, not always as a result of KIRIS, also had supports. As McGee as well as Jones and Whitford document, if the teachers were already "doing" KERA, then KIRIS supported their efforts. As Kannapel et al. write, "Many teachers saw the benefits and reported that they would continue to emphasize writing even if KERA were not in effect. This seemed especially true of the teachers in our study who had served as writing portfolio 'cluster leaders'—teachers who received regional and state-level training." Mary Jo, the math teacher in the Jones and Whitford chapter provides a specific example:

> She states that her professional experiences have been a greater force in her changing than any state mandate or national standard. . . . She has spent part of three summers with the Wilson Institute, a summer at the Fermi Lab studying fractals and chaos theory, and a summer as part of the Graphing Calculator Enhanced Algebra Project. She continues to take part in teacher networks, including the Louisville-based LATTICE (Learning Algebra Through Technology, Investigations, and Cooperative Experiences), a regional Technology Alliance, and a regional Goals 2000 curriculum-oriented initiative called Project SCIMATCH. . . . In addition, every Thursday, students are released an hour and twenty minutes early from school so that teachers may work together to plan and discuss lessons and plan the department's curriculum.

The lesson seems clear. Telling people what to do, even with threats of sanctions, is an insufficient change strategy. Coupled with the necessary protections for children (and the most necessary protection is the caliber of the educators working with students) must be the necessary opportunities for learning what it is one wishes educators to do. As Mary Jo Foster summarizes in the Jones and Whitford chapter, "I hate routines. I didn't used to hate them. I didn't know any better." To go about supporting educator support for student learning in a systemic way involves a set of five inter-related policy initiatives: (a) establish standards of learning for children and standards of practice for educators; (b) provide exemplary opportunities for teacher learning from pre-service through retirement; (c) recruit and retain high quality educators; (d) reward knowledge and skill; and (e) organize schools around student and teacher learning (NCTAF, 1996; 1997).

Mandating What Matters Most

The very essence of educational outcomes for children may be a core belief in the desire and capacity of children to learn (Snyder, Morrison, & Smith, 1996). Kannapel et al.'s chapter suggests that KIRIS is achieving some success in this regard: "Even though it did not appear that most educators believed that all children could achieve at high levels, there were instances when it appeared that student performance on KIRIS was convincing some educators that students were capable of performing at higher levels than they had imagined." When they looked for similarities among high-achieving schools they did not find a pattern of "things" schools did but rather a common sense of "right." "Educators in all three schools held high expectations for students. In addition, they had a relatively consistent instructional approach over time, with most educators in the schools adhering to a common approach (whether traditional or innovative)." In short teachers in high-achieving schools believed in children and had enough confidence in what they were doing to believe their actions could make a difference. In distinction is the teacher from their study who said that no matter what (s)he did, "I have kids who are novice students and that is all they will ever be."

There is a line among educational researchers used so often that one has a difficult time tracking down its inventor: "You cannot mandate what matters most." Of course, if the government followed this dictum, and simply waited for people to do on their own what matters most, this country could still practice slavery, women could still not have the vote, and so on. The core values that children want to learn, can learn, and must be provided opportunities for learning, may be precisely the appropriate state accountability role. They may be exactly what must be mandated. The Kentucky experience coupled with learnings from accountability efforts such as TAIP outlined in the Shelor chapter offer a path for a way out of this conundrum. It is the role of the government within a representative democracy to "mandate" core values ("self-evident" truths). This is not a new government encroachment, it is the very basis of the United States. It is neither the government's role, nor particularly effective, to mandate particular behaviors. The government establishes common values, the people enact those values. The same is true in education.

There is a "public" in public education and professional responsibility should not translate into individual autonomy (which in education is itself sometimes confused with autism). Therefore, when a state assumes its legal and ethical responsibility for public education it does not constitute an insult to professionalism. As a parent and citizen, I believe I have a right and a responsibility for public education. As a professional educator, however, I also have a right and a responsibility. In addition, as a professional educator I have both "abstract" educational knowledge and context-specific knowledge of my students that a nonprofessional does not possess.

TAIP provides an example of how state and professional/school responsibilities can work together. TAIP processes, in effect, mandate certain values (participation, time, matching responsibility with authority, educators as leaders rather than potential hamburger, etc.). Those values, however, by definition, must be enacted locally. In this same way, the either/or of state responsibility vis-à-vis professional responsibility may be transformed into a both/and. Again, where it "worked" in Kentucky, well supported professional educators did what they did best and children learned. KERA, in a sense, mandated values. Those values were enacted when teachers had support, worked in teams, and were allowed variability. Ruff, Smith, and Miller highlight the same successful ingredients in their Maine-based chapter. They point out that successful strategies for school improvement include such "mandated" values as: "academic focus, assessment and accountability, and community." They also include as essential ingredients such support factors as "helping schools and districts develop, developing and expanding teaching practice and designing local systems of accountability and assessment that drive instructional decisions, rather than certify, label and sort students." One might add, for that matter, schools.

The preceding chapters drive home one other essential component of balancing state and educator responsibility. When educators start with their students, rather than externally defined standards or assessments, those students learn the externally defined standards to a higher degree. The classroom based studies in this book provide compelling evidence that the professional confidence to serve one's clients first is essential to enacting professional responsibility and ultimately enhancing student learning.

Katherine Futrell in McGee's chapter feels she is primarily accountable to "the students in her classroom, their parents, the principal, and professional standards." Her Moving West unit covered every item on the KIRIS assessments, yet was not based on those assessments. Her students, "learn to spell a variety of words during their three years in this primary program and are generally considered good 'spellers'" by their fourth-grade teacher." She argues with professional confidence, "Whatever sanctions and rewards the state decides to attach to the testing procedure should not affect what I know to be good teaching strategies."

Mary Jo Foster in the Jones and Whitford chapter believes "These kids can do this. They just take time making connections." As the authors say of her, "Rather than operate as one who simply follows the prescriptions of authorities, she has taken it upon herself to understand the changing world of mathematics education; to stay informed about technology resources, and what other teachers are doing; to 'read' her students; and to rely upon her own judgment and creativity."

Demi Kidd and Jodie McKnight in the Brooks chapter "are not going to be governed by words. We're inventing Utopia for a bit of time for our kids. That business is too urgent to get caught up in politically correct notions. . . . We've got important work to be about." A parent of a child in their class pointed out, "With these teachers, I never get an excuse that 'So and so says we have to do it.' In fact, I have no doubt that they'd take on anybody if they thought it was the right thing to do." But Kidd may put it best, "I don't teach KERA, I teach what is best for kids."

References

Darling-Hammond, L., & Snyder, J. (1992). Reframing accountability: Creating learner-centered schools. In A. Lieberman (Ed.), *Changing context of teaching: Ninety-first yearbook of the National Society for the Study of Education, Part 1*. Chicago: University of Chicago Press.

Darling-Hammon, L., Ancess, J., & Falk, B. (1995). *Authentic assessment in action: Studies of schools and students at work*. New York: Teachers College Press.

Herzberg, F. (1996). *Work and the nature of man*. Cleveland, OH: World.

National Commission on Teaching and America's Future (1996). *What matters most: Teaching for America's future*. New York: Author.

National Commission on Teaching and America's Future (1997). *Doing what matters Most: Investing in quality teaching*. New York: Author.

Snyder, J. (1998). *New Haven Unified School District: A teaching quality system for excellence and equity*. New York: National Commission on Teaching and America's Future.

Snyder, J., Morrison, G., & Smith, R. C. (1996). *Dare to dream: Educational guidance for excellence*. Indianapolis, IN: Lilly Endowment.

Snyder, J., Chittenden, E., & Ellington, P. (1993). *Assessment of children's reading: A comparison of sources of evidence*. New York: National Center for Restructuring Education, Schools, and Teaching.

Tyack, D. (1974). *The one best system: A history of American urban education*. Cambridge, MA: Harvard University Press.

Waters, L. (1998). How to design a model standards–based accountability system. In Elise Trumball & Beverly Farr (Eds.), *Accountability in the age of standards: The role of grades*. Norwood, MA: Christopher-Gordon Publishers.

12

Success Needs Time
to Grow

A. RICHARDSON LOVE JR.

From the outside looking in, the Kentucky Education Reform Act is a remarkable accomplishment. Since 1990, it has shifted the state's often shrill public debate from "if" to "how" to improve education. Whether or not they fully agree with the vision or the plan, the players in Kentucky are focused on the same page, and impressive progress is being made. In national shorthand, KERA and the Kentucky Instructional Results Information System known as KIRIS have been synonymous with ambitious standards-based reform and efforts to develop and apply valid and reliable "authentic" assessment in which students demonstrate their capacities to recall, integrate and apply knowledge, using good judgment, in realistic situations.

The authors of this volume offer a closer, more sobering look at the inside of reform documenting the voice and experience of the doers responsible for implementing change day to day and assessing its impact on students. They show that KERA's goal of high achievement for all remains a formidable but no less compelling challenge, heightened by allocation of less than adequate resources to accomplish mandated change and by many societal factors outside of school that affect student development, motivation, and success. The cases presented here, however, show that there is not yet a confident, unrelenting commitment among Kentucky educators to pursue and refine authentic assessment, particularly in the course of messy transition from the comfortable inadequacy of multiple-choice testing and a tendency to relapse in that direction. With their documentation of the realities of reform in Kentucky the authors frame and equip us to ponder two fundamental questions about KIRIS and the broader issues of accountability and assessment: *Is it appropriate/realistic to hold teachers and schools accountable for education outcomes? And, if so, is KIRIS an effective means for holding teachers and schools accountable?*

Without expertise in assessment, the responsibility for a classroom or an obligation to help balance the interests of political constituencies, I can claim only to be a student of Kentucky reform, but an attentive one. My challenge as a grantmaker is to keep an eye on the larger frame and look beyond immediate need to find opportunities for small dollars to help leverage disproportionate future gains. As a statewide laboratory for reform, rich with lessons to document and share, Kentucky holds great appeal for grantmakers. Is KIRIS the first stage in the evolution of a valid and reliable system of authentic assessment of teaching and learning or is it a fundamentally flawed mechanism for assessment doomed to be discarded and replaced?

KIRIS has focused education on short-term rather than long-term goals. Jones and Whitford and the Appalachian Educational Laboratory (AEL) researchers observe that educators are more preoccupied with the test than with helping students achieve high standards. Teachers and schools resent being held accountable for what they view as unrealistic standards of performance. The need and opportunity are for this discontent about accountability and assessments to be channeled constructively to help evolve a system of assessment, by KIRIS or any other name, that challenges and nurtures rather than discourages teachers and students.

Generally, the authors report both increased use of the humanities and arts and more writing activity as discernable evidence of the impact of the reforms. Credit is given to the KIRIS assessments for the increased instance of writing in the schools, but caution is raised that it may be the right reaction for the wrong reasons. Increases in the amount and frequency of student writing that teachers are requiring is a desired change, although the cases illustrate circumstances where educators are simply going through the motions to comply. For example in chapter 7, the AEL researchers quote a physical education teacher and a science teacher who see writing as a distraction. These teachers are concerned that the requirement to teach writing is depleting rather than enhancing their capacity to teach their own subject matter.

Jonathan Monroe, who directs the exemplary writing program at Cornell University, is fond of saying "There is a synonym for good writing; it's THINKING." Kentucky teachers need time and assistance to discover that writing is not only a skill useful for KIRIS testing but also for life, and that it can be a highly effective method of teaching and learning *in any discipline.* Kentucky could accelerate reform and increase commitment to it by assuring now that future teachers learn both to teach writing and to appreciate why it is important for students to write.

Teaching to the test, normally considered bad practice, can be desirable, according to considerable literature cited in chapter 7, when the test is worth teaching to (i.e., "when performance-based examinations are closely linked to a 'thinking curriculum'"). Based on the information the cases present, KIRIS has had limited success in compelling compliance to KERA reforms, the best example being increases in student writing. It has failed to encourage and may well have discouraged the understanding of reforms necessary to move compliance to commitment. Further, the revisions to KIRIS seem to be diminishing rather than strengthening the role of assessment in advancing the substance of KERA reforms.

The memorable teachers profiled in these chapters—Katherine Futrell, Demi Kidd, Jodie McKnight, and Mary Jo Foster—certainly seem to be teachers who understand. Although they well illustrate the potential of the profession, my tendency is to view them as exceptional rather than typical. Reforms can often move rapidly to engage the best teachers but stall in the capacity to reach the majority. Linda Hargan of the Kentucky Collaborative for Teaching and Learning estimates that roughly 15% of teachers adapt instinctively and intuitively to reform, recognizing opportunity in change and how to make it work in their classrooms. The vast majority, however, need help with the process of change and particularly with incorporating changes effectively into their classrooms, as Grant Wiggins says, "to know what to do on Monday morning." So much of what we have discovered about teaching and learning (e.g., constructivism, learning styles, multiple intelligences, active learning) we fail to apply to adults and organizations who need to retool. Surely resistance could be reduced if KIRIS were more nurturing and less judgmental regarding the changes schools and teachers need to make. In concept, the "Distinguished Educator" strategy seems to have great potential for nurturing change. In practice, the focus seems to have been more on raising test scores than improving education. It and other components of the KIRIS system could benefit from a reconsideration of semantics. Rather than the use of such stigmatizing labels as "decline" and "crisis," could the system acknowledge that teachers and schools, as well as students, must develop through stages as novice, apprentice, proficient and distinguished learners?

The fact that teachers are preoccupied with the test rather than the goals of reform is not solely a commentary on KIRIS but also on teachers and the profession of teaching. Some teacher resistance to assessment is not aimed at the specifics of KERA or KIRIS, but grows from a fundamental discomfort with any system by whatever name that holds a teacher accountable for student achievement given the life circumstances of many of the students they teach. In chapter 3, McGee quotes fourth-grade teacher Katherine Futrell, "The givens for children are not being taken into account. . . . It is certainly our obligation as teachers to take each student as far as we possibly can during the time we have them in class, but to make us accountable to seeing that each child reaches the proficient stage is pretty unrealistic." The AEL researchers reported in chapter 7 that "the majority of educators either did not believe that all children can achieve at high levels, or believed that it was not within their power to ensure that all students scored proficient on the KIRIS test." From the perspective of the alternative Teacher Appraisal Invention Process (TAIP), Shelor observes in chapter 8 that "teachers understandably reject accountability systems that hold them responsible for factors in the learning process outside the teachers' control."

The reservations among teachers about whether all students can achieve at high levels documented in the case studies closely parallel findings of the Public Agenda Foundation's national survey of teacher attitudes, published in 1996 under the revealing title *Given the Circumstances: Teachers Talk About Public Education.* It found that "teachers support higher standards, but raising them is not their most urgent goal. Teachers focus on what they consider the foremost needs of their schools—pressures of social problems, lack of funding, overcrowded classes, and lack of parental involvement." Further, Public Agenda reports, "many teachers consider it inevitable, given the troubled backgrounds or students they teach, that some will be educational failures who slip through the cracks and graduate without basic skills."

The problem, of course, is the level of education that the future is defining as essential. Will there be any legitimate role in our society for adults who do not have the basic knowledge and skills that the technological workplace requires? *Ultimately, schools must be accountable to the future.* Their real assessment is long term in the adult lives of today's students and in the society they fashion. All of this begs the question: *who will stand for standards?* It seems essential for there to be a means for keeping standards high and the educational system focused on the student outcomes that the future is defining as essential. Linda Hargan believes that KERA and KIRIS offer that assurance and can accomplish "a comprehensive, inescapable raising of the bar, a new ambitious standard of acceptable performance for teachers and students."

The promise of KERA is that over time it will redress "the givens" that often frustrate student achievement through such strategies as youth service centers and efforts to nurture parental and community involvement, with the result being an increasing numbers of students who will be better able to achieve at high levels. The future urges educators to keep focused on where students *must* go rather than where they began.

As much as I respect the profession, I do not believe that we have yet seen teachers fully acknowledge their collective responsibility for improving student achievement or fully realize their collective capacity to nurture it. As a result, I do not believe that collectively teachers can say often with confidence and conscience "this child is beyond our capacity to reach." When teachers and schools make this statement the consequences are dire; society offers few alternatives— potentially only the mental health, welfare, and judicial systems. When education is premised on an individual's given circumstances, the students who are most dependent on schooling for the knowledge and skills they need to become productive citizens are the ones the system is least able to reach. In that regard,

KIRIS seems to confront and threaten teachers individually rather than challenge their sense of collective responsibility and capacity.

No one knows more about what a student is learning or how well he has been taught in the past than a teacher who observes and interacts with him day to day. When we speak of "collective responsibility," it is usually to emphasize the complementary roles parents and the community must play with schools and teachers to improve educational attainment. But there is need also for stronger collective responsibility among teachers so that their combined capacities can better strive to reach every child. Education needs *teachers who are accountable to each other*.

Several factors have traditionally limited the development of this sense of professional community and shared responsibility: the traditional isolation of the classroom, the organization of the teaching profession on a labor union model, a disjuncture between the preparation offered by teacher education programs and the changing realities of American society, schools and classrooms; and a teaching profession and education system that often insulate inadequate teaching rather than resolving to improve or replace it. Overcoming these and related barriers has been an agenda for reform in Kentucky and beyond.

A particularly effective way teachers can be critical and nurturing colleagues for each other and share responsibility for the quality of student achievement is through vertical collaboration: elementary, middle and high school teachers working to assure a system of teaching and learning that better nurtures student development and progress. It was encouraging to see McGee's report in chapter 3 that Katherine Futrell and her colleagues in the primary grades had begun to work with a fourth-grade teacher to ensure that their students were as prepared as possible for fourth-grade assessments. In addition, the chapters include scattered mentions of the benefits of professional development schools pointing to K–16 collaboration and efforts to improve the preparation of future teachers. But otherwise, I found little evidence that teachers and schools are collaborating to improve education as a continuum. This lack was notable in the portrait by Calvert, Gaus, and Ruscoe in chapter 6 of the "tortuous" struggles of West Middle despite the principal's clear acknowledgment that "we also knew that our students came to us from elementary school with very low basic skills." The school seemed to accept the challenge of providing substantial remediation rather than working collaboratively to improve elementary school achievement.

Another way to foster collective responsibility among teachers is opening opportunities for interdisciplinary teaching or reinforcement in one subject with teaching and learning in another. In their introduction, Jones and Whitford offer the vivid image of mathematics teacher Mary Jo Foster jumping into her chair "holding her arms at various angles to model shapes of different functions. She gets the whole class on its feet to follow her in these mathematical calisthenics." I thought immediately of the teacher quoted in chapter 7 grumbling about his students having to write during physical education, and if he might be inspired by this image of role playing mathematical functions to work with colleagues in other disciplines to help integrate some content-oriented physical activity into their lessons. I also thought of the principal quoted later in the same chapter concerned that "band's never going to do anything for us as far as reaching our threshold" and wondered how band practice might be used to illustrate the physical principles of sound or the selection of music used to reinforce history lessons.

Finally, fostering collective responsibility could also reduce a tendency for complacency among experienced and successful teachers, who may find unsettling the necessity in reform for a continuous process of change. I sensed a little complacency in the profile of the skilled teachers at Northtop Elementary in chapter 2. Although those teachers worked with their colleagues as mentors, it was not clear that there was a sense of a collective responsibility for nurturing student achievement. The type of collective accountability that KIRIS is intended to promote could both challenge the best teachers to inspire their colleagues and challenge the precarious assumption that what was once a good lesson, good teaching, good education will always be.

At the same time I was reading drafts for this volume, I also read an impressive article of similar ilk by Holly Holland, "The Brown vs. the Department of Education" in the December 1997 issue of *Louisville Magazine*. It describes the experience of Brown Middle School in falling from high attainment on early KIRIS testing to "in crisis" status, a school where some members admitted arrogance because they were "KERA before KERA." The article includes a memorable and revealing quote from Robin Lipsey, who teaches a fifth- and sixth-grade combination: "The evaluation process has absolutely made me rethink my teaching. It has made us look at evidence—what feels good may not be best for kids. It made us look at student work and student outcomes very differently . . . without accountability, I would not have looked as deeply."

In the final analysis, considered from a long-term perspective, the fundamental questions of accountability—by whom, to whom, for what—are answered with simple phrases for complex goals: education reform must be accountable to the future, teachers accountable to each other and students accountable to themselves. Well-educated students are prepared for productive, responsible and satisfying lives as both lifelong learners and effective team players. They are equipped to face a future in which change will be the constant. Much of the terminology of education reform is vocabulary long associated with undergraduate liberal education—the whole person, values and character building, thinking, reasoning, analysis, problem-solving, lifelong learning. Students need an education that inculcates what Sizer and Wiggins have called "habits of the mind." Students need to "know what to do when they don't know what to do."

The debates over school assessment echo in technical terms similar philosophical debates among liberal educators for decades, weighing the relative merits of measures of inputs, outcomes and the value-added by the process of education. This new emphasis on liberal learning points out a clear need and opportunity in Kentucky for more resourceful and committed involvement of liberal arts teaching faculty from the state's universities and private colleges with school reform, not just because of what they can contribute to refining a better system of student assessment, but what they can learn from the effort.

I have heard many teachers over time, skeptical about new reforms, describe the ways they focus on their classrooms in the belief that this, too, shall pass. To its credit, KIRIS seems to have signaled successfully that KERA is more than a "reform de jour," to borrow Public Agenda's phrase. At least in its formative stage, KIRIS has tended to focus too heavily on the immediate and in the process has alienated educators rather than engaged them constructively in the near term of longer-term reform.

At Knight Foundation, our survey of needs and opportunities growing out of KERA encouraged us to support efforts to help teachers see opportunity rather than additional burden in the reforms and to incorporate mandated change successfully into their own classrooms and styles of teaching. At the outset, we perceived tension between the philosophy of reform calling for student assessment to be a regular, ongoing, integrated component of classroom teaching and learning and the KIRIS system in which assessment in practical terms is a culminating event and a single score. In our experience, early teacher enthusiasm about a specific curricular structure and program of professional development led us to concentrate support in the work of the Los Angeles–based Galef Institute and the Kentucky Collaborative for Teaching and Learning and their efforts to introduce *Different Ways of Knowing* (DWoK) as a reform strategy for elementary schools across the state. I was encouraged to read about two DWoK teachers in Terry Brook's profile of Demi Kidd and Jodie McKnight of Northtop Elementary School in chapter 2.

With DWoK as my primary lens on Kentucky school reform, I have had an opportunity to see and appreciate what authentic assessment can look in a Kentucky when integrated thoroughly into standards-based instruction. DWoK helps teachers confidently blend the study of history and social studies with reading, math, science, and the arts, and use portfolios, open-ended questions, and "kidwatching" routinely in the course of their teaching. In addition, it encourages the use of performance events to punctuate intervals of study. For example, students studying a unit on the environment wrote and performed two songs about recycling on a local television broadcast, produced a puppet show on pollution for a local Earth Day celebration, and wrote letters to the editor with suggestions about how the local community could improve its environment.

My perception of the experience of teachers and schools using DWoK contrasts decidedly with the observations of four school districts reported by the AEL team in chapter 7. Those researchers observed that teachers were linking higher expectations for all students to the KIRIS demand that all students score proficient on the state test at some point, and as a result, "attitudes and beliefs about the new [accountability] system were quite negative, to the extent that they could become impediments to reform." They also note, however, that many of the KERA-mandated changes "may have a positive effect over time if teachers come to see the value of them and implement them for their own sake." I believe that we are seeing evidence over time that DWoK is helping nearly 3,700 Kentucky teachers move from compliance to commitment by nurturing recognition, according to their own values, of what KERA can mean for their teaching and classrooms, and how assessment can be a tool rather than a threat.

It was primary teacher Katherine Futrell in chapter 3 who used the metaphor of the "You Are Here" marker on a park map. Borrowing the image for a different twist, I would suggest that assessment in Kentucky, by KIRIS or whatever name, should and can provide an immensely useful "You Are Here" marker on the complex maze of KERA reforms for students, educators, schools, and communities. It can provide perspective, orientation, and bearing for moving toward a clearly defined, desirable destination. Although the marker may be puzzling and a source of frustration, it is only a representation, a messenger. Reform will never be linear, neat, or soothing. From my perspective, KERA's greatest risk is not in the uncertainties, vulnerabilities, or errors of change but the perils of impatience. Recently, much of that impatience has focused on KIRIS. It is important to remember that authentic assessment and a statewide accountability system based on it is new territory. Rather than the often cited analogy of "flying an airplane while building it," a more apt metaphor might come out of Kentucky's pioneering heritage: "creating the path by walking it."

Success needs time to grow. Less than 10 years into the effort, it seems early yet for confident expressions of either satisfaction or resignation. I view the tensions in Kentucky as evidence of dynamic, not troubled reform. A generation ago, John W. Gardner made an observation that could serve as KERA's motto: "The history of American education is the long, turbulent record of a nation that wasn't afraid to risk failure or trouble or confusion in pursuit of a goal that at first seemed widely impractical: to give every American child a chance to develop to the limit of his ability."

13

The Need to Broaden Accountability in Order to Foster Leadership

MARILYN HOHMANN

While I pledge my best effort to this reaction to the cases in this book, I must warn the reader that I am *not* a dispassionate, external reviewer of the events described in these chapters. My comments will reveal my role as a deeply involved participant, and I hope will reflect my profound commitment to the vision and promise of the Kentucky Education Reform Act.

Most educators and testing experts agree that the purpose of assessment is to improve instruction and thus improve student learning. Appropriate assessment tells teachers whether they are achieving their goals and really powerful assessments inform them about what to change in order to help students learn. Accountability refers to the obligation of teachers to be responsible to their communities for their work and the results of their work. Thus accountability requires teachers to learn from assessments as to whether they are achieving their goals, and to act on that learning by adjusting instruction appropriately.

These meanings became very clear to me about ten years ago when I was a Kentucky high school (herein named Lincoln High School) principal struggling to help teachers improve practice. In an effort to enlist and gain some ownership from a group of resisting athletic coaches, I asked them to reverse the familiar metaphor "Teacher as Coach" and to jot down some successful advice or strategies they used in coaching that could transfer to the academic classroom.

The result was an astonishing collection of simple, yet profound messages that were received by the faculty with such acclaim as to cause me to have it published and widely distributed. One powerful paragraph from "Coach as Teacher" went something like this: "Teach it, have kids perform, adjust; reteach it, have kids perform, adjust; teach it again, have kids perform, adjust, etc. The kids will never get the really important lessons that first time, and you will be able to figure out what you need to change to help them improve each time you watch the results of your previous tries." That coach helped all of us to understand the meaning of assessment and accountability and the relationship between them without ever using the words. Not surprisingly, we came to realize that we had to improve the quality of the work we gave to students if we expected students to improve their work and ultimately their learning. We recognized that self-assessment and self-adjustment were critical attributes in a valid, fair, credible, and useful assessment and accountability process.

That is the road we were on when the Kentucky Education Reform Act became law in 1990. As many reform-minded schools did, we celebrated that extraordinary event as a long overdue mandate to improve education in Kentucky and as affirmation and support of our four year struggle to change our school. The vision of KERA matched our own: that all students could learn more and at higher levels then they were currently learning and that it was our responsibility to ensure that they would.

Our teachers had become committed to that vision through a long process of clarifying our beliefs about teaching and learning, understanding what problems we were trying to solve, and participating in staff development activities that focused on their leadership in designing engaging work for students. We were informed and supported by Phil Schlechty, when as designer and leader of the Gheens Academy he issued an "Invitation to Invention" to schools committed to change. We immersed ourselves in the 9 Common Principles of the Coalition of Essential Schools and struggled to make them visible in our work, thus benefiting from the networking and shared learnings with colleagues from all over the country.

Those efforts were nationally recognized and numerous research studies provided external validation of internal results. The opportunity to work daily in a unique, mutually respectful, and beneficial Professional Development School collaboration with a local university provided us with constant support and challenges for our work while allowing us to contribute to the improvement of teacher preparation. Teacher commitment in a school can only be achieved through a process of developing shared beliefs and vision, leading to clear statements of mission, goals and actions, monitoring and measuring results, and providing the support and incentives such difficult work requires. Unless these fundamental capacities are constantly attended to in a systemic accountability design, the best efforts at reform cannot be sustained.

The Kentucky Instructional Results Information System (KIRIS) is the name given to the high-stakes assessments that drive the reform work in Kentucky. It seems quite a stretch to call it a "system" but the assessments have indeed been the engine of KERA to the degree that many citizens cannot distinguish between the two. The experiences described by Calvert et al. in chapter 6 eloquently and tragically spotlight the ironies resulting from KIRIS driving KERA:

1. Schools that had already begun major reform initiatives were forced to suspend or abandon them in order to teach to the test(s).
2. Schools with large numbers of low SES students who had already instituted reform practices aimed at supporting the social, emotional aspects of learning as well as the academic ones were more likely to fall "in decline" or "in crisis."
3. The leadership of the principal is sometimes seriously compromised by the very process intended to provide support.

For schools like West Middle and Lincoln, it was as if Kentucky had declared zero tolerance for any internal change efforts instituted by schools prior to 1990. Kentucky's mandates of external change, however well-meaning, often clashed with efforts already well advanced. KIRIS did not recognize or reward West Middle School or Lincoln High School for having initiated multiple efforts to change experiences for students by changing the system in fundamental ways. KIRIS could only accept quantitative data reduced to a single number that was legislatively decreed to equal the school's total educational performance. The heroic work of teachers and principals was reduced to that one number and published widely in annual rankings which have been termed "the pedagogy of public humiliation" by Larry Rosenstock, the president of Price family Charitable Fund in San Diego.

Leadership is a critical component in reform. The practices inherent in KIRIS in which the state tests the students, scores the tests, processes the follow-up, including placing "Distinguished Educators" in schools, has resulted in a state system that exerts greater influence, physical presence, and often outright interference with principal leadership than the framers of KERA could possibly have imagined or desired. KIRIS literally by-passes local school district offices whose support and involvement are critical to any long-term, sustained reform. The intent of KERA was to lessen the bureaucratic control of district offices to allow for innovation at school sites with the state providing guidelines. Instead, control over school sites has merely shifted from the district to the state.

And yet, shifting the locus of control to a higher governmental agency does little to improve the lot of teachers. Teacher leadership and commitment are essential to reform. Some positive changes have occurred as described in the AEL study (chapter 7). However, none of the changes relates to reforming the system; rather, they indicate slightly increased understanding of the current system and ways to improve it. That is the fatal flaw. The system we have is a sort and select system we cannot endure any longer. The data described by Kannapel et al. show teacher expectations of student performance rooted in elements of that bell curve–dependent system. Incremental improvement of the current system was not the vision and purpose of KERA. Leaders in our state never articulated the vision of KERA and the need for KERA in ways that could result in general understanding of the incredible leap in student performance and the changes in the systemic rules, roles, and relationships that would be necessary. Teachers were not provided the training and support essential for such change.

Still, there have always been and will always be outstanding teachers, despite changing external conditions. The classroom cases in part II of this book are vivid portraits of such outstanding teachers who are also, I suspect, "standing out" in their schools. By that I mean that these teachers are islands, often so very isolated from each other. Outstanding teachers also stand out in that they are sometimes criticized by other teachers.

In chapter 2, Brooks give us a thoughtful analysis of two teachers trying to build a curriculum together. Reading between the lines, I also suspect that these teachers suffered some barbs from their colleagues along the way. Outstanding teachers who stand out are also sometimes reluctant to share what they are doing with other teachers. Sometimes it is because of the barbs they anticipate or because they just don't want others seeing what they are doing.

To be sure, there are a few heroes among teachers who put in lots of time helping other teachers learn, but there are still way too few opportunities for them to affect others in their building. Principals can set up opportunities, but it's almost as if there is a virus out there that prevents teachers from wanting to learn from each other. Part of the reason may be that teachers get so little honor and recognition for their work. External support such as grants or university involvement can affirm what teachers are about and engender feelings of being valued and honored. Mandates and sanctions, such as those involved with KIRIS, only compound the negative feelings. And as the AEL data in chapter 7 indicate, teachers say that incentives such as those that have been part of KIRIS do not help them do better work.

A critical issue is how to build capacity, how to link the islands of outstanding teachers and create many more opportunities for outstanding teachers to work with other teachers. Fickel's case of the cohesive social studies department (chapter 5) describes one all too rare approach. Veteran math teacher Mary Jo Foster (chapter 4) demonstrates another approach—through participation in a range of substantial professional development and teacher leadership opportunities.

On a regional scale, the Southern Maine Partnership, described in chapter 9, provides many avenues for teacher support within a professional rather than punitive context. This partnership is primarily a grassroots approach, but because it links schools, districts, and higher education, it also provides external recognition and affirmation for teachers. This chapter is a powerful demonstration of how affirmation enhances teacher professionalism. We need to focus on a strategy that puts more teachers in such roles rather than a stance of having teachers fight to stay out of humiliation.

KIRIS relies on a coercive system of external rewards and sanctions to motivate educators to improve. What is needed is a system designed to develop local comprehensive assessment processes, build teacher capacity to use such processes and district-level capacity to support and sustain systemic change. The Southern Maine Partnership's School Quality Review process is rooted in such principles. It dares to trust local educators and communities to implement state accountability policies for student achievement, with a shared responsibility for monitoring and oversight. The School Quality Review design allows educators a way to examine their own practice and learn how looking at student work can inform teachers in designing work of much higher quality—thus resulting in higher levels of student learning. KIRIS reduces assessment to a number that purports to measure the total educational efforts of a school. The School Quality Review uses multiple indicators of student achievement such as Anne Wheelock describes in chapter 10.

In the beginning of this chapter, I described how one of our coaches taught us our first lessons about what we could learn by looking closely at student work (performances). It was, after all, direct evidence of what had happened as a result of the work teachers had given to students. The key to improvement of student work is designing, adjusting, improving the work teachers give to students so that the work is engaging and challenging and yes, relevant, as the curriculum so often cannot be to most youngsters. Phillip Schlechty, president and CEO of the Center for Leadership in School Reform (CLSR) and author of *Inventing Better Schools: An Action Plan for Educational Reform* argues that the way to improve schools is to improve the quality of the work provided to students, which requires that schools be organized around the work of students rather than around the work of teachers. He describes the capacities necessary for systemic reform in *Inventing Better Schools* with the key one being the ability of the entire system to focus on the student and the quality of the work provided to students. Schlechty sees teachers as designers of knowledge work and leaders in causing students to engage in such work.

Linda Shelor, my former colleague at CLSR, offers examples of systemic initiatives to build teacher ownership and commitment while developing leadership capacities. In chapter 8, she describes a continuous improvement model of teacher appraisal based upon reflective practice and systemic commitment to professional growth and development. In a bold departure from typical teacher evaluation processes, the TAIP focuses on student work and appraises not what that teacher is doing, saying, and so on but rather on what the teacher causes students to do.

In chapter 10, Wheelock proposes a hybrid management/professional model of accountability. Reflecting some realities of the conditions of teaching, perhaps that compromise is the best of both worlds. But I have to wonder, in the long run, if we can serve two masters. The Kentucky strategy in large part says teachers will do well only when there are incentives (and disincentives). Again, teachers say that this approach will not work.

One problem with accountability systems is that we seldom focus on how to measure processes. Inputs do not get you to outputs directly. The essence of good teaching is in the analysis of good teaching process. What is going on in the classroom among teachers and students? What tasks and projects do teachers assign? What characterizes this work? What characterizes the conversations among teachers and students? It is only by focusing on teaching processes that we understand how to promote learning.

Teachers need each other to engage in such analysis, to help solve particular problems in specific settings at a given time. This is nitty-gritty work. Teachers need to share all the quirky little things that happen with individual children when using a particular instructional strategy. What is glaringly missing from Kentucky's approach to accountability is what Wheelock calls "the stuff" of professional decision-making: such an approach requires professionals to describe the standards of practice they honor and account for decisions they make and actions they take in relation to those standards and the needs of their students. The setting of learning goals and assignments, selection of materials, balance of didactic instruction, Socratic discussion, and "hands-on" learning, grouping of students, scheduling of classes and use of classroom assessments are the "stuff" of such decisions.

The answers to the many important educational questions facing Kentucky must come from the teaching professionals. Their compliance can be coerced, but their commitment is needed. The Kentucky General Assembly has just recently agreed upon a new direction for KIRIS responding to the furor it has generated, and averting total abandonment of the process. Dare we hope that Kentucky policymakers—as well as policymakers in other states—will accept the wealth of knowledge and experiences of the last eight years and renew the vision of KERA for 2000 and beyond with a much broader accountability process that measures what really matters in reforming schools?

14

Reaching All Students

The Real Challenge of Reform

DICK CORBETT

Students in this country typically experience a "luck-based" curriculum. That is, whether students manage to find paths through their school experiences that are consistently of the highest quality is mostly out of their hands. Reformers and policymakers may tout learner-centered schools, performance-based assessments, and standards-based curricula as the means of enabling all students to succeed. However, beneath the rhetoric, the reality of reform is that improvement tends to occur in pockets—a third-grade team here, a social studies department there, and so on—rather than uniformly throughout an entire school or district. Thus, the particular district in which a student resides, the specific school he or she attends, and the individual teacher with whom he or she is placed still determine the student's chances of receiving an excellent education much more so than reform ideas and actions. From the students' point of view, that is luck, pure and simple, because they can do little to influence the assignment process.

We know, of course, that sociologically speaking, some groups of students are likely to have more luck than others. Oakes, Kozol, and Goodlad have taught us that. However, the uneven distribution of excellent schooling is a relative malady that afflicts all students. This is one of the more poignant and profound messages contained in the previous chapters.

Indeed, one could argue, based on the previous discussions, that reform efforts such as KERA actually increase the importance of student luck, for two reasons. One, when the swirling professional and political winds associated with reform come into contact with the prevailing patterns of teachers' pedagogical assumptions and actions, the interaction likely exacerbates rather than diminishes differences in practice that make a difference to students. Two, reform planning processes create an exclusive cadre of insiders who have opportunities to reflect on reform implementation and implications that are never available to other teachers, which in turn probably engenders wide disparities in capacity-building.

First, reform typically yields a predictably unpredictable response among teachers. That is, some innovative teachers use reform as justification for continuing their experimentation; other like-minded teachers become tentative and hesitant, unsure whether their explorations would be rewarded or punished. Similarly, a portion of the more traditional teachers may feel encouraged to alter how they work, reflecting a willingness to venture into somewhat uncharted territory, especially with the provision of professional development. Others, however, jaded by waves of initiatives, apparently strengthen their resolve to remain impervious to the perceived whims of politicians, administrators, and academics.

Such conjectures about teachers' reactions to KERA and the subsequent effects on their practice seem warranted, based on the evidence in the previous chapters. For example, McGee convincingly portrays the role that a teacher's individual decision-making capacity, willingness to stick with sound practice in the face of contradictory pressures, and ability to maintain a belief system that supports effective practice played in creating a classroom in which all children can learn. One wonders what was going on in the other classrooms if someone as dedicated to the profession as Katherine experienced such agony in constructing a path through a reform's maze of intentions. Did all teachers in her school manage to adopt this stance? Or, had they fallen prey to more narrow "test-prep" approaches? Or, did they simply resist any intrusion into their practice?

One could raise similar concerns about instructional unevenness with respect to the other case examples: Jones and Whitford's penetrating look at a math teacher's considered response to reform; Brooks' delightful depiction of the give and take between a pair of teachers; Fickel's cogent description of a high school department; Calvert et al.'s insightful portrayal of a principal's point of view; and the highly useful AEL cross-site presentation. In each case, the authors laid out how KERA alternately strengthened educators' resolve to engage in best practice, made them worry about how students and their schools would fare under a somewhat whimsical accountability system, and forced them to consider politically smart but educationally foolhardy actions. It is not far-fetched to assume that such uncertainty and pressure certainly could increase, rather than decrease, the professional distance between particular individuals, groups, and schools and those in proximity to them.

Second, the chapters' vivid glimpses into school life under the umbrella of reform highlighted an additional factor that could magnify classroom, school, and district differences in quality. Sprinkled throughout the cases are references to teachers who participated in advisory, planning, and other KERA leadership capacities. These opportunities enabled participants to consider what reform meant to them, to see how reform goals fit with their own professional purposes, to learn about alternative strategies to achieve those purposes and goals, and to judge the ultimate merits of KERA itself. They could fuss, cuss, and discuss at length the implications of the effort. This reflective process engendered understanding and commitment—or at least an informed accommodation to the inevitable.

Unfortunately, most educators do not have access to those opportunities. For them, reform becomes an informally acquired knowledge base, filled with rumor, hearsay, and innuendo. They do not wait unthinkingly for all the blue ribbon panels, leadership teams, and core planning groups to announce a direction before they act, nor do they blindly accept the consequences of others' deliberations to guide those actions. In other words, as the chapters show, reform creates new sets of insiders and outsiders, layering an additional aggregate of attitudes, beliefs, and knowledge on top of those that have accumulated collectively in peoples' work lives through the years. Brouillette has aptly demonstrated this process in one school district in *The Geology of School Reform* (1997) and the metaphor is applicable here as well.

So, what is striking in the chapters is not that reform can work or that reform can create contradictory pressures among those who earnestly try to enact it in their classrooms, schools, and districts. No. What is striking is that reform, or at least KERA, remains ineffective in reducing the luck factor in children's education, despite the massive amounts of time, money, and thought that went into its design.

That is to say, there is no doubt that the reform has left behind some pockets of high caliber instruction. I want my child in Mary Jo's, Katherine's, Demi's, and Jodie's classrooms; I want my child to attend West Middle School; and I want my child to study history in the social studies department. However, the glass is also half-empty. As long as it matters where my child is taught, then luck operates as a considerable influence on the quality of my child's education. Unfortunately, it is all too likely that KERA has allowed the traditional unevenness across classrooms to endure.

Of course, this is more an inference from the stories about KERA not told in this book than those that appear. But, combining what has been learned about reform elsewhere with the descriptions of the agonizing persistence of the teachers in the case chapters, a logical question to ask is: Are these journeys typical of most teachers?

It may well be that they are; and if so, that is grand. Given the differences in access to professional development, reform planning, and experience among the teachers in the buildings, however, the probability is that important differences across classrooms in these buildings and districts still exist.

And, that is my point. If all children are to succeed, then every single child has to have unfettered access to high-quality instruction. Improved mean scores are no consolation in this matter; I do not feel better that more students are graduating, attending, or even liking school more than they did before. You cannot predict the experience of a particular individual from group averages. For reform to be successful, every child has to be successful.

So, what I'm really trying to do is to offer a caution, or, perhaps, a challenge. If the rhetoric of reform is all children, then the standard by which we judge reform's success should also include all children. And the concern of practitioners and policymakers alike should become how to replicate the stories of a few teachers so that they in fact become the stories of all teachers.

Fortunately, the Wheelock, Ruff et al., and Shelor chapters offer a way for the often-rhetorical slogan of "success for all" to become a reality. Equally fortunately, they do not leave the solution to "market forces," as would the misguided advocates of school choice. That recommendation merely shifts luck to the aggressive. Instead, the common ingredient in these three very thoughtful chapters is an emphasis on reflection—the opportunity for all education stakeholders to examine their actions, evaluate the results, devise new strategies, and try them out, which sets in motion another round of reflection. This cyclical pattern, according to Senge, is the heart of an effectively evolving organization.

The above chapters do an excellent job of providing illustrations of how this reflection process can become inclusive rather than exclusive. Shelor describes the importance of having "invention teams" at the district and school levels within a system. This promotes both "big picture" and idiosyncratic thinking, both of which are necessary to enabling important ideas to become accepted within the context of peoples' daily work lives. Ruff et al. also emphasize the critical significance of local discussions, especially with respect to creating interpretations of reform that are setting-relevant. In addition, the authors provide wonderful illustrations of how critiques across sites can greatly improve the efficacy of reform-related actions. Wheelock provides a compelling justification for such processes, insightfully noting that accountability takes on much greater meaning when it becomes a professional rather than a managerial activity.

It is such processes that large-scale reform endeavors such as KERA must engender if they are to move beyond the all too familiar "pockets of success" pattern. Indeed, Fullan has long argued that reform occurs most abundantly when it becomes meaningful to educators. The illustrations in this book of local reflection on matters of accountability, assessment, curriculum, and instruction are ideal examples of what meaning-making looks and sounds like in practice.

It is this reflection that the system of rewards associated with reform should support. If state-level policymakers derive no message other than this from the authors then the writing effort will have been successful. The case chapter authors make clear that establishing sanctions and rewards associated with test score results do little to motivate educators; in fact, such incentives seemed to hobble implementation more than it helped. Holding people accountable in ways that contradict best practice and for results they have had little hand in defining simply does not make sense.

Instead, given what the authors have asserted as the core of being an effective professional, KERA in its subsequent iterations should promote reflection focused on the world class standards the state has deemed important for all students to achieve. This ultimate goal, success for all, is obtainable only if all districts, schools, and classrooms have in them educators who truly know about and believe in effective practice. That condition appears to be best created through continuous critique involving the whole school community. The consequence, one hopes, will be the disappearance of the luck factor in children's education.

Part V

Summary and Conclusions

15

The Next Generation of School Accountability

KEN JONES AND BETTY LOU WHITFORD

In our opening chapter, we pointed out how high-stakes accountability at the state level undermines the use of performance assessment. Kentucky's system of accountability, with its significant rewards and sanctions for teachers and administrators, has led to a state system of more traditional assessment, in large part because it can be scored more reliably for high stakes than can performance assessment formats. Thus, the perceived need for state standardization, measurement, and enforcement has superseded the call for greater diversity, authenticity, and local empowerment.

The 1998 legislative session in Kentucky went decisively further down this path of affirming a test-based high-stakes accountability system at the expense of a performance-based assessment system. KIRIS was officially terminated in favor of a new testing system, the Commonwealth Accountability Testing System (CATS). The statutory changes for the new system include:

- Deleting the requirement that the state test has to be "primarily performance-based," as was stipulated in KERA;
- Requiring the use of a norm-referenced test to provide national comparisons;
- Allowing the state board to decide whether or not to use open response questions;
- Scaling back the writing portfolio;
- Providing a longitudinal comparison of test results for the same students;
- Continuing the school accountability index mechanism;
- Retaining a system of rewards and sanctions;

- Creating a system of school audits to determine improvement needs for low-performing schools.

In the view of many KERA advocates, these changes continue a devolution of the performance-based curriculum vision. An important question is now whether there is a reasonable alternative that can satisfy the need for responsible public oversight of schooling while also protecting and insisting on the vision of performance-based classrooms and nurturing teacher commitment toward that vision.

This chapter takes the hopeful view that there is indeed a better way to design the system. The process of developing a "next generation" model of accountability entails taking an honest look at the effects of present policies, a clarification of vision and assumptions, and a collaborative rather than a commanding state posture.

Some Good News

It is important to acknowledge that KIRIS has had some very good effects. As noted by Love in chapter 12, Kentucky educational conversations are focused on important questions about direction and implementation, not on whether school improvement is even necessary. While the debate can be fierce, at least the topics of assessment, accountability, teacher professional development, and local decision-making are front and center in the public forum. Moreover, the significant increase in tax-based funding for schools that accompanied the passage of KERA has been sustained, something that cannot be said of many other states. The focus on and commitment to educational improvement in Kentucky are surely due in part to the high profile given to the assessment and accountability system.

Moreover, the state goals and standards that formed the foundation for KIRIS, as well as the professional development that has become available because of KIRIS, have served to validate, legitimize, and support a high-quality vision for teaching and learning, especially among those teachers who haven't needed to be convinced. The teachers portrayed in this book affirm that they have found support for their work in creating performance-based classrooms. Pockets of excellence have always existed in our schools and the statewide emphasis on writing, thinking, and applying knowledge has undoubtedly generated more and bigger pockets. The social studies department depicted by Fickel in chapter 5 is only one such example where critical masses of committed teachers are moving together to improve the work they provide to students.

Perhaps the most important positive effect of the KIRIS journey has been the increasing recognition that the complexity of schools, teaching, and learning cannot be easily addressed by test-based accountability schemes. Nor, for that matter, can human learning and motivation be easily manipulated through external "incentives." There simply is no quick-fix method of reversing existing beliefs and structures founded on the factory model of schooling. We may not yet have agreed upon a long-term strategy, but we can do a lot better job of "admiring the problem," as many are fond of saying. With respect to Kentucky's test-based high-stakes accountability system, the problem is that the intended cure has created a new illness.

The New Illness

As illustrated in the cases, the KIRIS "cure" for raising standards has proven to be naïve and simplistic. In fact, the ill effects of this approach, though only beginning to emerge, indicate that the cure may be creating a new illness as troublesome as the original problem. When good teachers complain that they are limited by a mandated curriculum and test, when thoughtful internal school improvement efforts are undermined by state takeovers, when the ends of schooling are reduced to the pursuit of test scores, something has gone terribly amiss.

It is too easy to simply blame "the state," as many are prone to do. Public opinion clearly favors holding schools accountable. And it may be that the most easily understood kind of school accountability is a system that mirrors what adults experienced in schools themselves: a grading system that uses tests to get numbers so that students can be "motivated," sorted, and classified. It is ironic that, in order to gain public approval, politicians have resorted to the very factory model of accountability that they have eschewed in terms of curricular vision. That is, policymakers are doing to schools the very thing that they say schools should *not* do to students. Therein lies the problem.

KIRIS and now CATS place the state squarely in the roles of judge, jury, and enforcer. Despite claims of increased local empowerment through school-based decision-making councils, the control of the state over education has grown, not lessened. The bureaucratic mechanism described so well by Anne Wheelock in chapter 10 has grown with KIRIS, as any principal or central office administrator in Kentucky will confirm. In fact, one of the lessons to learn from the Kentucky experience is that current statewide test-based accountability systems can be even more controlling than the old-style input-based accreditation schemes that preceded it.

The 1998 legislative session produced changes, yet the new accountability system will continue to work under the assumption that the quest for higher test scores can be achieved by using rewards and sanctions to get teachers to try harder. There seems to be the idea that if we can only measure the subject properly that the symptoms of illness will go away. However, as the first chapter explains and the cases document, the issues are far more complex than measurement alone.

The system designed to assure that schools were held accountable to a curricular vision of higher standards is killing the very vision it was meant to protect.

The term "higher standards" has come to mean higher test scores on a more and more conventional test, not more performance-based instruction and assessment.

Moreover, the state now essentially dictates *what* will be taught. Although state officials take great care not to officially call the *Core Content* or the regulatory *Program of Studies* a state curriculum, it is abundantly clear that these documents have become the basis for the rush in every district to "align curriculum." The bulk of teacher professional development time these days is spent making sure that schools are covering the prescribed state content. Moreover, that content is extensive enough to virtually dictate the entire school curriculum, despite disclaimers from the state that it is only meant to be "core." The state commissioner of education himself acknowledged in a meeting with university faculty that while we don't call it a state curriculum, "if it looks like a duck, and it walks like a duck, and it talks like a duck, it's a duck."

The state also greatly influences *how* the subject matter will be taught. The large amount of content specified by the state not only usurps the prerogative given in KERA to local school councils to determine curriculum, it also leads to instructional practices that further contradict the "performance-based" vision. This is because the amount of material required gives rise to a "coverage" mentality where breadth is favored over depth and direct instruction is the most expeditious means of delivery. In addition, as the resource teacher noted in the first chapter, open response questions have assumed such an emphasis that students lose interest in classroom work. Even with writing, which from all indications has improved at least in quantity around the state, students often report deadening repetition. Other parts of the teaching repertoire tend to be de-emphasized. When what "counts" is high-stakes, anything that doesn't "count" is marginalized.

Thus, a de facto state curriculum has emerged from the high stakes associated with the state test. As the pressure for coverage continues and the state test becomes less performance-based, how likely is it that teachers will continue to invest the time in the kinds of authentic classroom activities described in the classroom cases in this book?

The problem with the system is that it assumes one size fits all. Standardization and conformity are becoming the rule rather than diversity and individualization. The question the state is actually pursuing is not just whether all students can learn at high levels, but whether all students can master a particular body of content to a certain level of proficiency and score well on an external test given in a particular format on a given day. As the findings of Kannapel et al. in chapter 7 suggest, teachers in Kentucky have a lot more trouble believing that the latter expectation is realistic. Or equitable. KIRIS has lacked credibility with the very people who are meant to implement it. Since the assumptions have not changed, the same may be expected of CATS.

An equitable system of assessment and accountability should promote the kinds of opportunities to learn that allow students to use their individual learning styles, cultural backgrounds, expressive strengths, and intelligence profiles to demonstrate what they know or can do. Such individual differences cannot be very well accommodated from a large-scale testing perspective using multiple-choice or even open-response questions. This is why a range of local assessment strategies must be included in any fair accountability system.

Not only has the state of Kentucky assumed a monopoly in deciding for what and by what means schools shall be held accountable, it has raised the stakes for teachers by threatening public humiliation and even termination if student test scores do not improve at a predetermined rate. Creating this quota system and climate of fear has had exactly the classic repercussion predicted by Deming: goal displacement. It should come as no surprise that teachers and administrators zero in so tightly to the test. The test has become the end, not the means.

Ultimately, what is at stake in this accountability system is the decision-making role of those closest to the students: the local teachers, administrators, and parents. While the theory of the KIRIS/CATS approach is that local professionals and communities shall decide the "how" of raising achievement, the reality is that those cards are stacked by a state system of assessment that relies upon specific content and format. The role of the teacher is becoming more like that of a company technician than that of a professional who makes informed decisions depending upon the uncertain variables of context. As poignantly portrayed by the principal in the opening chapter, this change has had a negative impact on teacher morale. In his words, "The work is a lot heavier when it is someone else's work." The Kentucky accountability system not only ignores the need to cultivate teacher commitment, it erodes the base of teacher professionalism.

The new illness wrought by the KIRIS and CATS cure can be viewed as an abrogation of the democratic and intellectual values that have accompanied the current wave of educational reform. Much of the rhetoric of this reform movement portrays student-centered classrooms where students are empowered with choices and responsibilities, teachers facilitate open inquiry, and depth of understanding and ability to apply knowledge in meaningful contexts is of foremost importance. But an accountability system that undermines performance-based assessment and instruction, that narrows local concerns to the prerequisites of external test-taking, and that places teachers, administrators, parents, and students in the role of followers, belies this vision. The existing accountability system has eaten away the life of the original vision from within.

Teacher Commitments

As a starting place to address the illness just described, let us look at the vision for classroom work that KERA was meant to promote. What teacher commitment are we looking for? The cases in this book provide real examples for at least four kinds of teacher commitment that can give us perspective for developing an accountability system that can rekindle the KERA vision: commitment to certain goals and beliefs about learning; commitment to continuous improvement for everyone in the learning community; commitment to respectful relationships; and commitment to authentic and engaging work for students.

Goals and Beliefs about Learning

Above all, we want teachers to believe and act from the premise that all students can learn at high levels. As Kannapel et al. explain, this is not the same thing as expecting all students to test well on a state test. And, as Shelor argues in chapter 8, this belief must be accompanied by an approach where the teacher modifies the work to fit the student, without lowering standards, not vice versa. The factory model of sorting and selecting students is simply no longer acceptable. It is a matter of personal equity as well as social practicality.

Not only is this an issue about high expectations for all students, it is also about embracing learning targets that are essential and apt. The six KERA Learning Goals for students, listed in chapter 1, fit this bill nicely. Yet it is important to note that KIRIS deliberately does not address Goals 3 and 4, the personal and social goals for self-sufficiency and team membership. It is also arguable how well it addresses Goal 6, which is related to the integration of learning, since the test is subject specific and focuses on content snapshots. Thus, the KERA vision actually looks for teacher commitment that goes beyond the bounds of KIRIS.

The cases in this book give clear examples of teachers who are committed to such learning goals for all students, as a matter of belief, not mandate. Jodie McKnight and Demi Kidd have developed their own internal compasses that are tuned to these targets, especially the personal and social ones, which they see as moral issues. Katherine Futrell is fiercely committed to the seven Kentucky-defined attributes of the primary classroom, plus an eighth one, student empowerment, because she sees that such a learning environment helps students learn and to be good citizens. Mary Jo Foster is convinced that all of her students can and must learn mathematics at a high level because they will need it to be successful in life. The social studies department at Wilson County High School, despite differences in pedagogical styles, collectively have a strong desire to produce "independent learners who are reflective, critical thinkers who engage in reflection upon the social world in which they live." The West Middle School faculty makes a total staff commitment to making sure their students can read.

Continuous Improvement

The concept of continuous improvement is part of the KERA fabric, especially within the primary program. One might argue that it is also an intention of the school accountability system insofar as schools are expected to show test score improvements from baseline to threshold, over and over again. Yet the arbitrary nature of the threshold expectations and the comparison of different student cohorts create a less than continuous structure. What is needed is teacher commitment to the continuous improvement of each student in light of high standards as well as to the continuous improvement of their own teaching repertoire.

The cases illustrate how this looks in practice. Certainly Katherine, through her workshop approach and comprehensive set of assessment strategies, provides the kinds of opportunities to learn that can both cultivate and measure student progress. The criticism she levels at the state expectation that all students should be expected to reach proficiency on the state test is because she sees this as absolutism on the part of the state. It is not that she doesn't have high expectations for each student to show improvement. Rather, she is looking to move each student along from wherever they are on the standards continuum without prescribing what the gain has to be by a certain date or holding the bar in the same place at the same time for all students. She is committed to developmentally appropriate instruction, not having identical expectations for every student.

Mary Jo also looks for and allows her students to demonstrate continuous improvement when she stresses the revision of portfolio entries and when she gives students the opportunity to do work over again. "If a kid doesn't learn it today or tomorrow, all right, he learns it next week. That's wonderful!" The point is that her assessment is primarily formative. The learning cycle is ongoing and is not determined by the calendar date when her tests are set. Likewise, Mary Jo uses the data from the state test each year as an important, but not the only, source of information to help herself and her colleagues evaluate their own mathematics program.

As for teachers' commitment to their own continuous improvement, it is almost an adage of school reform that professional development is critical to change. Yet, too often, what occurs in the name of professional development is mandated training or formulaic approaches that give teachers a program to *adopt* rather than *adapt*. Much of this fails to model the vision of teaching and learning that the KERA vision espouses for the classroom. Indeed, much of it is geared towards "doing someone else's work."

What does it look like when teachers are committed to their own learning and are not simply passive recipients of state, district, or school programs? It looks like Mary Jo spending a lot of her time in summer institutes or local networks. Or Katherine doing in-depth and ongoing work with the Louisville Writing Project. Or Jodi and Demi learning from each other and serving as mentors for the student teachers who come their way through their school's Professional Development School affiliation with the local university. Or West Middle School's faculty learning from the UPS staff that their students can do more than they have been asking them to do. Or even the social studies staff at Wilson going out to dinner together. Too often in Kentucky professional development is defined as the four days required by the state. Teachers who are committed to their own continuous improvement will continue to find other venues as well. What is needed is many more opportunities for all teachers to be engaged in such substantive work and the school and district leadership to promote and support it.

Respectful Relationships

One of the striking characteristics of the teachers in this book is their commitment to establishing respectful relationships between themselves and their students, themselves and their fellow teachers, and among their students. As a whole, this might be seen as the nurturing of a learning community for all. While this concern may not be explicitly referred to in KERA documents, it comprises the very heart of the teaching-learning experience. Perhaps it goes too often without saying, but students learn best from people they care about and who care about them. Good relationships are not just about maintaining order and discipline in the classroom. They are essential to teaching and learning.

Look at how the teachers in this book work at developing respectful relationships. Jodie and Demi use the "throw-up incident" and the Golden Rule to instill self-awareness in students. Katherine fosters cooperative group discourse. Mary Jo openly expresses affection for her students and makes them laugh even as she maintains a firm grip on noise levels and work expectations. The social studies teachers practice what they preach as they work together to figure out how "their individuality strengthens and expands their collective work with students."

The comments of the principal at West stress how critical she felt it was that she help teachers establish a new school climate. "We needed to change our philosophy toward our students and toward each other. If we didn't believe in the promise of their future, how could they? If we didn't treat them with respect and dignity, why would they exhibit any?" Later in the year, after the science exhibitions where students demonstrated Newton's laws by describing the path of marbles down roller coasters they had designed, she remarks: "As I moved from group to group, nearly all students looked at me instead of hanging their heads, discussed their projects with interest, and attempted to answer my questions correctly. What struck me was how well they understood and valued their learning and how eager and proud they were to share it." Local leadership that recognizes and nurtures respectful relationships is critical to fostering teacher—and student—commitment.

Authentic and Engaging Tasks

Authentic tasks are those requiring substantial subject-matter understanding and thinking skills and having applicability or relevance to the real world. They take time to do well, more time than a two-page daily spread in a textbook allows. So they call for ingenuity on the part of the teacher and significant time and energy in planning, management, and evaluation. One big reason to do this is that such tasks are intended to be engaging for students. It is a good bet that engaged learners learn better.

It is easy to see what authenticity can mean in the classroom from the cases in this book. Mary Jo's balloon investigation provides an entry to study linear functions. She tries to "read" her students so that she can shift gears when attention wanes. Katherine's hands-on science and math activities, workshops, and thematic units allow students to explore their own interesting ideas. Jodie and Demi include in their repertoire the DWoK integrated, multimodality units in order to improve access and equity for learners. The high school social studies teachers bring in guest speakers, develop simulations, and even created a new course to address critical thinking. West Middle School obtains a grant so that students can explore careers, visit the university, work with employees of UPS, and have lunch with community members.

These four kinds of commitment—to certain goals and beliefs, continuous improvement, respectful relationships, and authentic and engaging tasks—ultimately focus on student needs. The task for designers of state accountability systems is how to create structures that honor and grow such commitments. It is time to move beyond compliance. As an instructional supervisor recently remarked, "We've gotten everyone's attention now and they are mostly doing what we say to do. But that is the low fruit and we have to go beyond that if we want to continue to show improvement."

Propositions for the Next Generation of School Accountability

When KERA was first being formulated, a great deal of thought and public discussion focused on what we should expect students to know and be able to do. This was a necessary first step in establishing the goals for a statewide assessment system. Never, however, was the following question similarly opened for discussion: *To whom, for what, and by what means should schools be held accountable?* It was accepted that schools should be held accountable by the state for the results of student testing. We know, however, that parents and communities have expectations about schools that are not reflected in test scores, such as order and safety, a caring atmosphere, effective communication, engaging and rigorous lessons, and equitable opportunities for students to learn. In order to establish a new system of accountability, these issues must be raised and assumptions regarding them made explicit.

The following five propositions about school accountability should be part of a new and recurring public discussion about what constitutes a successful school, and how we might construct a fair and comprehensive system to make judgments about individual schools, continuing to refine it over time.

1. *Schools should be primarily accountable to students, parents, and local communities, in cooperation with the state.* Without question, the state has an important role and responsibility in monitoring the quality of schools. But where is the balance between that responsibility and school constituents' rights for a school that is responsive to their interests and concerns? The constituents of the school are many, but students, parents, and local communities are primary. The role of the state should be a collaborative one, providing leadership and support rather than demanding compliance. Only in cases of educational malpractice, determined on the basis of multiple indicators, should the state move into an enforcement role. Coercive tactics from the state such as rewards and sanctions are inappropriate and counterproductive.

2. *The purposes of schools and the qualities of a successful school are multiple.* Therefore, a system of school accountability must look at more than test scores. In fact, as the saying goes, not everything that counts can be counted, so an information system for school accountability must include qualitative as well as quantitative data. Since the work of schools tends to be bound in local contexts, embedded in uncertainties, and subject to the dynamic complexities of human interactions, qualitative information must include data that are local in nature and high resolution in detail. Large-scale external tests can be valuable indicators, but they are far from sufficient. A quantitative accountability index that purports to tell the whole story about school success ignores many of the realities of schooling that matter.

3. *The purpose of a school accountability system should be to make public and support local commitment and continuous improvement according to agreed upon goals and standards and locally determined needs.* The KERA Learning Goals for students, being consensually derived and well established, can serve as an important core, but issues of school climate, professional practice, and opportunities to learn should be addressed by localities as well. Local districts and schools should engage in an ongoing planning and self-evaluation process based on these goals, standards, and needs. The state should monitor the quality of the local self-evaluation process, provide training and support, and provide valid and reliable data for local decision-making.

4. *Local districts and schools should be responsible for developing and implementing student assessment systems that include performance assessments of authentic work in formats such as exhibitions, projects, and portfolios.* This would help to restore the KERA curriculum vision and provide the basis for an individualized "value added" system that is capable

of charting individual student progress over time. Routine local use of performance assessment would also allow the state to test less, perhaps following Maine's lead in focusing on reading, writing, and mathematics for all, but using matrix sampling for other subject areas.

5. *The democratic and intellectual values that we hold for students should be reflected in the way schools hold themselves accountable.* For example, just as we want students to perceive and solve problems by making informed decisions in their own settings, so too must we allow schools the power to respond to their own conditions by making choices that are not circumscribed by the prerequisites of the state. This means that schools must be given the choice and encouragement to go beyond the norm, to reconceptualize the ends as well as the means of quality schooling. They should not be "motivated," sorted, and classified. Nor should their curriculum be dictated by the state. Standards must not lead to standardization.

Components for the Next Generation of School Accountability

Operationalizing a new school accountability system in Kentucky will not be easy, partly because few educators or policymakers appear willing to conceive of school accountability outside of the present index and rewards and sanctions. In the testimony and debates in the 1998 session of the legislature, the choice about accountability was to continue the existing approach with modifications or to have no state-directed accountability at all. There was no public consideration of alternative models.

Other models do exist. The alternatives described in this book are only examples. Toronto has developed an approach that honors local self-evaluation. Victoria, Australia, has developed a system based on local school goal-setting and data collection accompanied by a quality school review. European countries are exploring alternative models. It seems to be an especially American fixation to think that tests can tell the whole tale about school success.

Several existing structures in Kentucky suggest themselves as apt components for a new model: school-based decision-making (SBDM) councils, the consolidated planning mechanism, portfolios, locally designed performance standards, and the newly required school report cards and scholastic audits.

The SBDM councils created by KERA consist of the principal, teachers, and parents. Committees of the council may also include students, community members, classified employees or other interested parties. This governance body is legally charged with several responsibilities, one of which is to develop curriculum. It is this prerogative that has been pre-empted by the high-stakes testing system. If the rewards and sanctions were removed and the state adopted a more collaborative role, councils would be enabled to do the work they were charged to do: decide what curriculum fits the needs of their particular students.

The council could also work in collaboration with the district to establish improvement goals for which they would be held accountable. In fact, this already takes place in the form of the consolidated planning process, which includes a cycle of needs assessment (which requires local survey information from parents, teachers, and other stakeholders), action planning, resource allocation, and evaluation. As it currently exists, with high-stakes testing, school and district plans invariably target improvements in the KIRIS scores as the sole or primary goals. However, by broadening the parameters of accountability to include qualitative concerns related to school climate, local needs, professional practice, and opportunities to learn, this same process could be used to target and document progress on these essential elements of school improvement.

Collecting qualitative data for the planning and self-evaluation process could be well facilitated through assembling portfolios. All schools in Kentucky have considerable experience with student portfolios since writing and math portfolios have been mandated by the state. An ongoing problem with these portfolios has been scoring them with reliability for use in the accountability index. If portfolios were used as a qualitative data source instead, as a window into the curriculum and instruction provided to students rather than as a measure of individual student achievement, this problem would be eliminated. In addition, more and more schools are using teacher portfolios as a tool to show professional development or facilitate teacher evaluation. Using portfolios to document school improvement would not be a great stretch in Kentucky. It might even provide a "friendlier" purpose for portfolios that teachers and parents alike could more readily support.

In order for schools to show "value added" in terms of student performance, valid, fair, and reliable assessments at the school and classroom levels are needed. Clearly this would create a significant need for professional development since many teachers are not prepared to develop or use quality assessments in the classroom. But it also means considerable work on the part of districts to establish performance standards with indicators and benchmarks that can be used to measure student progress. While this would take leadership from state and district offices and time to put into place, it is feasible. Models exist already, for example, in the state portfolios, the New Standards Project, and a host of performance-based curriculum projects springing up around the country. Jefferson County, the urban district that encompasses Louisville, has already begun this work in a systematic way.

The school report card is a new requirement from the state, part of the changes made during the 1998 legislative session. It calls for schools to report publicly on indicators such as academic achievement, including the CATS results, attendance, retention, drop-out rates, student transition to adult life, and school learning environment, including measures of parent engagement. Other indicators could be included as a form of local accountability.

A scholastic audit was also included in the 1998 legislation. As it now exists, it will consist of an external team visiting a school that has failed to meet its projected test scores for the purpose of establishing improvement needs. The team will be composed of a teacher, administrator, parent, state designated "highly skilled certified educator," and university faculty member. If the high stakes were removed, such a visitation could be adapted to work in conjunction with local self-evaluation as a form of collegial feedback rather than a state sanction. It might look like the School Quality Review used in southern Maine that is described in chapter 9.

Together, these components that are already more or less in existence in Kentucky could create the foundation for a new generation of accountability, where the state truly adopts a posture of service, also a part of the KERA vision, rather than one of regulation and enforcement. The multiple measures used in such a system would provide the public with much more information on which to base judgments about its schools. This would not be a diminishing of accountability. In fact, schools would be accountable for more than they are in the existing system. It means trading in a low-resolution, high-stakes system for a high-resolution, collaborative one.

What's Best for Kids?

All of this talk about what adults should be doing begs the question about what is best for students. All sides of the school reform debate vouch for the fact that they are trying to do what's best for kids. Some reformers frame the discussion in terms of jobs, others in terms of international marketplace competition, others in terms of the democratic ideals of life, liberty, and the pursuit of happiness.

We see the issue as an immediate one. Too many classrooms are boring, with students asked to do the bidding of adults because someone else believes it will be good for them. Students, like adults, have very real needs for empowerment, choice, caring, relevancy, social contact, and fun. The reason we see a need to redefine the nature of how we hold schools accountable is twofold: we need to release students from the tyranny of test-taking and overly defined curriculum mandates and we need to promote classroom interactions that are more engaging and more centered on the needs of the students rather than the demands of the state.

In this age of information, when we are concerned about instilling the kind of lifelong learning orientation that we believe our children will need, it is contradictory of us to hold schools accountable for student mastery of a statewide curriculum with a high-stakes test. Instead, we should be looking for evidence that teachers are finding ways to engage students in meaningful intellectual work of all ilks, whether it be prescribed by the state or not, regardless of whether the learning and expressive modality is electronic, visual, or centered on writing short essays.

We live in a rapidly changing postmodern world that requires the capability of making quick local adjustments. The world of business knows this. And yet in education, we embrace large-scale solution strategies such as statewide testing that make local flexibility more and more difficult. For some reason, we place our trust in big arenas, as if scale confers effectiveness. Indeed, "scaling up" is considered desirable by many reformers. In a country and world of such immense diversity, it is troubling that authorities look into the future and predict that all students will need the same things. National standards proliferate and a national test develops momentum. And so it goes, on and on toward greater and greater centralization.

In the midst of this trend, we offer a countervailing plea for more local empowerment. Think globally, but act locally. The mission is to educate, support, and lead the local educators, and not undermine their professionalism. Undermining the professional in the classroom is bound to sap the energy and creativity of the teacher-learner relationship. And that cannot be what's best for our kids. What is best for kids, we believe, is a teacher corps that is knowledgeable, confident, and committed, not just one that is forced to comply with state mandates.

Moving from Kentucky's existing bureaucratic model of test-based high-stakes accountability to the model we suggest or one like Anne Wheelock's hybrid model, Southern Maine's Learner Centered Accountability model, or CLSR's Teacher Appraisal Invention Process will take a change in perspective on the part of state policymakers and other reformers. It will take a more complex understanding of the nature of schooling, child development, and the process of teaching and learning, not just disembodied "results." Political leaders must rely upon and promote teachers as professionals and seek to build the kind of teacher commitment that will serve the long-term goals of KERA and other similar state reforms.

Educational reform has come to be criticized for its pendulum swings, from one polar extreme to another. With school accountability, we have swung from a previous overconcern with inputs to the present overconcern with outcomes. The time has come to develop a next generation of school accountability, one that takes into account both types of concerns in a way that inspires the lasting commitment of adults to make the vision of authentic, engaging, and democratic classrooms a reality. This is what would be best for kids.

About the Authors

Lola Aagaard is a Staff Associate with the Appalachia Educational Laboratory (AEL), Charleston, West Virginia. She is a researcher for AEL's study of Kentucky school reform, which has been underway in four rural districts since 1991 and is ongoing through 2000. Her Ph.D. from the University of Oklahoma is in education with an emphasis in research methods and statistics.

Terry I. Brooks is currently principal of Anchorage School in Anchorage, Ky. He has worked as a teacher, principal, deputy superintendent, education consultant, and executive director of the Jefferson County Public Schools/Gheens Academy over the course of his 27-year career in public education. He completed his doctorate at the University of Louisville in 1995.

Jan Calvert has been an educator for over 25 years in middle school, high school, and alternative school programs. In 1986–87, she was principal of Maryhurst School, which was recognized as one of three schools in Kentucky for the School of Excellence Award from the U.S. Department of Education. In 1996, she was principal of Williams Middle School, one of five demonstration sites for a middle-level School-to-Work program funded by the US. Department of Education. This program also received the Wall Street Journal Employee Management Association Foundation Award. Jan is currently principal at Farnsley Middle School in Louisville, where she strives to minister to students, staff, and parents. She completed her doctorate in Educational Administration at the University of Louisville in 1996 writing a dissertation entitled, "The Principal as Minister: The Prophetic and Pastoral Roles of the Principalship."

Pam Coe is a Research & Development Specialist for the Appalachia Educational Laboratory (AEL), Charleston, West Virginia. She is principal investigator and co-director of AEL's study of Kentucky school reform, a study that has been underway in four rural districts since 1991 and is ongoing through 2000. She has an M.A. in anthropology from Columbia University and a Ph.D. in education, with an emphasis on ethnography of education, from Michigan State University. A previous vocation was community development, primarily with American Indians.

H. Dickson Corbett (Dick) is an independent educational researcher. He spends his time studying school reform, with a particular emphasis on interviewing students (K–12) about their experiences in such situations. He also conducts evaluations of innovative programs and practices. Currently his work includes examining teachers' assumptions about urban students as learners and the effects of those assumptions on instruction and student performance; following a cohort of urban middle schoolers through three years of a major city's reform efforts; studying the infusion of arts instruction into core academic subjects in rural and urban schools participating as pilot sites in a state's reform initiative; and conducting case studies of urban elementary science and math reform. He has published his research in books for Teachers College Press, Ablex, and the State University of New York Press and has written articles for journals such as *Educational Researcher, Phi Delta Kappan, Educational Leadership, Curriculum Inquiry, Urban Review,* and *Education Policy.* He also edits a book series on restructuring and school change with Betty Lou Whitford for the State University of New York Press.

Letitia Hochstrasser Fickel is assistant professor of education at the University of Alaska, Anchorage, where she is collaborating on the redesign of the elementary teacher education program and continuing her research on teacher culture and collegiality and school reform. She is co-author of *Knitting It All Together: Collaborative Teacher Education in Southern Maine* (with Betty Lou Whitford and Gordon Ruscoe, forthcoming from the American Association of Colleges for Teacher Education (AACTE). She completed her doctorate at the University of Louisville in 1998 with a specialty in teaching and learning.

Donna Gaus is co-partner in the evaluation consulting business in Louisville, Kentucky called "Inquiring Minds." She has been conducting research and evaluation related to equity, school change, and the resiliency of children since 1986. She has two children of her own, Kathryn and Jack Grundy, ages 7 and 5. She completed her doctorate in educational evaluation at the University of Louisville.

Marilyn Hohmann is a Senior Associate with the Center for Leadership in School Reform based in Louisville, Kentucky. She was a member of the Commission to Restructure the American High School, which authored *Breaking Ranks: Changing an American Institution.* Using practical experiences gained from her leadership at Fairdale High School in Jefferson County, Kentucky, and from her involvement with the Coalition of Essential Schools and the Commission, she engages CLSR's clients through keynote speaking and other professional development activities. She has also worked extensively to support the development of teacher leadership as well as leadership skills for principals, central office personnel, and superintendents in designing quality work for students.

Ken Jones is the Mathematics Specialist for the Jefferson County Public Schools in Louisville, Kentucky. When this book was being prepared, he worked for the Ohio Valley Educational Cooperative and served as the Director of the Partnership for Professional Development, a collaborative initiative with the University of Louisville. Since KERA was enacted in 1990, he has been closely involved in assisting Kentucky educators in implementing school reform, particularly in the areas of curriculum, instruction, and assessment. He completed his doctoral work at the University of Louisville in 1999 with a dissertation on performance-based classrooms.

Patricia J. Kannapel is a Research and Development Specialist for the Appalachia Educational Laboratory (AEL), Charleston, WV. She is co-director of AEL's study of Kentucky school reform, which has been underway in four rural districts since 1991 and is ongoing through 2000. She is completing work on a doctorate in educational anthropology at the University of Kentucky.

A. Richardson (Rick) Love Jr. joined the John S. and James L. Knight Foundation in Miami, Florida as Education Program Officer in 1990 and became Director of Education Programs in 1995. In that role he administers both national and local education grants and grants relating to literacy. Prior to joining Knight Foundation, Love served as Vice President of the Consortium for the Advancement of Private Higher Education (CAPHE) in Washington, D.C., a funder of small private colleges. Prior to his work at CAPHE, he was Executive Assistant to the President and Director of Institutional Research at Davidson College (NC).

Christy D. McGee received her doctorate in education from the University of Louisville. She is currently an assistant professor of education at the University of Arkansas, Fayetteville, where she serves as a Professional Development School liaison in the Master of Arts in Teaching program and continues her research of teacher practices at a local elementary school.

Lynne Miller is Executive Director of the Southern Maine Partnership (a school-university collaboration that is now in its fourteenth year) and Professor of Educational Leadership at the University of Southern Maine. The Partnership now includes thirty-three school districts and three institutions of higher education; it is closely aligned with the University's Extended Teacher Education Program, which Lynne developed and directed for three years. Lynne has written widely in the areas of teacher development and school reform and has served on a variety of local and national task forces, including the National Commission on Teaching and America's Future. Her most recent work (with Ann Lieberman) is entitled *Teachers Transforming Their World and Their Work* published in 1999 by Teachers College Press.

Beverly D. Moore is currently a member of the Board of Education for the public schools in Jefferson County, Kentucky. A doctoral candidate in Educational Supervision at the University of Louisville, she was formerly a staff associate with the Appalachia Educational Laboratory study of Kentucky school reform and a science teacher.

Cynthia A. Reeves is a staff associate for the Appalachia Education Laboratory (AEL), Charleston, West Virginia. She has been a member of AEL's Kentucky school reform research team since 1997. She is working toward a doctorate in educational anthropology at the University of Kentucky.

David Ruff is the Director of School Reform Projects at the Southern Maine Partnership. While at the Partnership, he has focused his efforts on helping teachers use various instructional, assessment, and accountability techniques to structure increased learning opportunities for all children. He currently serves on the Executive Board for the Coalition of Essential Schools and has worked extensively with the Foxfire Fund.

Gordon C. Ruscoe is Professor Emeritus in the School of Education at the University of Louisville. He recently moved to Florida where he is raising a Vietnamese pot-bellied pig, visiting the beach, and getting ready to be serious in the near future. His interest in school restructuring continues unabated.

Linda Shelor, a former Senior Associate with the Center for Leadership in School Reform (CLSR), is currently a Development and Assessment Consultant with the Holden Corporation. Based in Chicago, Holden works internationally on strategic alignment of sales, marketing, and human resources. Shelor has also worked in adult and middle grades education as a teacher and counselor. She completed her doctorate in education at the University of Louisville in 1989 where she was a Gheens Academy/University of Louisville fellow.

Debra Smith is Director of Curriculum, Assessment, and Technology for the Southern Maine Partnership. Her work with teachers and schools over the past few years has focused on assessment and collaborative inquiry. An experienced teacher, researcher and program evaluator, she is a doctoral candidate at Lesley College, Cambridge, MA.

Jon Snyder is the Director of Teacher Education and a faculty member in the Educational Leadership and Organizations specialization at the University of California at Santa Barbara. He is also a Senior Researcher for the National Commission on Teaching and America's Future. He began his career in education as an elementary school teacher where he worked with, at one time or another, first through sixth graders. He is serving as a member of the California Commission on Teacher Credentialing and as consultant to several states engaged in developing standards and assessments for beginning teachers. He remains engaged in researching teacher learning and the conditions of learning for teachers.

Patricia A. Wasley is Dean of the Graduate School of Education at Bank Street College in New York City. She has worked as a researcher for the Puget Sound Educational Consortium at the University of Washington, at the Coalition of Essential Schools, and at the Annenberg Institute for School Reform at Brown University. She is co-author of *Kids and School Reform* (1997, with Robert L. Hampel and Richard W. Clark) and author of *Stirring the Chalkdust* (1994) and *Teachers Who Lead* (1991).

Anne Wheelock is an independent education writer and policy analyst and author of *Crossing the Tracks: How 'Untracking' Can Save America's Schools* (New Press, 1992). She has a particular interest in understanding the impact of policy on schools and classrooms, especially in the middle grades. Her most recent publication is *Safe to Be Smart: Building a Culture for Standards-Based Reform in the Middle Grades* (National Middle Schools Association, 1998).

Betty Lou Whitford is Professor of Education and Director of the National Center for Restructuring Education, Schools, and Teaching (NCREST) at Teachers College, Columbia University. From 1981–1999, she was a professor at the University of Louisville where this book was prepared. Her research focuses on education reform, especially the work of school-university partnerships. Her most recent publications include "Assessment and Accountability in Kentucky" with Ken Jones in the *International Handbook of Educational Change* (1998, Kluwer Academic Publishers), *Knitting It All Together: Collaborative Teacher Education in Southern Maine* with Gordon Ruscoe and Letitia Fickel (forthcoming from AACTE), "Kentucky's Conflicting Reform Principles" with Ken Jones in the December 1997 *Phi Delta Kappan*, and "Of Promises and Unresolved Puzzles: Reforming Teacher Education with Professional Development Schools" with Phyllis Metcalf-Turner (1999, in the *Ninety-Eighth National Society for the Study of Education Yearbook*, University of Chicago Press).

Name Index

Subject Index

ability grouping, 62
academic: achievement, 150; expectations, 4, 11, 97–100, 106; focus, 169
Academy, Gheens. *See* Gheens Academy
Accelerated Reader Program, 122
Accelerated Schools, 191
"access to knowledge," 184, 188, 190, 194
accountability, 4, 103, 130–136, 139–140, 143, 150, 153, 159, 161, 167, 169, 179–195, 208, 211, 216, 220–224, 228, 234–237, 245; as a process, 186; authentic, 195; collective, 106; high resolution, 23; high stakes, 1, 3, 10, 23, 109–110, 130, 140, 142, 177, 185–186, 179, 193, 205, 233, 235, 245–246; index, 4, 11–12, 14, 23, 131, 233, 242, 244; learner-centered, 167, 174–177; model, 22, 180–183, 185–188, 194–195, 223, 246; professional, 22–23; school, 1, 14, 53, 161, 169, 177, 179–195, 212, 233, 235, 238, 241–243, 245–246; state, 45, 201–204, 207–208, 218, 223, 233, 241; student, 14, 17, 83, 216; systems, 85, 150–161, 167, 174, 184, 214, 218, 220, 224, 226; teacher, 17, 150–161, 187, 212–213, 216, 219; test-based, 234–235
achievement: academic, 150; student, 164, 167, 173–175, 177, 179, 184, 193–194, 214, 223

action: policy, 44; research, 194
activities: group, 78–80, 83, 104; hands-on, 78, 140; school-based, 156
Administrator/Teacher Team, 157, 160
Advanced Placement (AP), 92, 173
Advisory Committee. *See* District-wide Advisory Committee; Kentucky Mathematics Portfolio Advisory Committee; Kentucky State Advisory Committee
algebra. *See* Graphing Calculator Enhanced Algebra Project; Learning Algebra through Technology, Investigations, and Cooperative Experiences; mathematics
Amnesty International, 94
anecdotal notes, 54–55, 62, 65, 67
Annie B. Casey Foundation, 164
Appalachian Educational Laboratory, 3, 12, 212
Arizona, 180
assessment, 2, 18, 61, 85, 139, 140–143, 165, 167, 169, 174, 176–177, 180, 190, 193, 203–208, 213, 220, 223, 228, 234–246; authentic, 49, 204, 211–212, 217–218; classroom, 173, 181, 192, 224; district, 157; high stakes, 10, 77, 106, 125, 140, 165, 220, 243–244; individualized, 66; KIRIS, 4, 129–144; multiple-choice, 12, 140, 211, 237; multiple techniques, 61;